Praise for *Daughters of Daring*

"Chris Enss has done it again. For years and with many, many books, she has brought us wonderful stories and insights about the women of the West. These heroines of calico helped shape, define, and build the frontier. Now we step into the early days of filmdom with strong, independent women who helped create the magic of the movies. The weaker sex? Not in a heartbeat. These women mastered feats far beyond those of mortal men. An exciting book about women with an iron will, determination, and skill, *Daughters of Daring* belongs in every western lover's library."

—Peter Sherayko, actor, producer, author

"Chris Enss shines a much-needed spotlight on the unsung heroines of cinema history: the early stunt women. These daring ladies of the silver screen risked their lives without any publicity—until now. Enss carefully explains how they accomplished their stunts long before the use of wires or computer effects. *Daughters of Daring* is lovingly dedicated to these ladies."

—Michael F. Blake, Emmy Award–winning makeup artist and film historian

"Once again, Enss has unearthed hidden cinema secrets. In *Daughters of Daring*, she tells the remarkable story of women who, from the dawn of movies, risked their lives—mostly in secret. Finally, their names are shared and their incredible achievements are told. No one does it better."

—Rob Word, producer and host, *A Word on Westerns*

"Writing books about show business is truly difficult. The research is enormous, and you have to find a topic that hasn't been done to death. What Enss has accomplished with *Daughters of Daring* is remarkable: She has honored the great (many of them unjustly unknown) stunt women of the first movies ever made. Tracing their histories from Wild West Shows to the earliest silent films and beyond, Enss shines a much-deserved light on the great careers of expert sharpshooter May Lillie and serial queen Ruth Roland and even includes the tragic end of actress Mary Wiggins, among many others.

"These were the ladies who could ride, shoot, and rodeo without fear, and they have been unfairly ignored for more than a hundred years—until now.

"The daughters of daring were entertaining audiences when show business traveled in tents from town to town and then found themselves in the new medium of the movies. Enss's amazingly researched and highly readable record of their lives brings them the attention and applause they've so richly deserved for so long."

—C. Courtney Joyner, award-winning author and screenwriter

DAUGHTERS OF DARING

HOLLYWOOD COWGIRL STUNT WOMEN

CHRIS ENSS

Essex, Connecticut

An imprint of The Globe Pequot Publishing Group, Inc.
64 South Main St.
Essex, CT 06426
www.GlobePequot.com

British Library Cataloguing in Publication Information available

Library of Congress Cataloging-in-Publication Data available

ISBN 978-1-4930-8786-0 (cloth)
ISBN 978-1-4930-8787-7 (ebook)

∞™ The paper used in this publication meets the minimum requirements of American National Standard for Information Sciences—Permanence of Paper for Printed Library Materials, ANSI/NISO Z39.48-1992.

Contents

Introduction

An out-of-control team of horses races past a tremendous vista of desert, framed against mountains and a massive sky with a glimmer of dawn on the horizon. The buckboard roped to the animals lurches and shakes violently. The lone passenger desperately struggles to hang onto a metal bar under the seat of the vehicle. Her grip loosens when the wheels of the buggy slam into a rock, and the wooden tongue hitch snaps, allowing the team to break free. The horses gallop away from the buckboard, now rushing toward a steep embankment. The passenger leaps out of the vehicle moments before it hurtles down the hill. There is a grinding crash as it smacks into the ground, turning over and over, finally coming to a halt on its side, a mass of tangled wreckage.

Moments after the buckboard is destroyed in the accident, an imposing cowboy in a white hat spurs his horse to the spot where the woman who escaped the wreckage lies on the ground, unconscious. He scoops the heroine up into his manly arms and brushes a few flecks of dust from her cheek. She smiles, opens her eyes, and their lips meet in a passionate kiss.

Few moviegoers watching the scene on the big screen in this fast-action Western, wondered how the beautiful heroine didn't have so much as a misplaced hair as she lay in the hero's arms. They took it for granted that it would simply happen that way.

That scene and nearly every other thrill the audience witnessed in early motion pictures where a lovely girl was in danger was made by one of Hollywood's forgotten, fearless stunt women doubling for movie stars. She didn't double for the star because the star lacked courage. She did it because, if she were maimed or killed, it would make little difference to the cost of the picture. If the star tried to wreck a buckboard and suffered even a split lip, the cost of delayed production would have amounted to thousands of dollars. Using a cowgirl stunt woman in Westerns was insurance for the studios. While beautiful movie stars were expensive, courageous lady equestrians were more common and well within the studio's budget.

One of the first showmen to recognize the true value of talented and daring horsewomen was William F. Cody. Buffalo Bill Cody's Wild West Show was a leading source of entertainment for more than thirty years. During that time of worldwide travel and countless presentations, a myriad of performers captured the hearts and imagination of fans everywhere. Among those popular entertainers were a number of bold, highly skilled women who were horseback riders. Cody went to great lengths to hire the finest, most adventurous lady riders to be part of his well-known show.

In January 1885, Buffalo Bill sent a talent scout to San Antonio, Texas. The goal was to recruit more than forty women in the area known as the "cattle girls." The cattle girls lived in the hills between San Marco and San Antonio. Some of them were from the most respected families in the state; others from the least. Regardless of their backgrounds, they were known throughout the region as the finest riders in the West. Their leader was a statuesque brunette from Oklahoma with long black hair—legend had it that her hair cracked like a whip when she was riding. The women owned and operated a large ranch with more than five hundred head of cattle.

Cody's scout ventured into the region to visit the cattle girls and invited them to join the Wild West Show. He explained how much in demand women with their skills were. He also told them how much they could earn performing. His offer was politely declined. The leader of the cattle girls doubted the scout's claim, citing as her reason the fact that they'd been forced into the hills to run their own ranch because most people insisted women had no place in such a profession. "We can stick to a calf like a burro on a sheep's tail, but I don't believe anyone but us would ever be interested in seeing what we can do on the back of a horse," the head of the cattle girls told the scout.

The popularity of riding stars in Cody's show such as Della Ferrell, Lulu Parr, and Georgia Duffy proved that people were indeed interested

Buffalo Bill Cody employed many cowgirls who inspired the first stunt women in silent films.
DENVER PUBLIC LIBRARY S.TIF243

in what women could do on the back of a horse. They became even more accepted in 1904 when rodeo star Bertha Kaepernick became the first woman to ride a bucking horse at Cheyenne Frontier Days. By the time silent films were produced in Hollywood and Western movies were being made weekly, women who could ride a horse at breakneck speeds and leap over mountainous chasms were in high demand.

Among the earliest and most renowned cowgirls-turned-Western-stunt women were Nell Jones, Mabel Strickland, and May Boss. These women, and many other former cowgirls who worked on ranches, performed in Wild West Shows. They competed in rodeos and risked their lives daily as "insurance policies" for early film studios such as Monogram, Mack Sennett, and Republic Pictures.

Many cast as stunt women were fated to spend a considerable amount of their motion picture career accumulating a large variety of cuts and bruises. Even when they were granted a small speaking part, there was always a fall, a dive, or a wagon collision to go with it. Talented stunt women took backward, forward, headfirst, and feetfirst falls into water, ditches, and nets, over chairs and tables, from the tops of pianos, out of high windows, through trapdoors, and down haylofts. Some rode wild horses; worked with bears, goats, pigs, and cows; and chased donkeys and steers. They doubled for such luminaries as Joan Crawford, Barbara Stanwyck, and Jean Arthur.

A number of early Hollywood's most capable stunt women perfected their riding techniques at the Miller Brothers 101 Ranch in Oklahoma. Like Buffalo Bill Cody, the ranching brothers Joseph, George Jr., and Zack had their own Wild West Show that made its debut in 1907. Among the popular 101 Ranch Wild West Show cowgirls-turned-stunt women were Goldie Griffith, Bessie Herberg, and Helen Gibson. Recognized by film historians as the first professional stunt woman, Gibson performed the stirrup drag for the camera—deliberately falling off her horse with a leg still in a stirrup so that her horse would gallop, dragging her across the ground. She also leaped from a pair of horses to a rope dangling from a bridge, which she would then use to swing onto a moving railroad engine.

Trained, brave stunt women specialized in certain stunts. Ione Reed and Aline Goodwin were both expert bareback riders who rode their

Many of the first cowgirl stunt women began their careers in the 101 Ranch Wild West Show.
AUTHOR'S COLLECTION

horses off bridges and over automobiles. Mary Wiggins was a gifted high diver, but she accepted assignments of almost any stunt, including jumping from a moving train and then paddling a canoe down fierce rapids. In case of injury while doing a stunt, those plucky women were without sufficient insurance. In the early 1930s, California state law provided they receive $25 a week for the time they were unable to work. That was their only compensation.

"Every stuntman or woman I know is a fatalist," stunt woman Betty Danko told newspaper reporters in 1936. "How could they go on with their work if they were not? If your number is up, that's that and if it isn't, you can walk away from even the most dangerous stunt with a grin. We people who take desperate chances to earn a living will never live in a Beverly Hills mansion or drive a Rolls Royce. There is no future worth thinking of ahead of us. The work is a terrible strain, both mentally and physically, and you must know your business if you are ever to hold your grandchildren on your knee."

In 1938, equestrian stunt woman Frances Miles helped found the organization Riders and Stunt Girls of the Screen. The association's purpose was twofold: to provide studios with a list of the best trained stunt women in the industry, and to make sure members of the organization were adequately provided for in case of injury, sickness, or hard times. As president of Riders and Stunt Girls of the Screen, Miles created a booklet for casting directors to refer to whenever they needed a daredevil. The booklet included the specialty stunts the ladies were known for, a photograph of the double, and their contact information. Whether it was crashing through a windowpane or wrestling with a mountain lion, producers knew Miles's booklet would lead them to the right stunt woman for the job.

In the early days of the film business, stunting was the only strictly "piece work" field of wage-earning in the entire movie industry. Prices depended on the difficulties undertaken, so each stunt became a separate negotiation with the studio. The booklet Miles created featured a price list for various stunts. Ordinary riding was $11 a day, the same wage stock contract players received. Chases on horseback were listed at $16.50 per day. The minimum for a wagon crash was $50, $100 for a turnover, and $100 for being a standing target. Transfers from automobiles and trains varied from $50 to $230. General rough work, trick riding, riding bucking horses, and net falls were $35 per day. Handling wild animals was also $35 per day. High diving was $25 per day, but the price went up one dollar for every foot over 25 feet. Extremely high dives were paid per dive, and the price was negotiated.

In 1919, long before Frances Miles created the booklet and the stunt price list, trick and relay rider Vera McGinnis was earning a mere $8 for the stunts she performed in the romantic comedy *Nobody Home*. By 1938, thrill-seeking equestrian Alive Van Springsteen was one of the highest paid stunt women in the business. As the stunt double for Olivia de Havilland in the *Adventures of Robin Hood* and for Dale Evans in a handful of films with Roy Rogers, she earned between $45 and $60 per stunt.

The longevity of cowgirl stunt women varied. Polly Burson, known as the "premiere stunt woman in Hollywood," remained in the business for more than three decades, retiring only when she felt it wasn't safe for her to continue. Stunt doubles such as Betty Miles gave up the profession early to pursue a career as a teacher. After a couple of close calls, she believed teaching would be less hazardous than stunt work.

The danger and risk associated with the job enticed many cowgirls to become stunt women, but the reality of the work prompted many to consider leaving the trade. Aline Goodwin was an expert at horse stunts—riding, jumping, falling from horses, etcetera. She enjoyed the work but often suffered injuries that took months to heal. While filming a Western series in 1930, she suffered three fractured vertebrae when the horse she was riding ran her into a tree. "I was lucky," Goodwin recalled sometime after the incident. "I never knew I was hurt. Twenty-five specialists told me it was a miracle I could walk, and that I'd probably soon not be able to do so. They said I'd be paralyzed."

Betty Danko was performing with a cougar when the stunt went wrong. The animal grabbed her leg with his front paws and sank its claws deep into her flesh. He then clamped down with his jaws and stared to chew. "The pain was incredible," Danko shared with the press. "Each bite was torture. I wanted to pass out, but I couldn't."

The cougar managed to bite her thirteen times before the animal's trainer was able to pull him away from Danko. The bites were extremely deep, and doctors told her the scars would never disappear. "I have fallen into lakes, poles, over chairs and tables, down laundry chutes and stairs," she said. "I have fallen over backwards from a height of 25 feet into 32 inches of water and into a pool fully clothed, though I can barely swim. I've been yanked around on wire, had pies and knives thrown at me, have lain amid flames and gasoline—all for the sake of art and a paycheck."

The highest price paid for a dangerous stunt performed by a woman in the early 1930s was $50. Long before Aline Goodwin needed surgery to repair her fractured vertebrae, she stood in for actress Jean Parker in the film *Have a Heart*. The stunt Goodwin performed involved falling out of a window backward. It required fifteen takes before the director was satisfied with the result.

Unlike leading actresses of the day, most cowgirl stunt women were not going to amass a fortune for their work or receive awards for their perilous feats. Their contributions to the early film industry are obscured in the shadows cast by the studio lights that illuminate the stars. Their solace was the knowledge that Hollywood couldn't have gotten along without them.

Pioneer stunt woman Helen Gibson performs a daring feat in one of the first episodes of the silent film series *The Hazards of Helen*.
AUTHOR'S COLLECTION

Drawings of stunt woman Aline Goodwin at work appeared in a variety of advertisements.
AUTHOR'S COLLECTION

BEFORE THE CAMERAS

When the Superintendent of the Census Robert P. Porter published the department's annual report in 1890, he announced that the Wild West no longer existed. According to Porter, the country beyond the Mississippi River had been so widely populated there was no longer a clear distinction between frontier and settlement.[1]

At about the same time, and despite (or perhaps because of) the remarkable and ongoing innovation of the Industrial Revolutions, Americans grew intensely nostalgic for the Old West and its heroes. Writers churned out dime novels about cowboys and Indians, outlaws and quick-draw marshals, vast herds of bison, and intrepid scouts and frontiersmen. Other entrepreneurs recognized a mass market hungry for grander, more exciting, and more authentic portrayals of the West. So began the era of the Wild West Shows.

The first indication that the public in the East was interested in legendary characters who inhabited the rugged West came about in July 1843. The occasion was the dedication of the Bunker Hill Monument in Boston, Massachusetts. The organizers of the celebration arranged for a herd of buffalo to be exhibited, along with a mounted cavalry unit and members of the Pequot and Wampanoag Indian tribes. Thousands of people congregated at the event and were mesmerized by the display. The interest in the buffalo wasn't lost on businessman, showman, and New England politician P. T. Barnum. Barnum purchased the herd and hosted what he called A Grand Buffalo Hunt in Hoboken, New Jersey two months later.[2]

Sells Floto Circus publicity poster promoting a daredevil woman performer. AUTHOR'S COLLECTION

Crowds flocked to the grounds where the so-called "hunt" was to be held. Interested participants were provided with a rope to lasso the buffalo of their choice; that was Barnum's version of a hunt. The expert roper and rider he'd hired to show the multitudes how it was done, and the band that entertained between animal roping, were well received. The enthusiastic response demonstrated to the businessman that audiences were fascinated by the Wild West. And, if they weren't able to travel there themselves, they were willing to pay to experience the West if it came to them.[3]

Seventeen years would pass before P. T. Barnum officially launched his first traveling Western program. Other businessmen entered the trade, but it wasn't perfected until William S. Cody established the Buffalo Bill Wild West Show in May 1883. By including hundreds of Indians in his program atop magnificent horses, cowboys, scouts, stagecoaches, the United States Cavalry, and a mounted concert band, he helped further impress upon the American imagination the great, romantic legend of the West.[4]

Offering a new form of entertainment, the era of the Wild West Shows fed the appetite of audiences longing to immerse themselves in a frontier setting. People of all ages swarmed fairgrounds and vacant lots where elaborate programs were held to witness animals, bronc busters, sharpshooters, and reenactments of historic events, such as the Battle of the Little Bighorn and the Mountain Meadow Massacre. Some performers from various shows, such as Adam Forepaugh's New and Great All Feature Show and Wild West Combination, the Sells Floto Circus, Texas Jack's Great Wild West, and Pawnee Bill's Historic Wild West became celebrities. Dr. W. F. Carver, the Champion Shot of the World, the Cherokee Kid (better known as Will Rogers), and trick roper Mexican Joe were fan favorites.[5]

Among the thrill-seeking women who captured the hearts of those who attended the action-packed programs were Senorita Rosalie, Kitsipimi, Plenty Shawls, and Mamie Francis. Senorita Rosalie was the Mexican star of the Wild West Shows. She was a stunning, black-haired woman who had achieved fame as a trick rider. She would jump over barricades and ride holding the reins in her mouth while standing on the

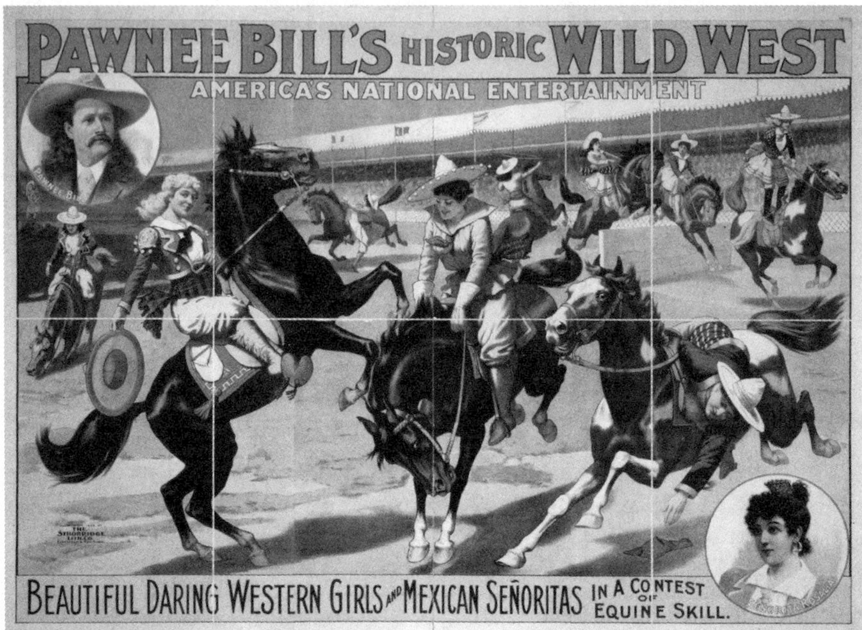

Pawnee Bill's Historic Wild West advertisement promoting the Beautiful Daring Western Girls and Mexican Señoritas. LIBRARY OF CONGRESS

back of her horse. With her feet firmly placed on the ground, she spurred her horse on and jumped on its back. While the animal was in full gallop, she would fling her body in and out of the saddle and dangle precariously off the sides of the horse. Rosalie could even lie down in the saddle and retrieve items left on the arena floor.[6]

Kitsipimi Otunna, a Sacree Indian from Alberta, Canada, portrayed either a devastated Indian maiden whose husband had been killed in battle or a gracious Indian interpreter who helped Cody communicate with the braves. As with the other Native Americans in the show, Kitsipimi played her part in and out of the arena. Dressed in her traditional apparel, she greeted patrons at the show's opening and closing.[7]

Kitsipimi wasn't the only standout female Indian performer with Cody's program. A Sioux Indian known as Plenty Shawls was front and center as well. She was an expert rider and served as one of the participants in the program's re-creation of the famed Ghost Dance ritual.[8]

Mamie Francis and her horse Babe were part of California Frank Hafley's Wild West Show as a diving equestrian act. In the summer of May 1908, Mamie and Babe could be seen perched on a wooden platform thirty feet in the air above Coney Island, New York, looking down at the audience in the grandstands. Directly below the platform was a forty-foot tank filled to overflowing with water.[9]

Mamie gently urged Babe to the edge of the platform. Both stood like a statue surveying the landscape before them. After receiving the signal, Mamie coaxed Babe forward. The horse pushed away from the boards and lunged outward into space. Moments later, horse and rider entered the water in the tank with a tremendous splash. When they rose to the surface, the audience erupted in applause. Mamie patted Babe's neck as the horse carried her up the ramp and out of the tank.

When Mamie stopped horse diving in 1914, she turned her attention to sharpshooting, trick riding, and training horses to compete in dressage events.[10]

Miss Mamie Francis atop her horse, Napoleon. AUTHOR'S COLLECTION

When (male competitors in a shooting competition) saw me coming along they laughed at the notion of my shooting against them. . . . It kind of galled me to see those hulking chaps so tickled in what was no doubt to them an impertinence in daring to shoot against them—and I reckon I was tickled too when I walked away with the prize.

—Annie Oakley

Annie Oakley was the greatest personality developed by the Wild West Show. She inspired many young women to break with tradition and enter fields of endeavor reserved primarily for men. In 1885, she rushed into the Wild West Show arena in Louisville, Kentucky, riding a brown and white pony. As she spurred her ride around a straw barrier at a high lope, Annie waved and blew kisses at the excited audience. The cowboy just ahead of her waited until she slowed down her ride down and then began tossing glass balls into the air. She raised her rifle to her shoulders and aimed. The balls exploded as she shot them, one by one.[11]

Putting her gun away for the moment, she quickly dismounted and raced over to a table at the far end of the grounds. Another cowboy juggling glass balls was waiting for her. Annie jumped over the gun table and scooped up a weapon just as the cowboy tossed up four balls. Two balls were obliterated. She picked up another gun. Those two balls blew apart. The timid women in the audience who screamed with fright at the initial sound of the loud firearms broke into enthusiastic rounds of applause.

Annie bowed to the delighted crowd, searching the table for the prop she used in her most famous stunt, the Mirror Trick. Using a knife blade for a mirror, Annie pointed her gun over her shoulder. Frank Butler, Annie's husband, stood behind her in the distance, holding up an ace of spades. After sighting the card in the knife blade, she squeezed the trigger. The gun barked. A hole appeared where the spade had been, dead center in the card.

The crowd burst into cheers. Annie smiled, swung onto her horse, and hurried out of the arena. As she rode past Buffalo Bill Cody, he shouted, "Sharp shooting, Missy!"[12]

The Sioux Indian chief Sitting Bull greeted the five-foot-tall performer backstage. Impressed with her skill and aim, the warrior proudly

Annie Oakley's famous rifle shot. LIBRARY OF CONGRESS

called her "Little Sure Shot." Sitting Bull believed Annie Oakley to be possessed by the Good Spirit.

"No one can hurt her," he told friends. "Only one who was supernaturally blessed could be such a dead shot."

Throughout the 1880s and 1890s, Annie Oakley was the biggest box-office attraction in Cody's show. Most historians consider her the first female star of the Wild West. She earned more than $1,000 per week, second only in pay to Buffalo Bill himself. Cody's press agent, Dexter Fellows, boasted that Annie was "the consummate actress, with a personality that made itself felt as soon as she entered the arena."[13]

Annie Oakley was born Annie Moses on August 13, 1860, in Darke County, Ohio. Her father's untimely death when she was still a child forced Annie to find work to help support her mother and her brothers and sisters.[14]

Annie learned to hunt with a rifle when she was eight and used her natural sharpshooting ability to provide food for their evening meals. She became such a good shot that she was hired by a merchant to supply his store with fresh game. By the time Annie turned nine, she was a major provider for her family.[15]

A shooting match between Annie and Western showman Frank Butler in 1875 forever changed her life. The challenge was for each marksman to shoot twenty-five clay pigeons. Frank hit twenty-four of the twenty-five targets. Annie hit them all.

Frank was so taken by the young woman's expertise and femininity that he invited her to see him perform in one of his Western programs. She was impressed with his kindness and proficiency with a weapon. After a short time, their mutual fondness and admiration blossomed into love. They were married on June 22, 1876. Frank was twenty-nine and Annie was fifteen.[16]

Frank and Annie took their shooting know-how on the road, giving exhibitions at theaters across the country. By this time, Annie had changed her name to Oakley. She decided on that name because she'd liked the sound of it ever since her sister told her of the Ohio district with the same handle.[17]

Butler and Oakley were well received wherever they performed. People were not only amazed by the teenager's shooting, they admired the pluck of a girl who could hold a coin steady until it was shot from her fingers. By December 1884, Frank and Annie had become the top shooting act in the country.[18]

Buffalo Bill Cody hired the popular duo to join his Wild West cast in 1885. Their first appearance with Cody was in Louisville, Kentucky.

Annie was working more as a solo act at this point, and Frank was her assistant. Frank judged that audiences preferred the novelty of a woman shooter to a husband-and-wife team. He decided to limit his role to be that of Annie's promotion manager and talent coach. The glowing reception Annie received from the more than seventeen thousand people at the program opening night proved Frank's judgment was right.[19]

Billed as the Peerless Wing and Rifle Shot, Annie Oakley nightly packed the house with her trick riding and shooting. Cody called Annie "the single greatest asset the Wild West Show ever had."[20]

Annie was as popular in England as she was in the United States. Throughout her London engagement, her tent was filled with flowers and gifts from admirers.[21]

Letters poured in from people everywhere who marveled at her showstopping stunts. One such stunt featured Annie riding while standing up on the back of her horse and shooting at targets set up around the arena. Fans wrote asking for those targets and for signed photographs of the sharpshooter in action. As a courtesy to her devotees, she supplied them with a short list of facts about herself.[22]

Answers to Ten Questions I Am Asked Every Day

1. *I was born in Woodland, Ohio.*

2. *I learned to shoot in the field.*

3. *I do not think I inherited my love of firearms from my parents, for they were Quakers, and were very much opposed to my using such weapons.*

4. *Having traveled in fourteen countries, and having hunted in almost all of them, I have shot nearly all kinds of game.*

5. *While I love to shoot in the field, I care very little for exhibition shooting and only do it as a matter of business.*

6. *I never use the word "champion" in connection with my name and always request my friends not to address me as such.*

7. *My guns weigh about six pounds each and are of many different makes. There is no such thing as the best gun maker. The best gun is the gun that best fits the shooter.*
8. *I use pistols, rifles, and shotguns. I do not believe in using cheap guns. To me, the use of a cheap gun is like driving a Star Pointer with a clothes-line—you never know when the line is going to give way.*
9. *I like pigeon shooting when the birds are first-class flyers, but I am very much opposed to shooting pigeons from the trap during the three summer months.*
10. *I use 39 grains of Schultze Smokeless Powder and one ounce of shot, loaded in the U. M. C. Smokeless shells. I don't say that this is the only load, but it is good enough for me.*[23]

After seventeen seasons with Buffalo Bill's Wild West Show, Annie retired from the program in 1902. Injuries she sustained in a train accident the previous year had caused trauma to her spine and made it too painful for her to continue riding.[24]

Annie and Frank settled in Greenville, Ohio, where for two decades they gave shooting lessons and provided short demonstrations of marksmanship to soldiers and rodeo folks. Annie lived to be sixty-six years old.[25] Bold women like Annie Oakley who were arena entertainers from 1843 to 1904 paved the way for the cowgirls who would make the move from Wild West Show to silent films.

Lucille Mulhall

Little Miss Mulhall, who weighs only ninety pounds, can break a bronc, lasso, brand a steer and shoot a coyote at 500 yards. She can also play Chopin, quote Browning, and make mayonnaise.

—*New York World*, July 7, 1900

A pair of large, mean steers charged out of the gate and raced onto the parade field. Seventeen-year-old Lucille Mulhall bolted after the beasts atop her trained horse, Governor. The beautiful blond with petite features and blue-gray eyes quickly tossed the lasso she was twirling and snagged one of the animals around its neck. The steer jerked to a stop as Governor planted his feet firmly on the ground. Lucille leapt at the steer with another rope and began to tie its feet together. In thirty seconds, she had completed the task, breaking the steer roping record at the rodeo grounds in Denison, Texas.[1]

On a hot September day in 1903, Lucille won the Grayson County Fair's roping contest, beating out two of the county's top cowboys in the process. She was awarded a gold pendant with a raised star in which a diamond was embedded. In the center of the pendant was a steer roping scene set in blue enamel. It was a prize she wore with pride for the rest of her career.[2]

Two years prior, Lucille Mulhall demonstrated her talent for the future president of the United States. She was fifteen when Vice President Theodore Roosevelt was in Oklahoma City in July 1909. He was in town to attend a reunion of the Rough Riders, a regiment of men who fought with him during the Spanish-American War. Lucille's father, Colonel Zack

Lucille Mulhall, the first cowgirl COURTESY OKLAHOMA HISTORICAL SOCIETY

Mulhall, owner of the expansive Mulhall Ranch and a traveling Wild West program, had arranged for the Rough Riders to see an exhibition of roping and riding by cast members from his Mulhall Wild West Show.

Among the performers was his teenage daughter. Lucille had been a favorite in the cowboy exhibition for two years. Her riding talent and skill with a lariat were the envy of women and a fair number of men, who had seen her work at fairgrounds and amphitheaters in the Mulhall Wild West Show. Newspapers noted she was a "remarkable girl for her age" with "wonderfully developed muscles and hands as hard as those of any cowpuncher."[3]

More than twenty-five thousand people filled the stands where the Wild West show was held. After a brief introduction, Lucille rode Governor into the center of the arena. She then led her horse through a series of tricks she had taught him, including picking up the wooden handle of a dinner bell with his teeth and shaking his head to ring it; rearing on his hind legs and walking; falling to the ground and "playing dead"; and bowing to the audience.

At the conclusion of Governor's act, Lucille retrieved the lariat hanging from his saddle and began spinning the rope. She twirled the lariat with ease, expanding the loop that was created with each rotation. When it was just the right size, she jumped in and out of the loop. Without missing a step, she twirled the lariat into a wider loop and swirled it out over the heads of the first few rows in the grandstand. Jerking the rope back to her, she shrunk the size of the loop while continuing to twirl it. Dropping it to her leg, she kicked the loop high, and it fell neatly over Governor's neck.[4]

The crowd went wild, cheering and applauding. Vice President Roosevelt jumped to his feet, whistling and clapping. Lucille smiled, waved at the audience, and then leaped onto Governor's back—and the horse took another bow. The pair raced from the arena as the crowd continued applauding. The vice president introduced himself to her after the performance and complimented her on her talent. "Not a Rough Rider here could have done better," the politician told her.[5]

The young woman, recognized by historians as America's first cowgirl, was born on October 21, 1885, in St. Louis, Missouri. Neither she nor her parents could say for certain when she began to ride, but all agreed she lived more or less on horseback "ever since she was a little baby." Her mother, Agnes, was always quick to point out that, growing up, there wasn't a horse of any kind Lucille wouldn't attempt to ride. She had immense patience working with animals and, if she did encounter a horse that seemed too difficult at first, she could tame the mount quickly with a quirt and a lasso.[6]

In addition to possessing a gift with horses and learning how to ride and rope from her father, Lucille was also a talented pianist. From her mother, she learned to appreciate the poetry of Robert Browning. She would have preferred to limit her education to her horses and riding across the more than five thousand acres of the Mulhall ranch, but her mother insisted she attend school. Before being enrolled at the St. Joseph Academy in Guthrie, Oklahoma, Lucille attended a school at a convent in St. Louis, Missouri. Agnes had hoped her daughter would outgrow her desire to ride and stop spending all her free time practicing roping everything from a wolf to a steer. She dreamed her daughter would eventually choose ball gowns, cotillions, and midafternoon teas with girls who preferred more refined tasks. But Lucille couldn't imagine herself anywhere except the wide-open range.[7]

Zack Mulhall encouraged his daughter's love of ranch life. Lucille accompanied him during cattle branding. She rode astride after the stray, wild steers hurrying away from the branding iron. Her father often boasted that she was equal to any two cowboys on the ranch, both in the measure of her ability and usefulness. When riding around the homestead, Lucille carried a heavy pocketknife, a hammer and nails, and saddle tools. The hammer and nails were brought into use whenever she noticed a board loose in the fences about the ranch. She was so good at maintaining the property and corralling runaway calves that her father made her a lucrative business proposition. For every yearling calf she roped and brought in, she could brand the animal with her own initials to build her own herd. The system worked well for a time, but Lucille's ambition increased with her skill, and her private herd kept pace with both. Zack rescinded the offer he'd made to his daughter after he returned from a short trip and learned that she'd roped and branded more than twenty of the finest and wildest steers on the ranch.[8]

Mulhall's Congress of Rough Riders and Ropers premiered at the St. Louis Fair in 1899. In addition to the bronc riders, steer ropers, and cowboy band members who performed in the program, there was a nineteen-year-old man from Oologah, Oklahoma. His name was Will Rogers. Will, or Billie as the Mulhall family called him, was the son of Clem Rogers, a wealthy Cherokee rancher and politician and a friend of Lucille's father.

Zack's association with Clem wasn't the only reason Will was invited to be part of the show. He was an exceptional trick and fancy roper and the winner of a highly competitive roping contest in Claremore, Oklahoma. Lucille was enamored by Will's talent. The two became fast friends, and she watched him practice for hours, learning his technique. In time, Lucille incorporated everything Will had taught her about twirling a lasso into the act she performed in her father's popular exhibition.[9]

In addition to entertaining the crowds that flocked to the Wild West shows with her trick and fancy roping routine, Lucille played the part of a bandit holding up a stagecoach with a group of other wild riders. She enjoyed the work but wanted desperately to participate in the steer roping event with the boys. She pleaded with her father to give her a chance, reminding him of the calves she lassoed on the ranch. Zack felt his daughter was too young for such a challenge. Lucille would have to wait two more years before she could rope steers for an audience.[10]

An article in the May 17, 1901, edition of the *Pryor Creek Clipper* reported that fifteen-year-old Lucille Mulhall was scheduled to "take part in the contest of roping steer" on May 24, in Memphis, Tennessee. Among the other contestants participating in the event were professional cowboys Dick Parris, Clem Musgrove, and Will Rogers. Lucille would be the only female to compete. Although she didn't win any of the top prizes, she gave a respectable showing and proved to her father she could hold her own in the competition. Lucille rode and roped in other contests in Washington, D.C., and Des Moines, Iowa. Those events set the stage for her steer roping debut at the big carnival in El Paso, Texas.[11]

Promoters for the El Paso carnival were thrilled to announce that the "lady roper" had entered the roping contest. They anticipated Lucille's presence would be a big draw. "She has roped at the leading events of this kind all over the country," an article in the December 20, 1902, edition of the *El Paso Herald* noted, "and has never failed to make a hit or draw good crowds."[12]

Lucille traveled to the carnival with her brother Charley and her father. Under the direction of Zack Mulhall, the Mulhall Cowboy Band was performing at the festivities, and Charley was going to take part in the bronc riding competition. After the trio settled into their hotel rooms, they took a tour of the rodeo grounds. Charley was taken aback by the fierce-looking steers selected for the event in which his sister was to take part. Lucille, however, was unfazed and looked forward to the challenge. Their father was more annoyed than worried about his daughter. Word had reached him that the oddsmakers were betting against Lucille; no one believed she could ride and throw a rope. Zack assured Lucille that he believed in her ability and was betting that the only woman competing in the steer roping event would finish on top.[13]

The day of the contest, Lucille waited patiently on top of her horse, Robin, near the chute at the arena. When her name was announced, she moved into place at the starting line and gave her ride a pat on the neck. When the chute opened, a steer bolted out of the stall. Lucille urged Robin away from the starting line, and he raced after the animal. Lucille quickly spun her lasso around and tossed it out. The loop dropped down over the steer's horn, and the rope snapped in two. Charley watched from the sidelines and, acting quickly, leaned over the fence around the arena and held out a fresh lasso.

Lucille and Robin sped toward him, and Lucille grabbed the rope. As Robin hurried after the steer again, Lucille spun the lasso. In a flash, she flipped the loop over the steer's horns and placed the slack under the animal's right hip. The horse ran until the rope snapped tautly, then stopped and dug into the ground. The steer went down with a thud. Lucille jumped out of the saddle with the tie, roped in her hands. She dropped to her knees next to the steer, and, with a quick flip, she wrapped the "piggin" strings around three legs and then got to her feet with her hands in the air.[14]

The crowd cheered as the announcer proclaimed, "Lucille Mulhall, twenty-nine and a half seconds. Best time for the day!" The applause from the stands suddenly changed to shouts and screams. The spectators rushed toward the fence surrounding the arena, jumped over the barrier, and ran to Lucille. Before she knew what was happening, the crowd pushed and grabbed her, shouting that she was a man. The angry mob jerked at her blouse and pulled at her skirt in a frenzied attempt to find out if she was a woman. Lucille tried to break free from the crowd but was overwhelmed. Thankfully, her brother and father rode in on the scene with their horses, and the crowd parted. Charley grabbed his sister by the waist and hoisted her onto his mount, and the three hurried away.[15]

Newspapers from St. Louis to San Francisco reported on Lucille's performance. They called her the "Female Conqueror of Beef and Horn" and "The Ranch Queen." It was Will Rogers who gave her the name by which she would most be remembered. "Lucille was just a little kid when we began working together," Rogers recalled in his memoirs. "She was riding and running her pony all over the place. . . . It was the direct start of what has since come to be known as the cowgirl."[16]

Cowgirl Lucille Mulhall became a lead attraction in her father's Wild West show. With Lucille as the star, Mulhall's Congress of Rough Riders and Ropers was a rodeo in high demand. The group toured extensively through Colorado, Montana, Washington, and Texas. Billed as the "Champion Lady Rider and Roper of the World," Lucille was continuously competing, winning gold medals, belt buckles, and trophies for steer roping and cutting horses.

She appreciated the attention she received as a woman competing in a man's sport and was humble and gracious. Reporters often remarked on her lack of vanity. An April 19, 1903, article in the *Butte Miner* reported:

> *She has earned the title, wears it with delightful modesty, and is the idol of the cowboys throughout the country. At seventeen, she has the unique distinction of being the only professional woman ropist in the world,*

with sparkling jewels, by way of medal testimony, to bear witness to the fact. She has won these medals fairly and squarely in roping contests with the most skillful knights of the spur and lariat in Texas.[17]

All men admire her grace, her courage and her dexterity, and all women envy her the possession of her equestrienne accomplishments. They admire her and envy her the more because they know that her pretty head cannot be turned by praise, nor her frank, girlish ingenuous and honest nature spoiled by the attention that she receives.[18]

To lasso a steer running at full speed and throw and tie the struggling animal is not easy work for strong men who have spent most of their lives in the saddle. When a pretty, modest young woman rides with the same skill, throws a frantic steer, and ties him with the same dexterity, it is no wonder the world applauds. . . .[19]

Few women would have the courage to attempt roping, even if they had the strength and skill, as considerable danger accompanies such reckless riding. Miss Mulhall is the only woman ropist in the world recorded in cattle land. She is not the least masculine in appearance. So very girlish is she in looks and in manner that one would scarcely credit her with more than sixteen years.[20]

Lucille had many admirers, but her first allegiance was to her father and the rodeo. Zack often ran interference between his daughter and the young men interested in courting her. He was protective of Lucille and didn't want her settling down too soon. She didn't enter into a serious relationship until she was twenty-two years old and, even then, kept the romance a secret from the family.

In 1906, Mulhall's Congress of Rough Riders and Ropers disbanded. The show had become tiresome for many of its participants, and they decided to go in different directions. Lucille returned to the family ranch for a while, but she was soon lured back into show business by her father—an offer came for her to join a vaudeville revue. The announcement of her return to the spotlight appeared in newspapers across the country. "Miss Lucille Mulhall's engagements will begin on January 20 in Orpheum at Kansas City where her father has completed a contract for her appearance in a number of cities," the January 18, 1907, edition of the

St. Louis Dispatch noted. "The vaudeville act will be modeled after the Wild West shows in which she has taken part so often."[21]

Lucille's new show was billed as "Lucille Mulhall and Her Ranch Boys." In addition to Lucille, the troupe consisted of her two sisters, her brother, and a cowboy baritone named Martin Van Bergen. Several horses and props were part of the entourage as well. Theaters had to be adapted to accommodate the show. A unique portable fence, designed to hang from the fly loft and fasten between the stage and orchestra pit, was installed in each venue. Several inches of dirt had to be spread out over the stage floor.[22]

Martin Van Bergen opened the show by riding out on a white horse and singing *My Lucille*. During the song, a spotlight followed Lucille as she rode slowly across the back of the stage. At the end of the song, Martin would hurry off, then Lucille and Governor would perform a variety of stunts.[23] Lucille and Martin were smitten with each other from the start. He was impressed with Lucille's beauty and talent as a horsewoman. She fell in love with his appealing sweetness and captivating singing voice. The two were married on March 22, 1907.[24]

Their son, William Logan Van Bergen, was born on January 29, 1909. Unfortunately, Lucille did not enjoy being a wife and mother. That spring, she left her son in the care of his father and her in-laws and returned to the rodeo program. Her show played in every major city across the United States, and she spent so much time away from home that it took a toll on her marriage. Then her professional career began to falter.[25]

During a matinee show in Chicago, Lucille accidentally killed a steer in the arena, prompting the Society for the Prevention of Cruelty to Animals to press charges against her. The May 19, 1910, edition of the *Chicago Livestock World* reported:

> *Several hundred men, women and children saw a badly frightened steer killed yesterday at the Coliseum by the woman roper, Lucille Mulhall. When the animal, struggling feebly as it was dragged about the ring by the young woman, gave a convulsive gasp and became unconscious, a cry of disgust and horror arose from the audience, and a dozen cowboys rushed forward and dragged the carcass from the arena.*[26]

Lucille Mulhall, daughter of the proprietor of the show and herself noted as one of the best women ropers in the country, was giving her exhibition of roping a steer when the accident occurred. Usually during the conduct of the show, a small, well tamed steer has been selected for use in that part of the performance. The usual steer has been so accustomed to being roped that there was little of excitement to the act. Yesterday, however, a new steer was brought into the ring.

Scared by the cries of the audience as well as by the strangeness of its surroundings, the steer darted about the arena at the coliseum until Miss Mulhall threw her rope at it.

Instead of submitting to the roping as the property steer had been wont to do, the new animal started to break away. Miss Mulhall, seated upon her pony, tightened the noose, and in a moment the steer had fallen to the ground. As the steer was thrown to the ground, there came a sharp crack as if a bone had been broken, and the animal made a few convulsive kicks and then lay passive in the sawdust.

. . . It was declared last night that members of the Humane Society would take action against the owners of the Wild West show in an effort to prevent a similar accident.[27]

A judge ultimately dismissed the charges against Lucille, but public opinion had turned against her. The incident wounded her reputation and promoted a state law against steer roping in Illinois.[28]

Hoping to distance herself from the bad publicity, Lucille abandoned her program and joined a troupe called California Frank's All Star Wild West Show. By 1911, she no longer spent any time with her husband or son. William grew up knowing little about his mother. Martin had held out hope that Lucille's devotion would shift from rodeo life to domestic life, but it never happened. In fact, while with California Frank's troupe, Lucille became romantically involved with an accomplished cowboy named Homer Wilson. Martin filed for divorce on March 28, 1914.

"Martin Van Bergen, baritone, and formerly a cowboy, has filed suit in Johnson County, Kansas, for a divorce from Lucille Mulhall (Van Bergen) charging desertion, and also naming Homer Wilson in other serious charges," an article in the March 31, 1914, edition of the *Manitoba Free*

Press noted. "Mr. Van Bergen asks for custody of their son, William Logan Van Bergen, five years of age, living with his grandmother in Kansas.[29] The petition alleges that Miss Mulhall deserted the defendant over a year ago and has since been traveling about the country with a Wild West show in the company of Homer Wilson."[30]

Between theater engagements that same month, Lucille entered a roping contest in Walla Walla, Washington. She was twenty-eight years old and still quick with a lariat. Her best steer roping time was thirty-three seconds.

By 1916, Lucille had graduated from being strictly a performer to producing her own Wild West show. She was business partners with Homer Wilson in producing the first indoor rodeo at the coliseum building in Fort Worth, Texas. Lucille was the first female producer of Wild West shows.

Her popularity was on the rise, but it slowed again when World War I sidetracked the nation. Still, Lucille continued to perform in rodeos and showed no sign of wanting to give up her profession, even if audience numbers weren't as high as they once had been.[31]

In 1919, she married a prominent cattleman and oilman, Thomas L. Burnett. She proved to be no better a wife the second time around, choosing again to travel with a rodeo she managed. Burnett filed for divorce two years later. The reason cited for the action was listed as "incompatibility." When their divorce was finalized in May 1922, she received $200,000 in cash and deeds to about five thousand acres of Texas land.[32]

From 1920 to 1930, Lucille continued to perform in both her own vaudeville productions and with established troupes like the Miller Brothers 101 Ranch Wild West Show and the Passing of the West program.[33]

Then in 1932, Lucille suffered several devastating blows. Her beloved parents died within less than a year of each other, and the Great Depression depleted the resources of the family ranch. Brokenhearted and in poor health, Lucille found herself living in poverty and turned to alcohol for solace. By the spring of 1935, she had pulled herself together and accepted an offer from her hometown of Guthrie, Oklahoma, to lead its annual Frontier Celebration Day parade. An excerpt from local newspaper reporter Noel Houston's column described the aging cowgirl's return to the saddle:

> *Once she was a vivacious, devil-may-care blonde in a divided skirt and white silk shirt as she passed in review before kings, presidents, and worshipping throngs. The thoughtless observer might see her now as only a gray, time-penciled old woman. But as she rode at the head of the frontier celebration in her traditional costume—beaded jacket over white silk waist, red corduroy skirt draping below her boot tops—Miss Mulhall was beautiful to me.*[34]

Encouraged by the crowd's response to her parade appearance, Lucille agreed to join her brother's Wild West show. Now fifty years old, she participated only in special acts and didn't take part in the rodeos as a contestant. With her life and career back on track, she worked steadily, entertaining audiences and training horses. After more than forty years in the saddle, she was one of the most revered and fearless horsewomen in the world.[35]

On December 21, 1940, Lucille was on her way back to the family ranch when a truck broadsided the car she was riding in, killing her instantly. On a cold, rainy day, she was laid to rest alongside her parents. Few attended her graveside funeral. A notice in the December 27, 1940, edition of the *Daily Oklahoman* newspaper described the sad, somewhat ironic scene. "A machine killed Lucille Mulhall, but horses brought her to her final resting place," the article read. "So deep was the mud and so slippery the road, that a neighbor's plow horse had to pull the hearse from the highway to near the house, and the car bearing the relatives had to be pulled back to the highway after the service."[36]

Lulu Belle Parr

Lulu is riding bucking horses with the 101 Ranch this season. Lulu and her accomplishments are too well known to the Billboard *readers for me to go into details any further than to say she still has her swell wardrobe and is "Wild Westy" as ever.*

—*Billboard*, July 20, 1912

An angry chestnut mare dashed out of the wire enclosure, bucking and twisting. The rider on its back gripped the reins with all her strength. The horse pitched, whirled, and kicked in an attempt to eject the passenger. Lulu Belle Parr, the tenacious cowgirl atop the animal, held on tightly, determined not to be thrown. Despite the bucker's best efforts, Lulu stayed put. The audience watching from the stands surrounding the rodeo arena in Harrisburg, Pennsylvania, erupted with applause. Lulu's strength, skill, and grip of iron in her thighs kept her in place, and the spectators were impressed with her persistence. Rides such as that had earned her the title Wild West show promoters bestowed upon her: "Champion Lady Bucking Horse Rider of the World."[1]

Her parents, William James Parr and Elizabeth Myers Parr, were reportedly homesteaders who worked the land in locations from Indiana to Ohio. In 1881, the Parrs moved to Springfield, Illinois, where Lulu and her brother Willie attended Lincoln Elementary School. She preferred riding her horse to school instead of walking.[2]

During a visit to her Uncle William Sheehan's home in Steubenville, Ohio as a teen, Lulu met and became romantically involved with a farmer

Buffalo Bill's Wild West Show performer Lulu Bell Parr COURTESY OKLAHOMA HISTORICAL SOCIETY named Frank Wheaton who was her third cousin. They planned to marry, until Lulu's parents objected. When Lulu called off the wedding, Wheaton became furious and brought a lawsuit against her to recover items he had given her in anticipation of their marriage. Among the things Wheaton wanted returned were parlor furniture and a watch. The jury that heard the case determined that Lulu "should keep the presents."[3]

Not long after the court case concluded, Lulu met twenty-two-year-old George Barrett of Jefferson County, Ohio. Barrett was a machinist or stationary engineer who maintained motors, boilers, turbines, and ventilators. The pair was married on March 31, 1896. For most of their marriage, he was abusive and frequently in trouble with the law. After six years, Lulu filed for divorce, citing extreme cruelty.[4]

The one constant in Lulu's life, since childhood, was horses. She owned more than five horses when she was married to Barrett and rode as often as she could.[5]

At twenty-seven years old, Lulu decided to pursue the life she'd been considering for several years. She wanted to use her love of horses and ride in traveling Wild West shows. In 1903, Lulu joined Pawnee Bill's Wild West Show. Because she was just starting out as a rodeo entertainer, she was simply one of the "congress of players" in the program.

An ad in the May 3, 1903, edition of the *Pittsburgh Press* explained what the cast of Pawnee Bill's production, which now included Lulu, would bring to audiences everywhere: "No country is too far away, none too inaccessible to the energies of the many agents who annually gather this strange ethnological congress together to tour our vast country. There are hundreds of them, and, coming as they do from many lands and various races, are an instructive feature and a marvel of perfect harmony. Pawnee Bill has been blessed with perspicuity to a lavish degree, and many reckon his show as the largest in America, and over a thousand men and hundreds of horses are actually seen in his grand historic Wild West exhibition."[6]

Before long, Lulu was featured as one of the top cowgirl acts in Pawnee Bill's show. Her specialty was riding bucking broncos. Lulu was grateful for the chance to work with the show's cast of skilled riders and performers from across the nation. The majority of her castmates were friendly and willing to share their knowledge of horseflesh with other entertainers. However, there were instances when the tension between the cowboys and cowgirls and the Russian Cossacks who rode in the show erupted into physical altercations. Such was the case in New York, mid-June 1906, when Lulu was injured in one of those disputes.[7]

An article in the June 24, 1906, edition of the *Standard Union* read:

> *There is no feeling of friendship existing between the cowboys and the Cossacks with the Pawnee Bill show at Brighton Beach Park. Both are excellent riders, and while the cowboys are not in the least jealous of the Cossacks, they don't like the way they try to run things around the show. They are overbearing and never lose an opportunity to try to impress the other members of the company with their importance. When riding out of the arena they do so with a careless dash regardless of whom may be standing in the dressing tent waiting to go on.*[8]
>
> *During a recent performance, Lulu Parr, one of the cowgirls, was standing in one of the rock-concealed entrances, waiting to go on as the Cossacks finished their act. Prince Lucca was in the lead of the Cossacks. Seeing Miss Parr, he swung his horse to one side to avoid her. All but the last two of the Cossacks followed him. These deliberately rode her down. The leading horse struck her full in the chest, knocking her down, and the second horse trampled on her, bruising her body and arms, and inflicting an ugly cut on her forehead.*[9]
>
> *Captain Jack Lear, of the Rough Riders, saw the occurrence and started after the Cossacks. As he passed the cowboys' quarters, he told them what had happened. Del Champion and Mamie Skeeper, two of the cowgirls, hurried to Miss Parr's assistance, while the cowboys took after the Cossacks. They had probably anticipated the coming of the cowboys and were bunched up with their ugly, heavy Russian swords drawn. They are experts with these nasty weapons, and the cowboys hesitated, but, for a moment. They rode down the Cossacks, knocking them right and left, and, before the latter could reach their horses, the cowboys had them on the ground and beat them unmercifully.*[10]
>
> *The Cossacks do not know how to use their fists nor defend themselves in a fistfight. They could only but shout for help as the cowboys*

rained blow after blow on their faces and bodies. Miss Parr recovered sufficiently to be in at the finish and with her riding whip avenged the wrong the Cossacks had done her.[11]

In June 1908, Lulu was asked to join Colonel Cummins' Wild West Indian Congress and Rough Riders of the World, traveling to England to perform at the New Brighton Tower Gardens. Among those who came to see her ride was King Edward VII. When she returned to the United States, the Wild West show was scheduled to appear in Steubenville, Ohio. Lulu was anxious to let those in the town where she'd lived for so many years see that she'd made good. With that in mind, she made a grant entrance riding her horse from Philadelphia, where Colonel Cummins's show was based, to Steubenville. The stunt made the front page of newspapers from New Jersey to Montana.[12]

According to the November 30, 1908, edition of the *Salt Lake Herald-Republican*, Lulu was to be in Ohio by early December. She would have arrived sooner, but inclement weather detained her. "It is a good six hundred miles from Philadelphia to Steubenville, although the roads are good during the entire distance," the article read. "She has several wagers with friends who have bet that she will abandon the pony before she gets home and finishes the journey by rail."

Lulu completed the trip on horseback with never a thought of giving up.[13]

Between 1909 and 1910, Lulu appeared in a variety of shows for the 101 Ranch Wild West program. She was honored to be part of the Oklahoma-based operation, and, when word reached the press that the "Champion Girl Bronc Buster" would be featured in the May 1910 Brooklyn show, reporters hurried to interview the cowgirl.[14]

"'The best fun in the world is to ride a bucking horse,' she assured the correspondent from the *Brooklyn Citizen* newspaper. 'It offers more fun than any pink tea or theatre party or tennis game ever yielded.' That is the promise given to her sisters in the city by Lulu B. Parr, whose home is the 100,000-acre tract of Oklahoma prairie comprising the famous 101 Ranch. Miss Parr is one of the groups of rollicking girl broncho "busters" who will be in this city all next week. She ropes, mounts, and subdues equine outlaws which even the lusty cowboys of the ranch hesitate to approach. She can shoot as quick and straight as the masculine adept and makes a lariat act as if endowed with reason.[15]

"The woman who rides, but who is not intimately familiar with equine species, does not appreciate that she [Lulu] is in as much danger on the back of an impetuous, spirited thoroughbred as in the saddle of a bucker. 'It is impossible ever to thoroughly tame the spirit of the thoroughbred,' Miss Parr shared. 'He may break out at any moment and at any place. Give me the avowedly outlaw horse every time rather than the thoroughbred who is docile one moment and a demand the next.'

"Lulu Parr has as much fun riding a bucker as the audience does watching her ride."[16]

When Lulu received an invitation from Buffalo Bill Cody to join his Wild West show in late 1910, she didn't hesitate. Cody was a legend, and his show was the first of the Wild West programs introduced to the American public. Lulu was associated with a variety of Wild West shows between 1911 and 1913. She rode for the 101 Ranch, for Buffalo Bill Cody, and for Cowboy Billie Burke's show. Cody's show was the most prestigious and well known of all the Wild West shows. One of the first locations she performed with his show was Waterloo, Iowa. The local paper covered the event, focusing on Lulu and how she was related to the famous showman. Much of the article was filled with misinformation that was later used by the Cody show to promote the lady bronc rider.[17]

"The presence in Waterloo yesterday of Wm. F. Cody, 'Buffalo Bill,' was of special interest to Mrs. George H. Myers, 622 Fowler Street, as the noted showman is a relative of hers, having married her mother's cousin," the August 11, 1911, edition of the *Courier* noted. "Her niece, Miss Lulu Parr, also a relative of Mr. Cody, is with the company.[18]

"Miss Parr was entertained at the Myers home for dinner last evening, but Mr. Cody was unable to come as he was busy at the grounds. Mrs. Myers had a good visit with him in his private tent earlier in the day, and the family all attended the performance.[19]

"Miss Parr, who rides the broncos and is the lead in the military tournament in the grand opening, has been with Buffalo Bill for twenty years, having started to travel with him when she was only eight years old.

She came from wealthy parentage but, being left an orphan in childhood, accepted the offer of her relative for a place in his show.

"Miss Parr's home was formerly in Canton, Ohio. She is a pretty, young woman, very intelligent and attractive. She is the last of her family as her parents, grandparents, brothers, and sisters are all dead.[20]

"When Mr. Cody, who is now 73 years old, completes this tour, which is his last, he will retire to his ranch near North Platte, Nebraska. At the same time, Miss Parr will retire from public life and will engage in business for herself, her intention being to open a store near her uncle's ranch."[21]

The press agent with the 101 Ranch Wild West show had his own way of promoting Lulu Parr's talent by calling her "one of the most daring and fearless riders with the company." An article that ran in the July 27, 1912, edition of the *Evening Times Republican,* and several other newspapers at the same time, was about Lulu's skill in the saddle. It was written by 101 Ranch promoter and cowboy Charles Mulhall:[22]

"Lulu Parr, one of the most daring of the intrepid girls who have won distinction as fearless riders, dauntless hunters, and skillful manipulators of the lariat, is to the manner born, for much of her life has been spent on a ranch, and the range life appeals to her as the only one that is really worthwhile," the *Evening Times Republican* story read. "At first sight, Miss Parr does not suggest the rough, often dangerous life of the range. She is physically made in a mold that suggests daintiness. Paquin gowns and society functions among the ultra-fashionable. As a matter of fact, these things do not appeal to her at all. The restrictions of the evening gown train and the bright lights of the society ball do not allure her in the least. Her greatest pleasure is derived in the saddle, dashing across the prairie on a wild, half-tamed pony, or mingling with the cowboys and doing her part in a thrilling and often dangerously exciting roundup.[23]

"Many times, both on the cattle range and in the 101 Ranch show, Miss Parr has flirted with death and narrowly escaped being a victim of her own daring. Last spring in Philadelphia, when dared to ride a vicious Indian pony which had injured several cowboys, she made the attempt and would have achieved an immediate victory if her saddle girth had not broken and precipitated her to the ground. Although momentarily stunned and painfully injured, she attempted the feat the following day and succeeded in thoroughly taming the 'outlaw.' It was for this victory that Miss Parr received the gold medal which she wears, and which was presented to her by the management of the cowboys as an acknowledgment of her cleverness and intrepidity."[24]

Charles Mulhall, brother to the first "cowgirl" Lucille Mulhall, found Lulu to be everything he noted in the promotional material and more. He fell in love with her, and the two were married in St. Louis, Missouri, on October 25, 1913. But then three days after the ceremony, Charles abandoned his new wife. Lulu filed for divorce on November 23, 1914, and the grounds for the action was listed as desertion.[25]

Lulu's personal problems did not keep her from continuing with her responsibilities as the world's champion woman bucking horse rider. In January 1914, she traveled with Colonel Cummins's show to South America. According to the February 21, 1914, edition of *Billboard Magazine,* Lulu made quite an impression on audiences in Buenos Aires, including the onetime president of Argentina, Dr. Jose Figueroa Alcorta. The politician showered her with gifts.[26]

When Lulu returned to the United States, she agreed to perform with the Barnum & Bailey Circus. She entertained ticket buyers in New York, Philadelphia, and several other locations throughout the year. During a show in Spokane, Washington, in August 1914, Lulu was thrown from her horse and sustained serious injuries. She wrote one of her relatives about the incident, describing in detail what happened. The letter was written on stationery specifically designed for her by the 101 Ranch Wild West Show staff. It featured an image of Lulu on a horse in the top left corner. The right corner included a list of other shows with which she was associated: Pawnee Bill's Wild West, Buffalo Bill's Wild West, and Colonel F. T. Cummins-Brighten Tours.[27]

"My Dear Ralph," her letter dated August 12, 1914, began, "Just a few lines to let you know I am still alive but came near to being sent home to you already for burial. My bucking horse was bucking down the line fine, his head between the fences. I had taken off my big black Mexican hat, and it spooked him. The horse slipped and turned a complete somersault over me. I doubled up in a ball and went under him for he went so quickly. I had no choice to jump—broke my arm—out my eye—doctor took stitches in it—hurt the top of my skull. I am bruised, and there is no feeling on one side of my head. My back cracked as he went over me, and I thought it was broke [*sic*]. He rolled over, and I rolled away for fear he would fall back on me.[28]

"I jumped up, run out with blood flowing down my face. Doctor sewed my face up, splinted my arm or done it up in boards and splints and bandages, and I am wearing big smoked glasses to protect the sight now and cover up those big, bruised eyes. I am a sight but glad I came out so lucky.

"Inclosed [*sic*] you a note card. Write me soon. Love to you and Aunt Mag. . . . Hope the time will soon fly away, and I will see you again soon. I will soon be all right again, and I get my money every week. Well, you never go till God calls you."[29]

Not satisfied with simply being billed as the "Champion Girl Bronco Buster in Wild West Shows," Lulu wanted to make the title official. In May 1915, she decided to register to take part in the World's Champion Bucking Contest at the Frontier Days Rodeo in Prescott, Arizona. She was informed by the rodeo director that there were no contests in the category of lady bucking horse riders but that she was welcome to compete against the men in that area if she so chose. Lulu's name was not listed among those in the event; she must have declined.[30]

Lulu returned to the Wild West shows and worked hard to prove she was worthy of being called a champion in her field. She took part in bronco busting contests in Cheyenne, Wyoming, and earned a number of first-prize medals.[31]

There was always a risk of injury when busting broncs, and Lulu had her fair share of injuries riding wild horses. In May 1915, at Pawnee Bill's Pioneer Days in Ohio, she suffered dislocated bones in her right knee when a bucking bronco fell on her. She was rendered unconscious for more than thirty minutes and, when she came to, she returned to the arena, got back into the saddle, and participated in the quadrille on horseback.

"The immense crowd cheered her daring," an article in the May 26, 1915, edition of the *Weekly-Journal-Miner*, reported. "The local physician who attended her after her injury told news reporters that the injury was of such a nature that she should not ride again for two or three weeks but, with her customary nerve and endurance, she insisted on mounting her horse and taking part in the program."[32]

Lulu's persistence extended to marriage, as well, which she gave a third try—marrying a sailor named Orth B. Barcus on November 14, 1917 in Washington, D.C. The time the pair spent apart working their respective jobs took a toll on their marriage and, less than three years later, they were divorced—to Lulu's surprise.[33]

"Dear Mother, I did not know Orth got a divorce from me," she confessed in a letter home. "I have never received any notification. I am indeed sorry to [*sic*] for I loved Orth, but if he has secured a divorce and don't care to live with me, of course I would not force him to live with me against his will. Nevertheless, I love him as well and ever more now but would like to have notification of the divorce and on what grounds I am sued, and I will never trouble him again with any correspondence. I never got a divorce, and I never will. . . . Pray for me, mother."[34]

Throughout the course of her career, Lulu distinguished herself not only with her riding style, but also with her manner of dress. From the broad-brimmed sombreros to the multi-laced riding boots, her look was unique to her personality. The April 1921 edition of *Billboard Magazine* noted Lulu was one of the "swellest dressed ladies in the Wild West game."[35] An article in the October 20, 1925, edition of the *Florence Morning News* echoed the sentiment, adding that few riders had such a stunning wardrobe or could look as good as Miss Parr in the garb. "She is the best dressed of all the cowgirls and girl riders with Miller Brothers 101 Ranch Real Wild West Show."[36]

The same month Lulu was being applauded for being such a well-dressed rodeo star, she married Tracy Thomas Andrews, a bull rider with the Cook Brothers Texas Ranch Show. They exchanged vows on October 31, 1925 in Newton, Iowa. This marriage, too, was short-lived.[37]

In the mid-1920s, Lulu performed in a variety of new Wild West shows traversing the United States. In 1926, she rode with the Mammoth Robbins Brothers Big Four-Ring Circus. An article in the July 4, 1926, edition of the *La Crosse Tribune* announced to the residents in La Crosse, Wisconsin, of her coming:

In the Wild West division is Miss Lulu B. Parr of London, England, of Paris, and other European continental places. She is a native of Oklahoma and will appear here and perform her thrilling act. She has appeared in most of the foreign countries as a bronco busting cowgirl rider. Only recently she appeared at the Intercolonial Empire Exposition before the prince of Wales. Later she appeared in the American Rodeo at Paris, France.[38]

She rides outlaw horses, does anything a man can do astride a cantankerous mustang, and has thrown more wild-eyed mavericks than the oldest "high-jacking," "hye-there" bronco buster to be found from the plaza of El Paso to the plains of Moosejaw. She is simply "it" when it comes to sailing along on the back of a horse. She appears in the Robbins Bros. Circus during the main performance and is an attractive figure at all times.[39]

The following year, Lulu was working for the Hagenbeck-Wallace Circus entertaining audiences in Dover, New Jersey. Among the other women representing the Wild West contingent in late May 1927 were trick riders Julie Rinehart and Hazel Hickey. Lulu was billed as "Ex-Woman Champion Bronc Buster and Bucking Horse Rider."[40]

In 1929, Lulu was still appearing in a number of Wild West shows, including King Brothers Rodeo run by Colonel Jack King. Prominent Westerners appearing under the King banner in addition to Lulu were Vivian Delmore, "Wild Cy" Perkins, Tommy Cropper, Jimmy Carson, and Tom Howard. The show included more than fifty riders, both men and women, twenty-five Sioux Indians, and more than a hundred head of stock.[41]

The Robbins Brothers Circus set up its tents in Dodge City, Kansas, on Wednesday, September 18, 1929, and Lulu was listed as one of the stars of the show. An article in the *Dodge City Journal* mentioned how excited residents were to have Lulu visit their town. "She stands without a peer and is the highest salaried rider known to the profession," the newspaper reported.[42]

Throughout the 1930s, Lulu continued to travel the country performing in any Wild West show or circus that invited her. She was in her fifties and still riding unmanageable horses that most men wouldn't dare tackle, and she survived bucking tactics without being displaced from the saddle.[43]

The May 17, 1938, edition of the *Gazette and Daily* reported that Lulu had retired to a ranch she owned in Nebraska. The story was only partially correct. She had retired but was living in Riverside, Ohio, with her brother William and sister-in-law Emma. Lulu might have been the "highest salaried rider," but she had little to show for her years as a bronc buster once her career ended. William and Emma were struggling financially as well. The three lived in a small tar-paper cabin with no water or electricity. Food was scarce, and either Lulu or William made frequent trips to the gas station across the street from their home to use the restroom and transport buckets of water back for cooking and bathing.[44]

Lulu's living conditions were not reflected in her disposition, though. She always had a kind word for neighbors and was happy to share stories about her days with the Wild West shows. She was seventy-seven when a burglar attempted to break into her feeble home and steal the belongings she had acquired while performing. Lulu leveled a gun at the thief as he entered, and he ran off before a shot was fired.[45]

On January 17, 1955, Lulu was transported to the Miami Valley Hospital in Dayton, Ohio, after neighbors called for help. Lulu was suffering from malnutrition and had suffered a stroke. Her sister-in-law, who was also ill, was taken to the hospital at the same time. Lulu died sixteen hours after being admitted.[46]

In the cabin where she had lived, trunks and cartons of memorabilia collected throughout her time on the rodeo circuit were piled ceiling-high. Among those items were costumes, hats, fancy cowgirl belts, and a pair of .45-caliber Colt pistols given to her by Buffalo Bill Cody back in the days she worked for him.[47]

Lulu Parr died on January 17, 1955 at the age of seventy-eight. Her death certificate listed her occupation as "housewife." She was buried in an unmarked grave in the Medway Cemetery in Clark County, Ohio.[48]

May Manning Lillie

Another feature worthy of special mention was the fancy rifle shooting of May Lillie. . . . She is young in years and with her large lustrous eyes and regular, sun-browned features, is very prepossessing, so that when she splits and cracked, or shivered in success with great skill and dexterity, the black glass balls thrown into the air by a seemingly careless cowboy, she commanded the encomiums of the spectators, and retired amid much applause.

—*The Tribune*, September 21, 1888

A bespectacled photographer emerged from under a black curtain draped over a massive camera and tripod. In his right hand he held an instrument that, when pressed, would take a picture. In his left hand he held a flash attachment to illuminate his subject. "On the count of three, Mrs. Lillie," he warned.

May Manning Lillie stared directly into the lens, her cowboy hat cocked on her head. She had a red kerchief tied around the neck of her white peasant blouse, a black split skirt belted around her waist, and leather gauntlets covering her hands. She wore a serious expression as the photographer began counting. Before he got to two, she raised a six-shooter and pointed it at the camera. One eye was closed, and the other looked down the barrel of the gun. Ka-Poof! The flash attachment fired, and smoke wafted into the air. "Perfect," the photographer said, smiling. And it was. The black-and-white image of cowgirl May demonstrating her skill as a marksman became one of the most widely publicized Wild West posters in the early 1900s.

May Manning Lillie COURTESY OKLAHOMA HISTORICAL SOCIETY

May's life as a trick rider and shooter in Wild West shows was far from the lifestyle in which she was raised. She was born in March 1869 in Philadelphia, to Dr. William R. Manning, a prominent physician, and his wife and aide Mary. Quakers, were quiet, unassuming people, reluctant to draw attention to themselves. If not for a chance meeting with frontiersman and performer Gordon William Lillie at a Buffalo Bill Cody Wild West Show in Philadelphia in 1885, May might have married a modest man from her faith, never venturing far from her birthplace. Lillie, better known as Pawnee Bill, was a twenty-six-year-old Pawnee Indian interpreter who was smitten with May the moment he saw her.[1]

"I was standing on the show grounds in front of the main tent when May came by," Lillie later recalled in his memoirs. "She was a schoolgirl then and carried her books under her arm. I thought I noticed her smile, and I turned and tipped my hat. She thought I was funny with my long hair, sombrero, and buckskin clothes, and just laughed out loud."[2]

May attended Cody's Wild West Show with her sister and her niece. Lillie sent a note to May letting her know he'd like to meet her. The two formally introduced themselves to one another after the program concluded. Lillie learned that seventeen-year-old May was studying to earn a Bachelor of Arts degree, and May learned Lillie was a former teacher and Commissioner of Indian Affairs. "It was love at first sight and I knew she was the girl for me," Lillie noted in his memoirs.[3]

May's parents were immune to Lillie's charms, at least at first. He walked May home the night they met, and it was only after they arrived at the Mannings' house that he realized the doctor and his wife were hosting a dinner party. May's mother and father were not pleased that their daughter had brought home a cowboy. Lillie tried to fit in and spent time talking with the guests about the West. Most had the impression that Native Americans were wandering the frontier, massacring white settlers. Lillie gently explained they were wrong and briefly shared what he knew of the Indians' plight. But he forgot to exercise good manners during the exchange and spit on the floor. May's father and mother were mortified by his behavior and urged her to see Lillie out of their house.[4]

When May returned to high school and Lillie to the Wild West show, they wrote one another often. A year after their first meeting, Lillie confessed his love for her and proposed. May graduated in the spring of 1886, and she and Lille married on August 31 of that same year. Lillie had assured Dr. Manning he would provide for his daughter with the earnings he made performing in the Wild West shows and from his cattle ranch in Kansas. Despite Lillie's long hair and strange buckskin-fringed clothing, which was another source of concern for the Mannings, the doctor and Mary gave the union their blessing. The Mannings arranged the ceremony, attended by numerous friends and family. The September 1, 1886, edition of the *Evening Telegram* reported that "a Quaker girl in pigtails was given in marriage, at Siloam Church to Gordon W. Lillie, of the plains country."[5]

Not long after the ceremony, the newlyweds boarded a train bound for their ranch in Wellington, Kansas. At first, May was apprehensive about the move. She'd never been West and worried she'd have a hard time adjusting to her new home. Sensing her concern, Lillie telegraphed his friends when to expect them and to make their arrival something special for his bride. According to Lillie's memoirs, "Fifty or sixty gentlemen and ladies turned out with a band to receive us and gave us a serenade." Lillie's sister held a reception for the newlyweds to celebrate their marriage and to introduce May to the family and townspeople.[6]

May was happy to be married to Lillie, and, although everyone went out of their way to make her feel welcome, she didn't feel she belonged on a ranch. Lillie traveled a great deal with the Wild West show, and May was left alone. She found work at the local bank and kept herself busy decorating their home, but she still felt homesick. In October 1886, she learned she was going to have a baby. Planning for the new arrival helped alleviate the loneliness, but the tragic event that would change her life was not far off.[7]

"In the natural course of events, a baby boy came to us in June 1887," May wrote in her journal. "Gordon was away. Babies were important only to the immediate parties most concerned in those days, so a country midwife was the only hope and consolation at the blessed event.[8] I was proud of my ten-and-a-half-pound son, and, when Gordon rushed home to see us three days after his birth, I foolishly arose from my bed to greet the proud father. The consequences of that rash act were terrible. To add to my suffering, our son lived only six weeks. A serious operation was necessary for me to correct complications which caused recurring illness."[9]

The surgical procedure May underwent left her unable to have any more children. She was devastated and, for several weeks, was too despondent to leave the house. From her bedroom window, she sat and watched the daily activities at the ranch. Oddly enough, it eventually provided her with the inspiration to move beyond the sorrow and find a reason to go on.[10]

When May finally felt well enough to leave her home, she made her way to the paddock to visit with the cowboys breaking horses on her husband's ranch. Lillie and the ranch hands taught May how to ride and to shoot. "She cultivated a taste for the rifle," Lillie wrote in his memoirs, "and at her first shooting match carried off the laurels by missing the object not a single time."

May practiced her newfound talent constantly. By the fall of 1887, she had joined Lillie on the road and became part of the Wild West show. The September 16, 1887, edition of the *Peabody Weekly Republican* reported on one of May's first performances. "Pawnee Bill and his famous Indian scouts and cowboys were, undoubtedly, the drawing cards this season," the article began. "Mr. G. William Lillie is the United States of Pawnee Bill's name, and the daring lady equestrienne rifle shot and heroine of the plains—May Lillie—was introduced to us as his wife. We found her to be all that is advertised on the bills and a perfect lady besides, educated and refined."[11]

May charmed crowds and the press in every city where she appeared. An article in the December 10, 1887, edition of the *Boston Journal* expressed the depth of feeling for the budding equestrienne and performer:

> *She took to them [cattle and horses] as most girls gravitate to ballrooms and pink teas. When her classmates were debutantes, entering upon the social whirl of conventional life, she was learning the tricks of the lariat. While they were making conquests of city hearts, she was roping steers and studying the art of remaining comfortable on the hurricane deck of a bucking mustang. Her recitals and soirees became target matches with the rifle and six-shooter. She brought the entire*

> *culture of the East into the cow camps of the West, and she exchanged her beneficent influence for the skill of her new companions.*[12]

The Pawnee Indians who lived near the ranch where the Lillies lived were also impressed with May's riding ability. To show their admiration for her skill and kindness to them, they gifted her with a colt she named Hunter. Hunter and May were inseparable. She rode him to an exhibition at the Pennsylvania State Rifle Range on November 12, 1887. In addition to demonstrating how well Hunter could perform various tricks, May participated in the shooting competition. The months of practice she put in paid off in a big way. Shooting at two hundred yards, she scored twenty-four points out of a possible twenty-five. It was the best score ever made by a woman at that distance. May was presented with a gold medal inscribed, "Presented to May Lillie Champion Girl Shot of the West."[13]

In the spring of 1888, Lillie organized his own Wild West program and made May one of the stars of the show. She continued to be well received by audiences. Newspaper reviews of her performances called the feisty equestrienne the "Princess of the Prairie." Her proficiency with a rifle earned her the additional title of the "New Rifle Queen." People who flocked to Pawnee Bill's Historical Wild West Show to see May were never disappointed. "Her work with the rifle is extraordinary," an article in the August 7, 1889, edition of the *Ashland Weekly News* read. "She is the only woman in the world able to break targets thrown in the air while riding at full speed on her mustang."[14]

The Lillies toured the United States and Europe for more than twenty years, performing for audiences of all types, including politicians and royalty. "It is remarkable that May Manning Lillie, bride, learned the show business, became an expert rifle shot, and was known as a champion horseback rider and marksman, one of the features of the show," an article in the January 15, 1928, edition of the *Oakland Tribune* read. "She is known throughout America for her skill as an expert shot and was one of the chief attractions with her husband's show, and later the combined shows of Buffalo Bill and Pawnee Bill. When not on the road, the Lillies make their home at Blue Hawk Peak, near the town of Pawnee, Oklahoma."[15]

Pawnee Bill's Wild West Show was a triumph in every respect, especially financially. May was not only responsible for the success of the show as a performer—she also contributed to its success behind the scenes. With May's exceptional business and money management skills, the couple was able to invest in many profitable ventures, including a two-thousand-acre buffalo sanctuary in southwest Oklahoma. But the couple didn't agree on every investment, particularly one Lillie made on his own in 1908. He purchased interest in Buffalo Bill Cody's Wild West Show from James Bailey of Barnum & Bailey fame. Lillie and Cody then decided to merge their popular programs and renamed the western exhibition Buffalo Bill's Wild West and Pawnee Bill's Great Far East. May was against the merger, believing Cody to be a poor businessman. She felt he overspent on everything for his shows.[16]

Throughout the many years May performed with the Wild West shows, the public remained fascinated with her daring accomplishments. Women wanted to know about her upbringing, her life as an equestrienne celebrity, and what advice she might have for those with a desire to be a trick rider and shooter. May addressed all those queries in an interview with the *Joliet News* on June 16, 1907. The publicist working for the Lillie's Wild West Show embellished May's background and her answers to the press.

"Miss Lillie was born in the East but, when still a child, went West with her parents and remained there until budding womanhood, when she returned East to complete her education," the article read. "While her European experience in school served to polish off the rough edges of Western life, it did not remove the self-reliance and confidence acquired in her Western home. Her early love for horses and horseback riding remained. The time that other women give to household and social affairs, Miss Lillie devoted to her horse, and her happiest hours were spent in the saddle. She never was happier than when off for a twenty-mile dash across the prairie or assisting in a roundup of cattle. She has roped and broke horses that men of greater experience would hesitate to approach.[17]

"She adds to her native talent, courage, determination, and love of her art, and endows her public performances with charming grace and finish of manner, movement, and method. Her equestrienne accomplishments range from simple to complex and from artistic and polite to intrepidly rough. No equine spirit is too wild or purpose too savage for her to quench and rule. She is an equestrienne empress whose throne is in her saddle and whose four-footed subjects are her devoted pride.[18]

"The apotheosis of high school revelations is seen in Miss Lillie's quartet of prize-winning steeds. Guided solely by the voice and gesture of their fair trainer, they executed a multiplicity of exacting feats that illustrate the extreme possibilities in equine expositions. Beyond this extraordinary performance it is impossible to go."[19]

According to May, "Let any normally healthy woman who is ordinarily strong screw up her courage and tackle a bucking bronco, and she will find the most fascinating pastime in the field of feminine athletic endeavor. There is nothing to compare to increase the joy of living, and, once accomplished, she'll have more real fun than any pink tea or theatre party or ballroom ever yielded."[20]

May retired from Lillie's Wild West show with Cody in the mid-1910s. She decided to shift her focus from performing to growing the buffalo ranch that she and Lillie had purchased on Blue Hawk Peak in Pawnee, Oklahoma. Despite her protests, May was never completely removed from the "Two Bills" program. Photographs of her graced playbills and posters exhibited throughout the West. In addition to overseeing the daily operations at the ranch, May became active in church and community services, including the National Women's Relief Corp and Auxiliary to the Grand Army of the Republic.[21]

In December 1916, May and Lillie traveled to Kansas City to adopt a baby boy they named Billy. Sadly, the boy died in a tragic accident at the ranch in 1925. May fought through the devastating loss by caring for the buffalo and other livestock.[22]

On August 31, 1936, May and Lillie celebrated their fiftieth wedding anniversary. To commemorate the special event, the couple decided to renew their vows. The special event was held in Taos, New Mexico. More than five hundred guests and spectators attended the ceremony.

"Pawnee Bill, the Indian scout and showman, wore the same buckskin suit he wore at the first marriage, but his wife dressed in an Alice blue gown of lace, with turban to match and silver slippers," the August

31, 1936, edition of the *El Reno Daily Tribune* read. "Preceding the ceremony on the plaza of old Taos, a tribe of Indians from a nearby reservation, twelve flower girls in Spanish attire, and scores of tourists assembled. Lillie recalled his long and nearly frustrated romance with the daughter of stern Quaker parents in Pennsylvania.[23]

"They met on a sidewalk in front of a theatre in Philadelphia where Pawnee Bill was appearing in the Wild West show headed by William F. Buffalo Bill Cody. Their first reaction, Lillie said, was that each looked twice. 'I thought she was the prettiest girl I ever saw, and I haven't changed my thought,' the white-haired Indian fighter said. 'My first thought when I saw Pawnee Bill,' Mrs. Lillie remarked, 'was what a funny man.' Lillie coughed and glowered at his aged wife, then said he was 'sorry I taught May so much about shooting irons.'"[24]

Less than two weeks after the golden wedding anniversary celebration, Lillie and May were driving back to their home in Oklahoma when they were involved in a head-on collision. They were both seriously injured, and May's injuries proved fatal.[25] She was sixty-seven.

May Manning Lillie was laid to rest at the Highland Cemetery in the Pawnee Indian hills of Pawnee, Oklahoma. But her memory lives on in the popular photograph she posed for when she was best known as the New Rifle Queen.[26]

Bertha Kaepernik Blanchett

I have ridden some of the worst outlaw horses in the West, such as Dynamite, Carrie Nation, Johnny-on-the-Spot, Tombstone, and Black Beauty. Any bronc buster will tell you what it means to ride those horses. How the crowd loves it, too.

—Bertha Kaepernik, 1906

It was said of cowgirl Bertha Kaepernik Blanchett that "she rode the worst of the animals with the best of men." Crowned the Champion Lady Rough Rider of the World in the summer of 1905, she earned the title by subduing bucking terrors that many cowboys refused to ride.[1]

In 1905, she demonstrated her much talked about ability to handle wild broncos at the rodeo arena in Cheyenne, Wyoming. The large crowd groaned, watching the fashionably dressed equestrian being thrown from the back of a big, gray horse. She picked herself up from the dust and mud, turned to the officials, and announced, "Why of course I'm going to ride him again." Bertha was determined to show the crowd and the rodeo judges that the hard fall she just received was merely a slight incident in the life of the only woman in the world who "busts" outlaw horses.[2]

The big gray was brought back, after a long chase down the arena, and Bertha once more swung into the saddle. Spurs were sunk and the quirk was brought down on the animal's flanks, but the buck was out of energy, and he merely stampeded . . . much to the disgust of the rodeo officials.

Urging her horse back to the judge's stand, the fair bronco buster called for another horse. The little roan now assigned to her contained the elevating powers of a volcano and charge of dynamite. The animal was brought

Bertha Blanchett winning the standing Roman race at the Pendleton Rodeo, 1916
SPECIAL COLLECTIONS & UNIVERSITY ARCHIVES, UNIVERSITY OF OREGON LIBRARIES

out and saddled, after a hard fight, in which the animal tried to kill the horse wrangler by striking the man down with iron-shod hoofs. Bertha wasn't dismayed by the fierce aspect of the roan, whose eyes were rolling and who was showing the craft of the wild horse. He bent slightly toward the ground, ready for the first wild, skyward jump when the rider mounted.

Grasping the saddle horn with one gauntleted hand, deftly inserting one food in a stirrup, and then swinging to the saddle with a nicety that left her well-balanced for any jump the horse might make, Bertha was away on her rough voyage. The roan proved to be a better bucker than the big gray. He pitched and jerked, but Bertha was in the saddle to stay, and she rode upright until the horse fairly wore himself out.[3]

After the roan had been turned back among the other buckers in the corral, Bertha told a reporter for the *Sunday Oregonian*:

> *Yes, I guess I have ridden more bad horses than any other woman in the world. It ought to be understood right at the start, however,*

> *that I don't advise other women to try this work. It is too hard for the average woman. Why even the strongest men who bust broncos kill themselves if they stick to the business long enough. It will bring hemorrhages to the stoutest pair of lungs in time.*[4] *But I will say, too, that I like the game and find it fascinating even if it is dangerous. I guess I am made of iron for I never feel any ill effects from the ride. Oh, yes, I get thrown sometimes and pretty hard, too, but I always make it a rule to climb right on any horse that gets me out of the saddle. It keeps up my own nerve besides letting the horse know that I am not to be beaten.*[5]

Born in Cleveland, Ohio, in 1883, Bertha Kaepernik made history doing her teenage years, becoming the first woman to ride a bucking horse at Cheyenne Frontier Days. She would go on to win the bucking championship at the Pendleton Roundup in Oregon in 1911, 1912, and 1914.[6]

"I really don't remember when I began to ride bad horses," Bertha admitted in a newspaper interview early in her career. "You see, I was brought up on a ranch near Sterling, Colorado. It is great cattle country around there, and there have always been lots of broncos that didn't like to be ridden.[7]

"I had a pony and saddle when I was a tiny girl, but soon that sort of riding didn't suit me. I saw the bronco buster at work taming the horses right off the range. I was a strong, hardy girl, and I knew I could ride as well as any of the men, so it wasn't long until I began to bust broncos. I had to ride the first one in secret, of course, but I tackled some pretty bad ones and subdued them, and then I went right into the corral one day when the men were at work breaking horses, and I showed them what I could do. After that it all came easy. Somebody heard of my ability to ride buckers and offered me an engagement at a Colorado fair. I took part in a bucking contest and rode a couple of outlaws, and since then I have been doing that sort of riding right along."[8]

Not only was Bertha an accomplished bronco buster, she also established the world record for the Roman race. Standing atop a pair of horses with one foot on each horse, she raced a quarter mile in eight seconds at Pendleton. She also set a record for a female Roman rider at the Washington Rodeo in Walla Walla.[9]

In August 1909 she married a trick rider for the Bison Moving Picture Company, Dell Blanchett, whom she met while riding the rodeo circuit. During World War I, he was killed in action.[10]

In addition to competing in rodeos, Bertha was a stunt woman working on some of the first Western films that starred Tom Mix and Hoot Gibson. She traveled extensively across the United States and Europe while working for Pawnee Bill's Wild West Show and the 101 Ranch Wild West Show. When her career in rodeos and motion pictures ended, she became a guide at Yosemite National Park.[11]

In July 1922, Bertha received an official commendation from the state of California for stopping a fire that threatened to burn thousands of timbered acres. The incident that led to the recognition occurred at the top of Yosemite Falls Trail while she was taking a horseback riding party to Eagle Peak. A manzanita thicket was blazing freely from a fire set by a hiker who had flipped a smoldering cigarette stub into the brush.[12]

Realizing the danger, Bertha unsaddled her horse in an instant and began to beat out the flames with her saddle blankets. Two men in the party followed her example. Bertha spied a trash can near the trail and, seizing the cover, she used it as a shovel and soon had a trench between the flames and the trees. Then she ordered one of the men to assist her and carried water in the trash can to wet the brush. In an hour, the flames were checked.[13]

Bertha Kaepernik Blanchett lived to be ninety-five. She passed away on July 3, 1979, in Porterville, California.[14]

Adele Von Ohl

Miss Adele Von Ohl, of this city, attracted considerable attention on Broadway, New York, yesterday afternoon as she rode through that busy thoroughfare astride a horse on her way to Bridgeport, CT., to join the Buffalo Bill Show.

—*The Courier News*, April 14, 1908

Mesmerized onlookers lining the streets in Denver, Colorado, in 1913, were treated to a grand Wild West Show entourage. The crowd cheered as showman Buffalo Bill Cody proudly led his cast and crew down the thoroughfare toward the parade field where they would be performing. The lengthy caravan consisted of 181 horses, eighteen buffalo elk, donkeys, the Deadwood stagecoach, high-riding cowboys, brave Indian warriors, and a select group of women known as Cody's American Amazons.

The ladies who made up the American Amazon act possessed a variety of talents, all of which were guaranteed to "thrill and entertain" audiences. Among the popular Amazons was the charming Goldie Griffith. Griffith was a gifted horsewoman with a flamboyant reputation. She was a steer wrestler as well as a rider. Often called a "heller in skirts," she fascinated the public with her bronc-riding stunts. In a display of independence, Griffith boldly rode her favorite pony up the steps of Grant's Tomb during a Wild West Show parade in New York. A delighted crowd wildly applauded her audacious act.

Lillian Ward was another daring bronco rider with the Amazons. Born in Brooklyn, New York, Lillian learned to ride after relocating to Texas while she was in her twenties. Her equestrian skills were discovered

Adele Von Ohl DENVER PUBLIC LIBRARY SPECIAL COLLECTIONS

by Cody himself. After watching her ride a particularly disagreeable horse that most men refused to sit, Cody recruited her for his show.[1]

The most famous of the Amazons was a scrappy cowgirl from the East Coast named Adele Von Ohl Parker. In promotion material for his show, Cody noted that Adele was a "mixture of feminine delicacy and masculine will," determined to entertain audiences with her exceptional equestrienne. Born on December 13, 1885, in Plainfield, New Jersey, she was the daughter of a rider with the New York Dragoons, a cavalry regiment with the Union army. Her mother and grandmother operated a riding school and trained horses. Adele, her sister, and brother were among the pupils who attended the respected academy.[2]

One of the first occasions when Adele was written up in newspapers involved an encounter with a horse. She was attempting to ride a small bay bronco, belonging to her brother, down Park Avenue in New Jersey. On this Saturday evening, July 18, 1903, the animal became agitated and attempted to run away. The horse stumbled and fell and then became entangled in the harness. Passersby helped Adele free the animal from its knotted harness. The horse bucked and plunged a bit but, in the end, Adele got control. The rider and bronco headed home.[3]

Simply saddling and riding her prized horse, Delmar, from one point to another would never do for Adele. She enjoyed riding fast and performing tricks on the back of her horse in the process. She jumped out of the saddle and back in again while riding at high speeds, and she could stand in the saddle and hold her position while the animal was cantering. She demonstrated these trick riding skills at several horse shows at Madison Square Garden.[4]

Adele was a favorite of horse show fans, both as an exhibitor and as a rider. Reporters referred to her as "a most charming example of the athletic girl" and followed her career religiously. The November 15, 1904, edition of the *Courier News* noted:

> *Her recent entry [in the Madison Square Garden show] is Daisy, a white pony. It is a handsome little equine, raised on the Von Ohl place. Its gifted and lovely owner is Miss Von Ohl Parker. It stands every chance of winning a blue ribbon.*[5]

> *Tomorrow Miss Von Ohl will ride a prize-winner, in the combination class, for another exhibitor. She is a perfect horsewoman, and none of the horse's good points will suffer by reason of her riding.*[6]
>
> *While an enthusiastic believer in the doctrine of outdoors, and a steady follower of her belief, she is exceedingly prepossessing and graceful and as engaging in manner, as the most babyish of the old fashion "clinging" type of girl.*
>
> *Not only does she excel as an equestrian, but she is an expert shot with the rifle, shotgun, and revolver, and during the hunting season spends much of her time booted and short-skirted out after game. While she has not done much trapshooting, she is interested in the sport and may take part in the tournament of the Gun Club Saturday afternoon. The committee in charge of the shoot are exceedingly anxious to have Miss Von Ohl add to the general interest in the shoot by an appearance at the traps, and have offered to put a special exhibition event on the program for a display of her skill. Miss Von Ohl, however, is not seeking notoriety and for that reason she hesitates to promise the gun club that she will appear in a shoot where all the other participants are men. Should she take part, there is no doubt that she will make some of the crack shots in trousers work hard to equal her scores.*[7]

In a short time, Adele's talent grew beyond what could be included in horse shows, and the trick rider and bronc buster was hired to perform at the Hippodrome in New York. Adele was billed as the "fair maid from Texas." The producers for the Western show that Adele was to star in believed patrons would prefer seeing a girl from Texas than New Jersey. The April 25, 1905, edition of the *Buffalo Courier* described the equestrienne in glowing terms:

> *She is a cowgirl with a complexion of peaches and cream, pretty as you like, with dancing black eyes. . . . Adele's long suit is doing things with horses—the meaner the better. She did things in yesterday's show that made people sit up and wonder what sort of girl this young person could be. She lariated a kicking stallion from her little pony, clapped a saddle on him before he knew what happened, and was riding him*

around the ring, clinging like glue, while he raved and racked and tied himself up into knots. Then she shied her sombrero into the ring, hung from the saddle with one foot in the stirrup, and caught up with the hat as easy as a cowboy.[8]

The riding and roping demonstration Adele offered at the Hippodrome was incorporated into the part that the entertainer played at the theater. She took on a comedic role in the show about an unsophisticated country girl who stays with her rich, proper relatives in the city. Laughter ensued when Adele's character tried to teach one of her cultured cousins how to ride a horse. Adele pretended the horse was spooked, at some point during the performance, and had to ride the animal until she brought it under control. In late October 1905, that scene was to be filmed in a park near the Hippodrome. The finished product was shown at nickelodeon theaters from coast to coast.[9]

The production did not go as planned, however. Adele nearly lost her life. The make-believe rescue of the horse became an episode fraught with danger when Adele's skirt got caught on the pommel of the saddle. She fell sideways, her foot still in the harness. And she was unable to lift herself out of the saddle and stop the horse from running. The animal was truly frightened by what was happening and had gone wild. A mounted police officer managed to overtake the horse and, leaning down, grabbed Adele, swinging her up in front of him on his own horse.[10]

The camera captured the harrowing incident from start to finish, and it was featured at nickelodeon theaters everywhere. Patrons had no idea the drama was real. As a result, Adele was a horseback-riding sensation long before the screen stars Tom Mix or William S. Hart made their first film.

In addition to the tricks she performed in the saddle in various comedies, Adele appeared with her horse in a handful of tragedies. At the conclusion of a Civil War drama, she and her ride would dive off a high platform into a pool below. Audiences burst into applause at the daring feat. The perfect execution of the death-defying stunt earned Adele the title of "America's Most Daring Woman Rider."[11]

Adele also aspired to be an accomplished actress. At seventeen, she performed dramatic sketches at posh venues such as the Hotel Netherwood in Plainfield. She wanted to excel onstage as much as she did in the saddle. Toward that end, she attended acting classes and received voice training from reputable New York voice coaches. She didn't know where her career would take her, but she intended to be prepared.[12]

When Buffalo Bill Cody, arguably the most famous Wild West show producer in the history of such programs, heard about Adele, he hurried to hire her. Adele officially joined Buffalo Bill's cast in the spring of 1907. The show was touring the East Coast, and those in the region, familiar with the daring rider's routine, flocked to see her. Cody's cast of thrill-seeking women captivated audiences. Young girls admired cowgirls like Adele, women who broke away from society's traditional roles, jumped aboard a horse, and held their own in a predominately male profession. Adele was aware of the impact she had on those young female fans, and she took every opportunity to prove there was nothing a woman couldn't do.[13]

On April 13, 1908, she took to the streets of Broadway on her horse, promoting the ladies in the Wild West Show who had saddled up and followed their dreams. On her way to join fellow female cast members, Adele rode her horse down the busiest thoroughfare in New York City to their scheduled performance in Bridgeport, Connecticut.[14]

When Adele wasn't on the road with Cody's show, she was home performing onstage in various plays. In late spring of 1908, she starred in a farce comedy titled *A Box of Monkeys* in which she offered a humorous monologue and entertained the audience by singing a couple of popular songs.[15]

New Jersey residents, anxious for their star to return to Plainfield and stay for a while, were thrilled to learn Adele would be heading east from Memphis at the close of her engagement with Cody's program. Members of the press were waiting to interview her when she stepped off the Atlantic Coast Line steamer in New York on December 3, 1908.[16]

The December 4, 1908, edition of the *Central New Jersey Home News* reported:

> *Traveling over 22,000 miles in thirty weeks, Miss Adele Von Ohl returned home yesterday, enthusiastic about her wonderful experience*

as a member of Buffalo Bill's Wild West show. After exhibiting for three weeks last May at Madison Square Garden, the show traveled through Pennsylvania, and then jumped to the Eastern states going as far north as Maine, then on to the middle states as far as St. Louis. . . .[17]

Miss Von Ohl appeared at every performance on her celebrated pony Aristocrat, who executes many wonderful stunts, including the cake walk, that of jumping three feet into the air from a standing position and many other tricks which the owner describes as of the high school variety. Everywhere both rider and animal received a great ovation.[18]

Among the cast members Adele met touring with Buffalo Bill Cody's Wild West Show was a bronc riding performer named James Letcher Parker. Born in Cheyenne, Wyoming, on October 26, 1886, Parker was a lawyer prior to working in rodeos. The pair bonded over their mutual love of horses and travel. They married on July 29, 1909, in Kankakee County, Illinois. The Parkers remained with Cody's show through the first year of their marriage.[19]

In early 1911, the couple decided to join the vaudeville circuit and performed with Arizona Joe and Company in a series of Wild West shows titled *A Glimpse of Prairie Life and Cheyenne Days*. Replete with thrilling acts illustrating life on the plains, Adele was billed as the "Noted Wyoming Horse Woman" and performed with her high school broncos, Ditmar and Diablo. The show and the star riders were well received and critically praised from Tacoma, Washington, to Tulsa, Oklahoma.[20]

"All the audience needs to do to imagine themselves looking out of the ranch window and watching the cowboys and cowgirls in the evening frolicking with their horses, is to pay no attention to the walls and the lights, etc. of the theater," the April 29, 1912, edition of the *New York Times* boasted about the Wild West show.[21]

"Those who haven't seen the great act by Adele Von Ohl should make every effort to do so," an article in the January 8, 1912, edition of the *Press Sun Bulletin* announced.[22]

In the summer of 1913, Adele, her husband, and the rest of the cast of Arizona Joe and Company traveled overseas to perform for audiences in the most notable theaters in Europe. But not all of Adele's time would be spent working onstage. She had a legal matter to attend to in England and, if all went as planned, the Parkers expected to return to America millionaires.[23]

Sir Benjamin Laing Stites of Dundee, a distant relative of the Von Ohls, left an eight-million-dollar estate to be divided among his relatives. Adele planned to meet with Sir Stites's solicitors and lay claim to her portion of the fortune. The cowgirl actress hoped to use some of the money to produce her own Wild West show.[24]

Adele and her husband returned to New Jersey on December 27, 1913. The Wild West programs were successful and well attended. Adele celebrated both the positive response she received from European audiences and the small fortune she inherited.

Between 1914 and 1916, Adele lent her talent to several shows. Now billed as the "Champion Lady Bronco Buster of the World," she appeared at the Strand Theatre on Broadway, the Bowdoin Square Theatre in Boston, and the Pantages Theatres in San Francisco and Los Angeles. Theatergoers marveled at the way she handled a horse. She credited her parents for her ability to break wild horses. They had taught her how to train horses, and the prowess had become a passion.[25]

In 1916, when the United States was contemplating entering World War I, Adele suggested to government officials to put Red Cross nurses working in the field on horseback. She offered to train for the mission. The radical idea made the front page of newspapers across the country.[26]

An article in the July 13, 1916, edition of the *Los Angeles Record* read:

> *Here is the latest new project under the sun which is being wished upon Los Angeles by a woman who has been nurse, equestrienne, and society woman, by turn. And why haven't we thought of the plan before, you'll all say when you know the details. The idea originated in the clever brain of Adele Von Ohl who appears in a riding act at the Pantages this week.*[27]
>
> *"I think there are always many women who are living a social butterfly existence," said Miss Von Ohl today, "who would dearly love to go in for something worthwhile. The present war has awakened the*

spirit of doing among a number of rich women who have gone to the front in the service of the Red Cross. I think a great many more could be interested in this wonderfully human peculiarly woman's work, if it were promoted in times of peace and in countries at peace as well as at war.[28]

". . . I am in favor of the Red Cross mounted brigade being organized in every city in the country. I think the women who enter it might very well be women who are interested in doing something for others.

"They might not only become proficient as horsewomen, but they might be equally capable of handling a machine or driving a team. . . . I should like to see this organization of women make itself a first aid, not only in time of war to the soldier but in time of peace to the civilian, and it could answer emergency calls, such as in accidents, fires, or riots. Often on such occasions there is grave need of a woman's hand and a woman's care."[29]

Miss Von Ohl so firmly believes in her plan that she took the matter up with the Out West Riding Club in Los Angeles and continues her propaganda everywhere she goes.[30]

The years between 1917 to 1928 were filled with stage performances, dazzling crowds with fancy riding exhibitions and bronc busting demonstrations. The expert horsewoman was renowned from the Atlantic to the Pacific. When motion pictures became the rage, she was sought after by film producers who wanted her to work as a stunt woman in a series of Western films. She worked alongside some of the most popular film stars of the day, including Hoot Gibson and Buck Jones.[31]

By this time in her life, she had two daughters. No matter how busy Adele was with work and her family, she always found time to participate in horse shows. At the California Stock Horse Classic in April 1923, she rode a buckskin gelding to victory on three consecutive nights. She won first place trophies and one second place award.[32]

Adele joined the cast of Wild West entertainers with Ringling Bros. and Barnum & Bailey in the spring of 1928. At the age of forty-three she was still performing bold stunts on the back of a horse. She brought audiences to their feet at Madison Square Garden with tricks known as the "pickup" and the "death drag." The pickup involved leaning low, almost sideways in the saddle, to retrieve a kerchief on the floor of the arena. The death drag was a stunt where the rider hung upside down on the side of the horse as it galloped at full speed. Adele was among the first women to perform either stunt in a show.[33]

Shortly after Adele's mother died in May 1928, she decided to retire from working in vaudeville, circuses, and Wild West shows and turned her attention to establishing a riding school in Cleveland, Ohio. The Von Ohl Equestrian School opened for business in the fall of 1928. Adele believed northeast Ohio was the perfect location for her school of horsemanship because, according to her, the Rocky River Valley "provided the grandest riding range in the United States."

She eventually moved the school to North Olmsted, Ohio, on a six-acre parcel of land, changing the name of the institution to Parker's Ranch. In addition to teaching students how to ride and sit properly in a saddle, she also taught them how to swim horses. Adele's pupils were given a chance to demonstrate what they'd learned at the school by participating in the horse shows she produced at the ranch, in which the public was invited to attend.[34]

In an interview Adele did with the Great Falls, Montana newspaper, the *Great Falls Tribune*, in April 1965, she admitted that if she could live anywhere other than Ohio it would be in Montana. At one time, she and her husband had a ranch in Sheridan, Montana, and she fell in love with the state. She told the *Great Falls Tribune* reporter that Cleveland was home because, "the services of a horsewoman are more in demand in a heavily populated part of the country."[35]

For more than thirty years, Adele contented herself with running the equestrian school and reliving her days touring the United States and Europe by performing with her many students.[36]

The avid horsewoman and equestrian instructor passed away on January 21, 1966, at the age of eighty. More than three hundred of her pupils attended the funeral. She was laid to rest at the Brook Avenue Presbyterian Cemetery in North Plainfield, New Jersey.[37]

SILENT STUNTERS

THE FIRST MAJOR AMERICAN FILM WAS THE WESTERN *THE GREAT TRAIN Robbery*, released in December 1903. It was directed by the inventor Edwin S. Porter. Although only eight minutes long, the silent film greatly influenced the development of motion pictures, featuring such innovations as intercutting, or switching back and forth from one scene to the other, and climaxing in a chase.

In the production of his work, Porter developed one of the fundamental techniques of film creation—shooting various scenes at various times and places, then editing them together, quite arbitrarily, to shape a work possessing logic and consistency. *The Great Train Robbery* helped

Movie poster for *The Great Train Robbery* LIBRARY OF CONGRESS

enlarge the audience for motion pictures, especially Westerns. Those nostalgic for pioneers, mining rushes, the rise and fall of the cattle industry, Indians, buffalo, cowboys, and wagon trains flooded vaudeville houses and nickelodeons where the film was being shown.[1]

Newspapers across the nation praised the film, including the December 29, 1903, edition of the *Kenosha News,* which called *The Great Train Robbery* "a decided hit":

> *Patrons of theaters from one coast to the next have never before had the opportunity of beholding an actual train robbery as is reproduced in this motion picture. . . . The subject has been given every attention and shows in fourteen scenes, just what happens when the bandits proceed to hold up a train, rob the express safe and loot the passengers, it even goes further, it shows the bandits making their escape, it shows the chase and final battle, and with it all, presents the most spellbinding and realistic scene ever offered in a theater.*[2]

Theatergoers were enthralled by *The Great Train Robbery,* believing it mirrored frontier life and captured all the fascinating and colorful charm of those unruly times. The motion picture's success prompted other filmmaking companies to produce more westerns that focused on the action-packed, alluring side of the wild country beyond the quiet plains. Prolific production companies such as Edison Studios, the Selig Polyscope Company, Christie-Nestor Studios, and the Kinemacolor Company of America created a string of pictures featuring the same elements that had attracted audiences to the Wild West shows.

Most centered around valiant men who fought desperate outlaws and had six-shooters strapped to their hips. The films offered excitement, lessons in morality, and riveting entertainment. Theatergoers, cloaked in darkness and fixed to the screen, with no distracting sound to lessen the visual impact, delighted in revisiting a recent past that had passed into legend.[3]

Just as had been true with Wild West shows, there were silent picture stars that became fan favorites. Cowboys such as Ken Maynard, Tom Mix, William S. Hart, and Buck Jones were admired symbols of the Old

West. All four actors appeared in scores of films and made the white hat the flag of the good guy. They were capable actors, but they didn't do all their own stunts.

In the beginning, women in Western films were relegated to playing mothers, daughters, or love interests of the Western heroes. They were usually in need and too frail to help themselves. Off camera, women were seen differently by film producers. Because women sat lighter in the saddle than men, they were called on to perform stunts on horseback that were difficult for their heavier male costars. Many of the sensational feats, such as riding horses into a raging river, riding full gallop down a cliff face, or over a small chasm, were performed by cowgirls.[4]

When Max Sennett decided to feature those daring stunt women as stars in his pictures, placing them in perilous situations and filming their hair-raising escapes, other movie executives followed suit. Audiences proved their appreciation for the films by swarming to theaters to watch the heroines deal with danger. The female silent stars who dazzled fans in a series of fast-paced Westerns included Olive Fuller Golden, Bessie Barriscale, and Anita Bush.

When the five-reel western drama *A Knight of the Range* premiered in early 1916, critics praised the performances of silent film cowboy and cowgirl actors Harry D. Carey and Olive Fuller Golden. Audiences were dazzled by the equestrian tricks that had never been seen before in motion pictures. "Stunts that are inconceivable of execution are performed before the all-seeing eye of the camera," a review of the film in a Hollywood magazine read. "Lovers of riding will miss the treat of their lifetime if they fail to see Western stars Carey and Golden work their magic on horseback. Golden is one of the prettiest and most popular of film favorites. Her long golden curls droop over her shoulders and her bewitching smile is as golden as an Arizona sunset; golden also is her disposition. She will be a star as long as motion pictures are being made."[5]

Olive Fuller Golden learned to ride in upstate New York, where she was born on January 31, 1896. Before becoming an actress and stunt woman, she was a rodeo performer, specializing in trick riding and roping. At the age of sixteen, she traveled to Los Angeles, where she became an original stock player for director D. W. Griffith along with Mary Pickford,

Lillian and Dorothy Gish, and her future husband, Harry Carey. She appeared in her first major film in 1914, *Tess of the Storm Country*, starring Mary Pickford.[6]

Olive excelled in stunt work and was unafraid to try even the most outrageous feats. In the picture *The Inner Conscience*, she played the part of a runaway wife who had to escape her husband by jumping out of a boat, sailing around Catalina Island. While rehearsing the scene of her

Olive Fuller Golden Carey with her husband Harry Carey in one of their first films together in 1919 AUTHOR'S COLLECTION

character's drowning, cast and crew members who didn't know she was acting jumped in to save her.[7]

Critics were consistently impressed with Olive's riding skills and often pointed out her ability in their reviews, noting that "her feats of horsemanship never fail to thrill us to the core, and we have nothing but admiration for the daring rider, who performs remarkable stunts on the backs of treacherous cow ponies."[8]

In 1916, she signed a contract with Universal. It was during this time she made the acquaintance of an up-and-coming director named John Ford. After the studio hired him to direct pictures, he cast Olive and Harry Carey in many of his films. The first picture she did with Ford was *The Soul Herder* in 1917.[9]

Shortly after Olive and Harry Carey were married on January 5, 1920, she decided to retire from motion pictures and help manage her husband's career and raise a family. But then, after Harry's death in 1947, she appeared in a number of movies, including *Gunfight at the O.K. Corral*, *The Alamo*, and *Two Rode Together*. The most memorable film in which Olive appeared was Ford's *The Searchers*. She played the mother of Vera Miles and her real-life son, Harry Carey, Jr.[10]

Olive passed away in March 1988, after a brief illness at her ranch in Carpinteria, California. She was ninety-two.[11]

Between 1914 and 1926, roper, rider, and actress Bessie Barriscale amazed silent film fans in a series of fast-moving Westerns. Movie audiences were fascinated with the versatile and beautiful star's ability to outsmart and outshoot the outlaws in pictures such as *The Bells of Austi* and *The Gambler's Pal*.[12]

Named Elizabeth Mary Barriscale at birth in Manhattan, New York, on January 1, 1886, she acquired a love for acting from her mother, Jane. Jane nurtured her daughter's talent and helped with various auditions, which ultimately led to a supporting role in a stage play when she was just nine years old. Bessie acted in a number of theatrical productions, landing her first starring role in the play *Mrs. Wiggs of the Cabbage Patch* in 1905. She toured with the show for more than three years, traveling across the United States and London. During her time on the road, she

Bessie Barriscale adorned in woolly chaps for her starring role in silent film *Two-Gun Betty* AUTHOR'S COLLECTION

met a fellow actor named Howard Hickman. The two were married in San Francisco on October 17, 1906.[13]

The Hickmans settled in northern California for a time, and it was there they both learned to ride horses. Bessie quickly became an expert rider, competing in regional exhibitions and entertaining crowds with the tricks she could perform. At the time, she had no idea how important that skill would be to her career.[14]

Bessie and her husband moved to Los Angeles in 1913, and she was quickly cast in the silent film *Rose of the Rancho*. Having played the lead character in the stage play, she was familiar with the story and more than prepared to make her screen debut. The Western picture was based on a play by David Belasco and Richard Walton Tully, and it was directed by Cecil B. DeMille. Bessie's character, Juanita, was the feisty love interest of a government agent sent to help California landowners battle with an unscrupulous banker who threatened to take over the territory. Bessie showed off her horseback riding expertise in the film, and critics applauded her equestrian feats as well as her acting.[15]

A review in the December 12, 1914, edition of the *Daily Times* in Davenport, Iowa, reported:

> *The stage version of the story, with its life and color, was a most pleasing spectacle. Yet because of the story, because of good acting, especially on the part of the very personable heroine (Bessie Barriscale) and because of the charm of the actual California backgrounds, the offering is, as a picture, a decided success.*[16]
>
> *Eighteen Mexican vaqueros, a large equipment of Spanish accoutrements, and a number of Spanish girls were imported from Mexico for the film. The vaqueros riding techniques were superb and that goes double for the phenomenal Bessie.*[17]

One of Bessie's most popular films was *Two-Gun Betty*. The immensely talented actress was able to show her incredible range in the tongue-in-cheek comedy Western. The premise was an inspired and unique one in 1918. Bessie plays the role of a fashionable city girl who attempts to lead a cowpuncher's life on a western ranch, the result of a wager. She makes a bet with her companion that she can work on a western ranch for a certain length of time without disclosing her identity. She carries this out, arriving at the ranch accompanied by her best friend, whose brother is the owner. Then comes the inevitable initiation of the tenderfoot. The men readily see through her disguise. They stage some scenes of bygone days in an effort to terrify her. It is in one of these scenes that she earns the name "Two-Gun Betty." Later on, in an attempt to even up the score, she captures one of the men, who turns out to be a notorious bandit.[18]

Two-Gun Betty was directed by Bessie's husband. Reviewers praised *Two-Gun Betty* as her "best work yet" and "a most entertaining film that highlights her stupendous acting gifts along with her talent for doing stunts—all of which she does herself."[19]

Bessie and Howard left Hollywood in 1919 and crisscrossed the country for more than eight years on the vaudeville circuit. The pair performed comedy skits, Bessie adding rope tricks to the act she had perfected from the back of her horse.[20] "I want to be a truly good entertainer," she told a newspaper reporter in 1924. "Not a star grown up in a night because some manager took a special interest in me. I want to feel that I have won my place, not through the good will of an individual, but because of the favor of audiences who liked my work."[21]

Bessie passed away at the age of eighty-one at the Center Medical Convalescent Hospital in Kentfield, California, on June 30, 1965.[22]

Anita Bush was the first Black American actress and stunt woman to star in a Western. Born on September 1, 1883, she began her entertainment career as a dancer. She was only sixteen years old when she was hired to appear in Vaudeville with a comedy act known as William and Walker. Silent film director Richard Norman saw Bush perform in a Broadway play and sought her out to take part in a film opposite rodeo sensation Bill Pickett.[23]

"If you want an experienced rider, I can't say that I am one," Bush wrote to Norman about what would become her leading lady role in *The Bull Dogger*, a Western that was Pickett's first film as well. "But I have lots of nerve and learn anything quickly. I can row, drive, ride a wheel, sail a boat, dance, and do most anything required in pictures."[24]

True to her word, Anita did indeed have nerve. She learned how to ride a horse and rope a steer, both of which she did in the film. There were no stunt doubles for the fearless actress as she performed dangerous tricks, supervised by professional cowboy and bulldogger Pickett himself.[25]

Richard Norman was so certain *The Bull Dogger* and Bush would be hits, he cast her in his next film, *The Crimson Skull*. Billed by the April 21, 1922, edition of *The Afro American* "as the first genuine Western-photo drama ever produced with an all-black cast," advertisements promised audiences big fights, fast action, and thrilling love scenes.[26]

The May 5, 1922, edition of *The Afro American* reported:

> *The opening scenes of this epic of wildlife and smoking revolvers shows the peace-loving city of Boley, Oklahoma, snuggling itself on the great Oklahoma prairie. The city's peace has been disturbed by a band of outlaws. "The Skull" and his "Terrors" have sown mortal fear into the*

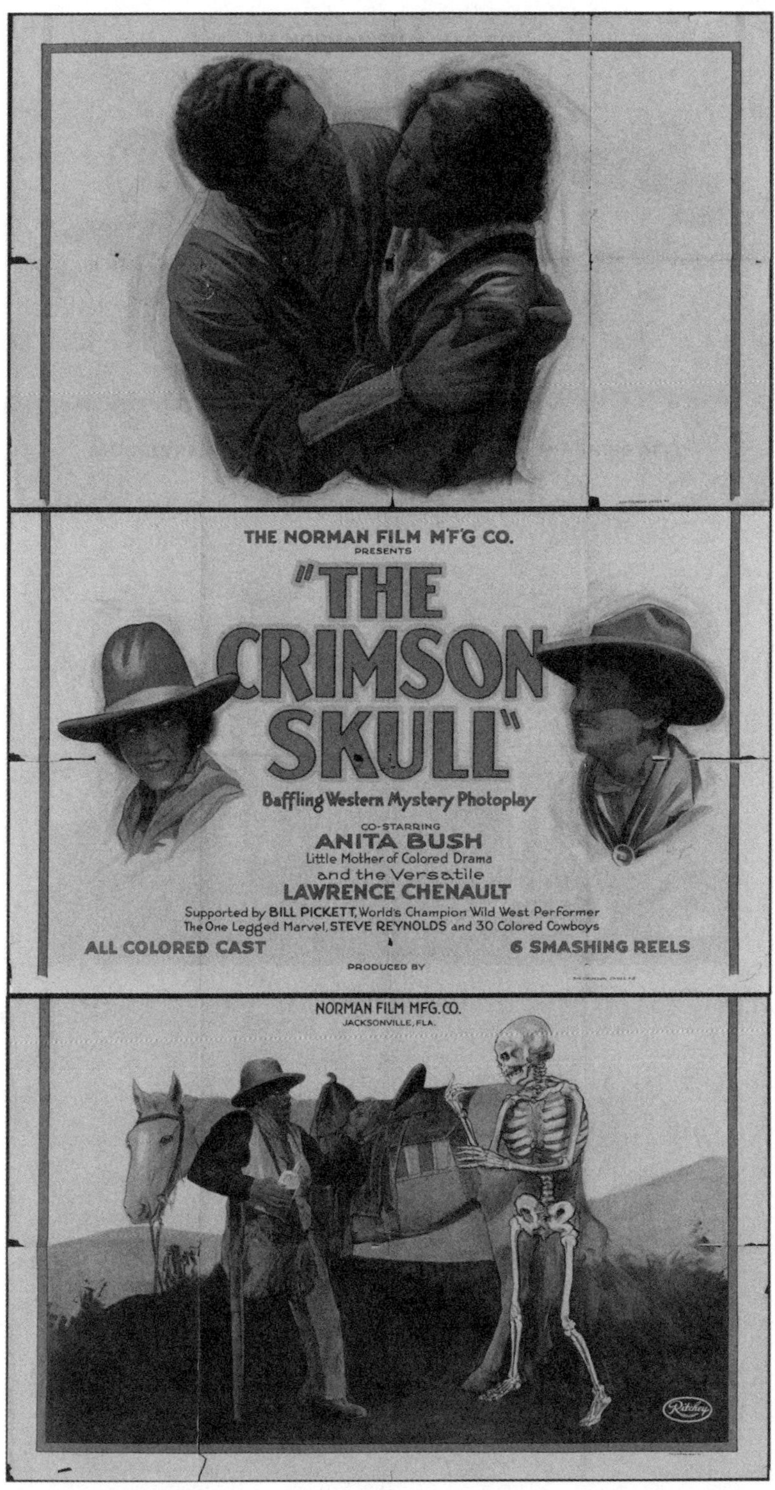

The Crimson Skull was one of cowgirl stunt woman Anita Bush's early films.
LIBRARY OF CONGRESS

hearts of the less intrepid of the countryside, and they have the sheriff in their power. The law-and-order league forced his resignation and offered $5,000 for the capture of "The Skull," dead or alive.[27]

Lem Nelson, fearless cattleman and owner of the Crown C Ranch is persuaded to take the sheriff's job. Bob Calem, his ranch foreman, is in love with Nelson's daughter, Anita, and he volunteers his aid to help capture of "The Skull." In order to affect the capture of "The Skull," Bob joins his gang.[28]

Anita and Steve Reynolds, a one-legged cowboy, are captured by "The Skull." Bob aids them to escape and is accused of being a traitor. As there is no definite proof of his guilt, and opinion is the test of equally divided between members of the gang, he is tried by the test of "The Crimson Skull." One drop of blood decides his fate—if he shall live or die.[29]

The Crimson Skull's lead actress received glowing reviews for her on-camera work. "Anita Bush proves she is as versatile on the screen as she is behind the footlights. She is captivating."[30]

Bush was proud of the two films she made with Norman because they went against type. She was tired of seeing Black Americans cast primarily in bumbling, comedic roles. She was determined to prove they were capable of taking serious, dramatic work. To that end, she founded the Anita Bush Players of Harlem, a famous acting troupe that later became known as the Lafayette Players.[31]

Bush was not only talented on-screen, she proved a tough negotiator with film and theater executives, sometimes demanding—and getting—a salary higher than her leading man.[32]

Anita Bush passed away at her home in New York on February 16, 1974, at the age of ninety-one.[33]

As Westerns graduated from one- and two-reelers into full features, more stunt women were needed to be part of the evolving medium. The new roster of talented ladies would improve upon the tricks their pioneering sisters introduced to spellbound crowds.

Helen Gibson

Daredevil Helen thinks nothing of riding full tilt down a steep mountainside or leaping from cliff to cliff on the back of one of her string of wonder horses; and her railroad feats, as shown in pictures on the screen, have made many a fan gasp with amazement.

—*Los Angeles Times*, January 10, 1918

Daring silent film actress, Helen Gibson, stylishly dressed in a leather split skirt, white blouse, kerchief, and cowboy hat, leapt on the back of her chestnut-colored horse. She spurred him to a fast run. The pair hurried across the open landscape toward a wooden water tower situated next to the railroad tracks. The horse and rider were on a rescue mission. The character Helen portrayed in the Universal railroad thriller *Mettle and Metal*, was a telegraph operator. The lines were down, and she couldn't get an urgent message to the engineer of the incoming train—the air brakes had been cut between the cars. The only thing she could do was ride out to intercept the vehicle somewhere along its route.[1]

Unaware of their perilous situation, passengers on the train watch the beautiful mountainous scenery pass by, visiting with friends and family also on the journey. But the audience knows that all will perish if Helen doesn't make it in time. She urges her ride across a rocky landscape peppered with coyote brush and manzanita. The horse gallops obediently onward, four hooves meeting the earth in full valor.

Helen slows the horse to a quick stop when they reach the isolated water tower. Jumping off her ride, she races to the stairs leading to the top of the structure and quickly climbs up. The train speeds by the tower. Helen studies the setting, trying to think how to get onboard. Suddenly she leaps up and grabs hold of the funnel that shoots water into the tank on the locomotive. With all her might, she swings the funnel away from the tower until she is hanging over the train rushing just below her legs. In an instant, she lets go and lands hard on top of one of the cars.

Making her way from the back of the train to the front is treacherous. Helen hurries along the top of the vehicle, jumping from car to car, until she finally reaches the engineer. She quickly shares the urgent message with him about the train's brakes. The engineer and brakeman waste no time addressing the problem. Once the crisis is averted, they turn their attention to Helen and express their gratitude for her heroic efforts. All is right with the world again.[2]

Helen Gibson is recognized by film historians as the first professional American stunt woman. Being a leading lady in serial pictures was the furthest from her mind when she became part of the Miller Brothers 101 Ranch Wild West Show in 1910. But her talent and fearlessness were too vast to be held in the confines of a single show.

Helen was born Rose August Wenger on August 27, 1892, in Cleveland, Ohio, to a Swedish father and German mother who immigrated to the United States in 1883. There was nothing out of the ordinary about her upbringing. She and her four sisters had a fairly happy childhood. Helen preferred playing outside and enjoyed sports of all kinds. Missing from her younger years was a horse. Unlike other pioneer cowgirl stunters, she didn't learn to ride until she was seventeen.[3] Her stage name "Helen" came from a film role she was offered in *The Hazards of Helen* in 1915.

In the summer of 1909, and employed at the local cigar factory, Rose Wenger and her best friend skipped work to attend a Wild West Show at Luna Park in Cleveland. Rose was captivated by the bronc riders, the galloping parade of cowboys and cowgirls, the steer ropers, and the trick and fancy riders. Consumed with a desire to be a part of the spectacle, she sought out the performers to learn how she could be one of them. The advice she received was to consult the back pages of *Billboard Magazine*, an entertainment and music publication first printed in 1894. Managers of various western shows often posted job opportunities.

The Miller Brothers organization had placed an advertisement in search of young women eager to learn how to ride, and Helen responded immediately. She was invited to audition for the show in the spring of 1910, and she made the cut. After learning about horses and riding, she went on tour with the well-known 101 Ranch troupe.[4]

Natural in the saddle and exuding charm, Rose won over audiences wherever she performed. She had a way with reporters, too. Recognizing the importance of promoting her work as a relay racer and trick rider in the Wild West Show, she never missed a chance to talk with newspaper correspondents. "She is a clever press agent," noted an article in the April 27, 1910, edition of the *Dayton Herald*.[5]

> *After the parade of the Wild West Show 101 Ranch, Wednesday, the* Herald *editorial rooms were visited by Miss Rose Wenger, who has the double distinction of being one of the champion cowgirl broncho busters and extremely smart when it comes to marketing. Miss Wenger covers the papers daily for the 101 Ranch and the space she gathers is the envy of many press agents, who devote their whole time to the newspapers.*[6]

In 1911, Rose and other entertainers with the show were hired to work for producer-director Thomas Ince. Often referred to as the "Father of Westerns," Ince was shooting a film in Topanga Canyon, California, for New York Motion Pictures. Rose received $8 a week to do what she loved best—ride her horse. Before Ince's project concluded, an ambitious actor and filmmaker who noticed Rose at the location persuaded her to do a screen test for the Kalem Film Company. She agreed, and the result was an offer to sign with the studio for $15 a week.[7]

Rose's new job called for her to be in California full-time, which meant she had to leave the Miller Brothers Show. She was grateful for all she had learned, but the chance to use her skills in silent pictures was intoxicating. The first film in which she costarred was *Ranch Girls on a Rampage*. Released in May 1912, Rose played the little sister of Kalem Film Company's lead actress Ruth Roland. The plot of the Western comedy involved a group of women from a Southern California ranch who travel together to the big city for a day of fun. Things get a little out of hand at an amusement park, and the ranch girls end up being pursued by the law. Critics called the film a "picture to please the masses."[8]

Encouraged by the response from her film debut, Rose was excited about the prospect of the studio casting her in future pictures. While between jobs, she competed in a few rodeos. She won third place in the trick riding contest at the Los Angeles Rodeo in February 1913. That summer she entered the girls' relay race at Stampede Days in Salt Lake City, winning the two-mile competition with a time of five minutes and eighteen seconds.[9]

Her equestrian skills caught the attention of entrepreneur Barney Sherry. Sherry liked to invest in talented riders and offered to back Rose on a rodeo tour, promising to pay her expenses in return for half her winnings. She agreed. Before leaving California with Sherry to travel to his ranch in Oregon to train for events using his horses, Rose appeared in her second Kalem Film Company Western production, *Girl of the Range*. The story involved the breakup of a cattle rustling gang by an Arizona ranger. Rose played the ranger's sweetheart, a woman exposed to a fair amount of danger from rustlers who were determined not to be caught. Reviewers called the picture a "real gem."[10]

While working at the ranch in Oregon, Rose met other riders employed by Sherry, including a cowboy named Edmund "Hoot" Gibson. Hoot rode bucking broncos for the Bud Atkinson Wild West Show as well as the Dick Stanley Congress of Rough Riders. Rose and Hoot got along well and enjoyed their time together, preparing to compete at various rodeos, including the Pendleton Roundup and Cheyenne Frontier Days. The two became even better friends as they traveled from one rodeo to the next. "He and I won everything. The relay race, the standing woman race, trick riding, and Hoot won the Pony Express race," she recalled in an interview for the magazine *Films in Review* in late 1967.[11]

Unfortunately for Rose, Hoot, and the other cowboys and cowgirls who rode in the Stampede Rodeo in July 1913, the promoters absconded with the prize money. The pair were forced to pool their money to get to the next rodeo event in Canada. There, she was unable to finish the cowgirl relay race, because her ride kicked her in the face and knee. Rose was rushed to the hospital tent at the rodeo grounds and was relieved to learn she would suffer no permanent damage.[12]

Still low on funds, the circuit riders put their money together again and managed to make it back to Oregon in time to compete at Pendleton. "When we arrived, rooms there were almost impossible to obtain," she noted years later. "People were sleeping in hallways, even on porch benches. When we learned that married couples were given preference, we decided to get married. The result, a landlady gave us her room."[13]

News of the nuptials was reported in the September 8, 1913, edition of the *East Oregonian*:

> *Fewer cowboys are more expert with the lariat than Edmund Richard Gibson, but Saturday he became a victim of an expert as great as himself, for Cupid, aided by Judge Joe Parkes, tied him by the holy bonds of wedlock to Miss Rose Wenger, relay rider and cowgirl, with scores of victories to her credit won in Wild West Shows all over the western half of the United States.*[14]
>
> *The wedding ceremony was performed in the office of Justice of the Peace J. H. Parkes and was witnessed by only a few of the friends of the young couple, some of them being T. D. Taylor, president of the Roundup association and sheriff of Umatilla County, Directors S. R. Thompson and Mark Moorhouse of the Roundup association, and Deputy Sheriff George Strand. They were immediately taken for a ride in an automobile decorated with a placard stating that the occupants of the machine were newly wedded and upon their appearance at the park where the bucking tryouts were being held became the butts of many good-humored jokes.*[15]

Both Rose and Hoot were twenty-two years old when they exchanged vows on September 6, 1913. On their marriage license he wrote "riding" as his occupation and Rose wrote "cowgirl." Husband and wife competed in the Pendleton Roundup. Hoot won the standing cowboy's race, and Rose bested Tillie Baldwin to win the cowgirls' Roman race.[16]

The couple continued their winning streaks at the Idaho Rodeo in Boise two weeks later. They ended the rodeo season the following month at the Wasco County Fair and Rodeo in Tygh Valley, Oregon. The Gibsons returned to Los Angeles in mid-October. Both in need of jobs, Hoot quickly found work at Selig Studios as a cowboy extra and stunt double for Tom Mix. Rose went back to the Kalem Film Company. No longer on the payroll, she worked as an extra here and there while waiting for a full-time opportunity. The first film the Gibsons appeared in together was *The Real Thing in Cowboys*. Hoot stunted for Tom Mix, and Rose was a background character.[17]

Between jobs as an extra, Rose kept busy participating in local and regional rodeos. In April 1915, she was the first contestant to enter the cowgirl relay race in the Los Angeles Rodeo. She would ride every day during the nine-day event, participating in not only the relay race but the cowgirl pony race. The relay race requires riders to make three laps of the track, changing horses at the end of the first and second laps. Rose hoped to win the $550 prize purse and the gold belt that went along with it.[18]

Fascinated with thrill-seeking women who preferred being astride careening horses than any domestic pursuit, the *Los Angeles Express* sought out Rose to ask her about her life in the saddle. She informed the reporter:

> *All cowgirls don't know how to milk. I'm not Rose of the Rancho. That sentimental line might go all right with some women, but I'm a businesswoman, and sentiment make a poor education when a woman is on the job.*[19]
>
> *No, my business is furnishing thrills, but I can't say it is a thrilling business. That is the penalty, I suppose, of efficiency. Because we are called cowgirls is no sign we know how to milk. Cowboys, you know, are men whose chief business is herding and branding steers.*
>
> *Next to riding bucking horses, I enjoy trimming hats. If I had a baby all the time I got out of the saddle I would be put in embroidering the laciest caps for its head.*
>
> *The only woman I might say I'm jealous is the one known as the lady lion tamer. Her perils, like most troubles, are mostly imaginary. If you are looking for understanding of our jeopardy, ask the life insurance man.*[20]

Rose won the cowgirl relay event at the Los Angeles Rodeo but lost the cowgirls' pony race to champion rodeo rider Vera McGinnis.[21]

As luck would have it, a representative of the Kalem Film Company was in the stands watching Rose ride. He couldn't wait to return to the studio to share his discovery. Rose was the thrill-seeker that the company needed to help them through a difficult time. Helen Holmes, star of the popular *Hazards of Helen* serial, had been seriously hurt on the set and was suffering with pneumonia. Filming had been briefly suspended while she recovered. Studio executives realized, even after Holmes got better, she would no longer be able to do the stunts necessary for the films, and they were desperate to find someone who could double for Helen Holmes on a permanent basis.

The Hazards of Helen was an exciting, edge-of-your-seat, railroad series in which the lady lead always found herself in mortal danger. After explaining the gritty part to Rose, she didn't hesitate to say agree. The studio offered to sign her to a contract at a rate of $35 a week. The stunts Rose tackled on screen ranged from racing horses down steep embankments to riding a bicycle off a collapsed train trellis into the ocean.[22]

When executives at Kalem Film Company offered Helen the lead in *The Hazards of Helen*, she was using the name Rose Gibson. The studio asked her to change her name, and she agreed. Helen Gibson's introduction to the public was in the episode "The Test of Courage," which debuted in theaters in October 1915. The plot involved Helen's character, a telegrapher, being locked in the closet of a railroad switch tower by two thieves who steal everything of value. The crooks accidentally upset a lantern. When the tower catches fire, they flee, leaving Helen in the closet. She barely escapes with her life and eventually brings about the capture of the culprits.[23]

The press material issued by the studio about the actress-stunt woman, in her debut performance, included a sensational story about her background created to attract audiences. "Although Miss Gibson is new to the screen, she has taken to motion picture work just as naturally as a duck takes to water," the creative release read. "The daughter of a veteran railroad engineer and having lived in a railroad atmosphere all her life,

Helen Gibson with dueling cowboys in the film *Broken Brake* AUTHOR'S COLLECTION

Miss Gibson is especially well-qualified to appear in the role of Helen of the many hazards.[24]

"It is her father's boast that his daughter can run a locomotive as skillfully as any engineer in the country, while the chief dispatcher of one of the roads running out of Los Angeles has pronounced Miss Gibson to be one of the best telegraphers he ever met. Of course, the accomplishments are among those which the heroine of the *Hazards of Helen* railroad series should possess.

"It is her remarkable courage, however, which is this young miss's most valuable asset. Think of the nerve required to leap across the chasm separating the two sections of a broken train! The slightest miscalculation would have meant her death beneath the wheels of the oncoming section, but Miss Gibson never faltered an instant when this scene was being filmed for the upcoming episode "A Test of Courage." Nor did she falter when in an earlier scene she came within an ace of being burned to death in a switch tower set afire specially for this episode."[25]

In more than 130 episodes filmed between October 1915 and February 24, 1917, Helen Gibson exposed herself to a variety of dangerous situations, portraying the feisty telegrapher who fought to save railroad passengers, brakeman, engineers, and other crew members, as well as the trains themselves. One of the most harrowing stunts Helen performed was in series episode #59, "The Boy at the Throttle." She is manning her post at the telegraph office at Long Point, somewhere in a remote area along the rail line. It's just another day in the life of a railroad telegraph operator. Down the road a freight train is standing at a station waiting to move out when Bobbie, the son of an engineer, climbs into the cab when no one is looking. He accidentally pulls the throttle open.[26]

Helen Gibson hangs from a railroad bridge in a scene from *Boy at the Throttle*.
ACADEMY OF MOTION PICTURE ARTS AND SCIENCE. IMAGE IN PUBLIC DOMAIN.

"Helen Gibson, whom Photoplay fans have christened 'the most daring girl in motion pictures,' calls the feats performed in *The Boy at the Throttle*, her birthday thrill," reported the *Hutchinson Gazette* on February 5, 1916. "It appears that on the day the scene was to be filmed in which she was to hang perilously from a steel girder of a bridge while a train passes under her feet, one of the players in the company suddenly remembered it was the first-year anniversary of her being hired.

"Once Helen dropped from the steel girder onto the freight car the runaway train came to a stop. The crew applauded her work and presented her with flowers to commemorate her special day. Although she received a slight shock from the impact of the landing on the racing train, it was remarkable to note that Helen performed the feat without serious injury."[27]

Not long after *The Hazards of Helen* came to an end, the Kalem Film Company created a new series called *A Daughter of Daring*, which was also a railroad drama. Audiences would be able to witness Helen's pluck and nervy ability in these one-part dramas (*The Hazards of Helen* was made up of two-part dramas) filmed to look more like a feature presentation than a serial.[28]

The first chapter in the *A Daughter of Daring* series was *In the Path of Peril.* Executives at Kalem promoted the *A Daughter of Daring* star from coast to coast, letting readers know that Helen's work on screen was genuine and that she could handle a locomotive as well as any seasoned train engineer. They assured theatergoers that all the messages she sent via telegram in the film were real, and that she tapped the keys herself. She could also make flying switches—a maneuver in railroad operations where a set of railroad cars are detached from a locomotive while still moving, then directed onto a different track to reach a desired location using their own momentum, essentially "flying" to a new track without the locomotive pulling them the entire way.[29]

Just as she had done in *The Hazards of Helen*, the fearless actress performed death-defying stunts that left audiences breathless. During the new short-lived series, she leapt from a velocipede (a three-wheeled railroad handcar) onto a moving train, raced an automobile down the tracks leaping onto the caboose just as she caught up with the vehicle, and fought her way through a fire in the engine cab to rescue the engineer.

The most ambitious stunt she ever dared to attempt was in the seventh chapter of the program *The Railroad Smugglers*.[30] While working at her telegraph office in Lone Point, Helen's character stumbles across information about Mexican bandits raiding an American border town and killing several people. She shares the information with her rancher friend—he is at the office to send a message regarding a carload of farming equipment he's expecting. He leaves to do some work in a nearby freight shed and asks Helen to keep him up to date on any further news about the bandits.[31]

Moments later a message comes in and Helen quickly jots it down. Unbeknownst to her, a mysterious man is milling around outside the office listening to the telegraph machine. When she exits the building to tend to some business, the man hurries away on a motorcycle.[32]

The message that the man, who is really a secret service agent, deciphered for himself was an official order to hold the limited train for a special car containing a party of naval officers. The agent's job is to make sure nothing happens to them. Meanwhile, Helen uncovers a plot that her rancher friend and the Mexican bandits have devised to blow up the train as soon as it arrives. They've kidnapped the secret service agent and are going to kill him as soon as the explosives take out their target.[33]

Acting quickly, Helen commandeers the agent's motorcycle and hurries to stop the inbound train. She rides up the freight incline onto the loading platform, through the open doors of an empty freight car, and leaps the motorcycle to a flat car on a passing train. Crawling back over the tops of the intervening cars, she gives a warning to the officers. The train comes to a stop just in the nick of time.[34]

Not only were moviegoers mesmerized by the outrageous stunt, but the makers of the motorcycle she drove took notice as well. The manufacturer approached Helen, asking her to endorse their product. She agreed. The ads always included the tagline "the motorcycle Helen Gibson uses to run down wild locomotives."[35]

The *A Daughter of Daring* series was canceled in late 1917 after eleven installments, and Kalem Film Company decided not to renew Helen's contract. Hoot had joined the Army earlier in the year and was serving overseas as a tank commander. Temporarily out of work and alone, Helen retreated to her home in Glendale, California.

But before Helen realized any downtime in her career, Universal Film Manufacturing Company signed her to a three-year contract paying her $125 a week. The first action pictures she made for the company were Westerns. *The Perilous Leap*, *The Dynamite Special*, *Saving the Fast Mail*, and the *End of the Run* all had a railroad setting in common. In each one, Helen's amazing stunts were key to the films' success.[36]

When she wasn't making movies, she was riding her horse. In January 1918, she agreed to participate in the Douglas Fairbanks Wild West Show in Los Angeles. Helen, as well as popular cowgirls Prairie Rose Henderson and Marietta Gregory, gave a trick exhibition. They rode standing and in tandem, whisked bandanas from the ground, and performed flying mounts (a trick in which a performer is propelled through the air by a hidden mechanism, often a rope or wire system, to simulate flying or leaping great distances).[37]

In addition to her film work and rodeo performances, Helen volunteered to help with the war effort. She and many of the other contract players at Universal adopted recruits and furnished them with tobacco, basic necessities, and specialty items like cookies and candy.[38]

Westerns were the most popular film genre in 1918, and filmmakers produced several pictures a month. Helen worked steadily. She played a detective investigating a series of train robberies, the daughter of a railroad tycoon who tries to stop a runaway engine cab, and a gunfighter out for revenge. In each, she performed risky stunts that enabled the characters she played to prevent great catastrophes.[39]

After being separated for eighteen months, Helen welcomed her husband home in February 1919. Although Hoot was quickly back at work filming a movie with Harry Carey and John Ford, he struggled with the notion of having to rebuild his career and was intimidated by his wife's popularity. The couple made six pictures together, but his feelings for her had changed. He was distant and sullen. Even after his star was on the rise again, he couldn't make himself feel the same about Helen. "His attitude toward me was quite different, and the success of these Universal Westerns further inflated his ego and ended our marriage," she recalled years later.[40]

More than Helen's marital status changed in 1920. After more than nine years making movies for Kalem, Universal, and then Capital Films, she decided to launch her own production company. The first Western made under the Helen Gibson Production banner was *No Man's Women.* Sadly, Helen lacked the funds to complete the project. All the filming had been done but she needed money to pay for the title cards—the pieces of printed text that appear during the silent film in lieu of dialogue. Helen had to return to stunting and rodeo riding to supplement her income. *No Man's Woman,* the story of a heart-of-gold dance hall girl who saves a rancher's daughter, was purchased and completed by another studio. It was released in March 1922 with a new title, *Nine Points of the Law.*[41]

Spencer Productions signed Helen to appear in *The Wolverine* in late 1921. This film about a rancher who comes to the defense of a hired hand accused of cattle rustling, received rave reviews for its cinematography and its action sequences. Helen, who played the rancher, was singled out for her equestrienne skills. The overwhelming positive response prompted the studio to offer Helen a contract to star in another picture. But, just before production was to start, the actress's appendix ruptured and she was unable to do the job. Production continued on the film, ironically with Helen Holmes, the woman Helen Gibson had replaced years before in the serial *The Hazards of Helen.*[42]

As soon as Helen recovered from emergency surgery, she sued Spencer Productions for breach of contract. The case was settled out of court.[43]

Work as a stunt double or actress slowed to a stop after the highly publicized lawsuit, forcing Helen to seek full-time employment elsewhere. In late April 1924, she signed a two-and-a-half-year contract with Ringling Bros. and Barnum & Bailey Circus. She traveled the country, entertaining audiences with her trick riding exhibitions. Once her time with the circus ended, Helen joined a Hopi Indian Vaudeville Act, playing engagements from Washington, D.C. to California.[44]

The famous daredevil of the movies made her return to film in the summer of 1927, stunting for Marie Dressler, Majorie Main, Ethel Barrymore, and several other screen stars. Helen occasionally played bit parts in serials such as Mascot Pictures' *Heroes of the Wild West* and *Rin Tin Tin,* but she primarily concentrated on stunt work. When she wasn't shooting pictures, she was riding in rodeos competing for prizes in trick riding and roping.[45]

Helen made the transition from silent pictures to talkies with ease, along with her friend and fellow stunter Yakima Canutt. The two appeared together in the Western *Cyclone of the Saddle*, released in April 1935. Helen portrayed one of the women on a wagon train heading west and under attack by a pair of unscrupulous characters looking to rob travelers.

Less than two months later, she was cast to play Calamity Jane in a fifteen-chapter serial, *Custer's Last Stand*. According to the September 26, 1936, edition of the *Clinton Daily Journal and Public*, the production was one of the most spectacular films of its kind that had ever been made. Thousands of Indians, two troops of cavalry, three herds of buffalo, and hundreds of covered wagons were employed for the series.[46]

While filming *Custer's Last Stand*, Helen met and married Clifton Johnson. Johnson was employed by the Petroleum Oil Company, supervising the maintenance of an oil rig. He later became an electrician for Universal Studios.[47]

As an actress and stunt woman, Helen worked steadily from September 1936 until 1941. Universal Studios kept her busy with various serials, and Herbert Yates at Republic Pictures hired her to play bit parts in a number of John Wayne films, including *The Lawless Nineties* and *Stagecoach*.[48]

In the RKO Picture *Condemned Women* released in March 1938, Helen performed a dangerous stunt that made the front page of newspapers everywhere. The headline read, "Movie 'Daughter of Daring' Still Does the Hazards." Helen's role in the film was that of a prison matron overseeing female inmates at an institution in the San Francisco area. She is shot during a riot. The forty-five-year-old stunter tumbled down a flight of stairs after taking a bullet to the stomach. The stunt required two takes to get it right. She was paid $50 for the first take and $25 for the second. She suffered abrasions and bruises, but the result was a realistic scene that she noted was the toughest she'd executed in many years.[49]

Through the 1940s and '50s, Helen worked with Western stars Roy Rogers, Audie Murphy, and Glenn Ford. She drove stagecoaches, fell off runaway horses, and leapt clear of out-of-control wagons. She appeared in *Cheyenne Cowboy* with Tex Williams, *The Blocked Trail* with Bob Steele, and *The Horse Soldiers* with William Holden.[50]

In 1957, a reporter with the *Sacramento Bee* interviewed Helen about her extensive career in motion pictures. She was living in Eldorado County and was happy to have a chance to share her story of the days when movie villains pursued her on screen. "The heavies were always trying to kill me," she told the journalist. "I was always the girl at the railroad station, or the one they caught alone at the ranch house, and believe me, it was pretty rugged."[51]

She expressed her gratitude for the opportunity to have worked in the industry for so many decades. She noted that among her most prized film keepsakes was the trophy she received from the Hollywood Chamber of Commerce in 1951, which read: "For outstanding contribution to motion picture art. For the pleasure you have brought millions. For your help in making Hollywood the world's film capital. In grateful appreciation."[52]

"I don't know which was the part I enjoyed most," she told the reporter. "I think the one I liked best was playing Calamity Jane in *Custer's Last Stand*. But that's just one, you know."[53]

Helen Gibson made her last film in 1961. It was the John Ford film *The Man Who Shot Liberty Valance*, starring John Wayne and James Stewart. She was an extra who drove a team of horses.[54]

Helen and her husband of twenty-seven years left Hollywood in 1963 and moved to Roseburg, Oregon. The couple spent their retirement years fishing and visiting family. The pioneer stunt woman died on October 10, 1977. She was eighty-five years old.[55]

Tillie Baldwin

There are those ready to wager $10,000 that in all-around ability she [Tillie Baldwin] is superior to any woman in America today and they are also willing to bet a good round sum that there is no trick or stunt performed by any rider, man or woman, cowboy, circus riders or Russian Cossack that she cannot duplicate upon first trial.

—*Elmore County Republican*, September 7, 1912

Hundreds of rodeo fans filled every available seat at the Pendleton Roundup in northwestern Oregon in late September 1912. They cheered loudly for bronc buster Tillie Baldwin, who sat atop an outlaw horse named Spike. The gate was moments away from opening, and the bronc was already bucking wildly. Tillie ground her hat down tightly on her head and then clenched the thick reins. The chute opened, and Spike darted out into the arena. Holding on with all her might, Tillie bobbed up and down in the saddle as the horse worked violently to throw her off his back. At last, a horn sounded, and the ride was officially over. Tillie had survived the long trek around the arena on top of an animal who had been unsuccessful in tossing her. The crowd enthusiastically applauded the twenty-four-year-old, and the remarkable ride earned her first prize in the women's bucking bronco contest. She was awarded a $350 saddle. In addition to winning the bucking bronco championship, Tillie also won the trick riding competition and its $150 purse.[1]

Tillie Baldwin was born Anna Mathilda Winger in Arendal, Norway, in 1888. She was fourteen years old when she immigrated to the

Champion Cowgirl Tillie Baldwin SPECIAL COLLECTIONS & UNIVERSITY ARCHIVES, UNIVERSITY OF OREGON LIBRARIES

United States with her family in 1902. Six years later, Mathilda spoke English fluently and had become a hairdresser with a healthy clientele of New York ladies wanting the newest look.[2]

Mathilda made friends easily, and the group of young women she spent time with enjoyed regular trips to Staten Island. One day, near the beach the ladies liked to visit, there was a troupe of actors making a film called *Red Wing and Young Deer*. Husband-and-wife filmmaking team James Red Deer and Lillian St. Cyr were members of the Winnebago tribe in Nebraska who starred in one-reel Westerns during the first part of the silent era. They were respected professionals and the first Native duo to produce films for the New York Motion Picture Company.[3] Native Americans were then primarily portrayed as a peaceful people and a symbol of integrity and virtue.

Mathilda and her friends were dazzled by the wonderful costumes and what seemed to be the colorful lives of the actors and actresses. The young hairdresser immediately wanted to learn to ride a horse and join the troupe. After the outing, she returned to New York with a dream she couldn't shake. Determined to ride a horse like Young Deer, Mathilda returned to Staten Island to talk with cast members about her ambition. She offered to pay one of the cowboy actors to teach her to ride. They worked together for weeks, turning her into a competent equestrienne. Mathilda learned how to ride and perform a couple of tricks in the saddle, including snatching up a handkerchief lying on the ground.[4]

Shortly after learning to ride and perform additional tricks, Mathilda approached the film producer and asked if she could join the cast. He agreed, and she was paid $6 a week for her efforts. She was one of many extras on horseback, filling in the scenes where needed.

From silent pictures, the eager young woman signed a contract to join Captain Jack Baldwin's Western Show. The March 20, 1912, edition of the *Daily Report* in Ontario, California included Mathilda—billed as "the bravest girl in the West"—in an article about the Western cowgirl, pointing out that the initial impression most people have of women performers in Wild West shows isn't entirely accurate.[5]

> *She is not the hoiden that has been pictured in fiction and by artists whose only knowledge of this beautiful type of the American woman is imagination. She is a beautiful composite of perfect woman reared in the lap of nature whose rough edges have been smoothed down by a college education. A fearless muscular and graceful daughter of the plains in lingerie, possessing just enough of the mannish to bring the*

gender traits of her sex and conspicuously set forth the unadulterated types of her perfect womanhood.

There is no more perfect type of the American woman that is the western cowgirl. Serious flirtations—she has no knowledge of. Matrimony to her is a sacred institution that once indulged in is a venture for life. Flattery to her is obnoxious while any allusion to her personal charms would be met with deserved resentment. It must not be inferred from this that she is entirely devoid of all the charms that make women attractive. Far from it. It is her extreme honesty to herself and to others that makes her taboo. . . .

It is a silent admiration that is bestowed upon her social functions of the other ranches or at the more pretentious gatherings in the cities. She does not become fascinated with the swell society man. His blandishments are all lost on her. He is just endured. In her little suit of buckskin or corduroy when the cowboys are rounding up the cattle and showing their expertness with rope and gun; when they are dashing with neck risking speed over the prairies, she will show interest and confer more compliments than to the society because of the drawing room. It is the real that appeals to her and not the artificial.[6]

Though the *Daily Report* story was misleading, too—not all cowgirls had attended college—the publicity was appreciated.

During Tillie's time with Jack Baldwin's show she perfected her riding skills, met her husband Johnny Baldwin, and changed her name from Mathilda Winger to Tillie Baldwin.[7]

Her big break came months later when she met Will Rogers. The cowboy humorist was passing through the city en route to Philadelphia. There he was to give an exhibition at the National League baseball park. Tillie took advantage of the chance encounter, and shared with Rogers that she was a trick rider. He hired her to perform with him in Philadelphia. Tillie remained with Rogers's program until the Miller Brothers 101 Ranch Wild West show visited Brooklyn.[8]

It was while watching the parade of entertainers marching down New York Avenue that Tillie made up her mind to join their cast. Just as she had been swept away by the costumes and impressive men and women seated tall in their saddles, preparing to be filmed, she was awestruck by the horses and riders in the show. Without a moment's hesitation, Tillie approached Joseph Miller, one of the show's producers, and informed him that she wanted to sign up as a trick rider. Miller appreciated her boldness but wanted a demonstration of what she could do.[9]

It was a rainy day, but Tillie wasn't going to let the weather keep her from showing off all she'd learned. She borrowed a horse from one of the show's cast members and performed many of her tricks. Miller thought Tillie had talent and invited her to be part of the program. During the two seasons Tillie was with the 101 Ranch show, she became more and more proficient at trick riding and was schooled in bronc busting and bulldogging.[10]

After Tillie's success at the Pendleton Roundup in 1912, she decided to focus on a rodeo career. From Oregon, she traveled to Southern California to participate in the International Rodeo in February 1913. The world's champion woman bronco buster attracted a large audience, and she did not disappoint patrons who waited to see if she could add to her title. She could. At the Los Angeles event, she was named best woman rider and top cowgirl trick rider.[11]

Between rodeos, the celebrated equestrienne appeared in a few stampede shows. (A stampede show features more acts and riders than a rodeo. Riders can win trophies, medals, or other prizes, but their participation is more an exhibition of their skill than a competition.) In early July 1913, Tillie rode some of the wildest horses on the stampede circuit. She also took part in the women's relay pony race. In such a race, the women rode one horse, just one lap, around the track. They switched to another horse for a second lap, rode a third horse for the final lap, and then sprinted to the finish line. Tillie won the woman's relay race at the Tacoma Stampede in Tacoma, Washington, on July 3, 1913. Then, at the Winnipeg Stampede in Winnipeg, Manitoba, Canada, in August 1913, she gave a bulldogging exhibit and won both the trick and fancy riding event and the Roman standing race (where the rider stands with each foot on the back of a pair of horses).

Tillie told reporters with the *Spokesman Review* that she was a real cowgirl and she was going to wrestle a steer to prove it. She practiced on a tame, half-breed cow, but, for the actual performance, she did indeed wrestle a steer from the Texas longhorns.[12]

Newspapers and advertisements across the country heralded the legendary Tillie Baldwin. Her daring feats inside the rodeo arena had made her well known. But, according to her friends and family, that fame didn't change her at all. She held tightly to her conservative values, refusing to drink or engage in any questionable behavior. As male fans sat in clubs, hotels, and at home in the early hours of the morning and smoked gilt-wrapped cigars bearing the picture of Tillie Baldwin, Tillie was sleeping soundly, conserving her strength for the next day's riding schedule. While smokers of the night before were soundly sleeping the next morning, Tillie was beginning her next day's program. She was a firm believer and follower of the early-to-bed and early-to-rise theory.

In September 1916, the former New York hairdresser, who had defeated the best cowgirls in the country and won bronc busting and rough riding championship contests, shared her secret for capturing those titles. In a September 9, 1916 article in *The Times,* she is quoted as saying:

> *Bronco-busting depends mainly on the knee-grip. You hold on with the lower part of the thigh, being careful to keep the legs curved in, so that the calves cling to the animal's flanks. And you don't try to sit erect in your saddle. I lean back and keep my chin down so that when the animal bucks he doesn't jerk my head back and hurt my neck.*[13]
>
> *For straight racing, such as we do in the relays, you naturally need a different seat. Then you stand in your stirrups, cling with the knees only, and bend the body over the horse's neck. That's the jockey seat. I guess that's about all there is to riding except practice and lots of strength.*[14]

When Tillie wasn't riding in rodeos or stampede shows, she lent her talent to county fairs. She and her husband gave rough riding exhibitions and performed death-defying tricks atop their horses. The couple had settled in Connecticut, and many of the carnivals and fairs they took part in were close to their home. Tillie enjoyed life in New London, a coastal town that overlooks the Thames River, but she preferred being on the road competing.[15]

The Calgary Stampede, held in August 1919, gave her the perfect opportunity to show off her riding skills, earn a top spot in the festivities, and take a shot at a piece of the $25,000 cash prize. One of the contests Tillie entered was the women's bulldogging event. She was prepared for the competition, but the steer was not. It wanted nothing to do with the performance and fought to get back to the corral. "Cornered by horsemen, it [the steer] made three escapes over the fence of the enclosure, and at one time tried to find a place in the boxes among the audience," a report in the August 28, 1919, edition of the *Calgary Herald* read. "Another animal was procured and Tillie, leaping from the back of her grey mount, put the huge black beast down in splendid style and very good time."[16]

At the rodeos and stampedes where Tillie appeared in 1920, she was routinely billed as the "fearless rider who had never been thrown from a bucking bronco." More than a decade after entering the profession, she continued to astonish crowds with her clever riding. In June 1921, rodeo fans from coast to coast named Tillie Baldwin, along with Ferry Sperry and Bertha Blanchard, as three of the best women riders in the country.[17]

By 1925, Tillie had retired from rodeo competitions, divorced John Baldwin, and married William C. Slate, a landowner residing in South Lyme, Connecticut. She might have been out of the bronc busting spotlight, but neither the press nor her fans had forgotten the champion equestrienne.[18]

On August 23, 1925, the *Hartford Courant* reported:

> *It was not more than two years ago that the name, Tillie Baldwin, glittered upon the horizon of fame. Only yesterday did the critics spread far and wide the story of her success. Jammed were the curbs of many cities, while spectators awaited the approach of her bespangled figure as she smartly reined her pony through their ranks on circus day.*[19]
>
> *Large and glaring were the posters advertising the coming show and featuring Tillie Baldwin, fearless, intrepid, rough rider horsewoman. Throughout the West and in some sections of the East gentlemen were pleased to select from plate-glass showcases, cigars labelled "Let em, buck," encircled in wrappers of gilt with a picture of Tillie Baldwin on either side.*

And then the curtain dropped upon the colorful career of Miss Baldwin. The shrill and enthusiastic cries for "Tillie" softened, and the hoofs of her pony were not heard at anymore stampedes. Not that the proficiency of this buxom girl is not spoken of now or that she at present does not hold a role in life as important as she did then—but today she is far from the eyes of her admiring world as she enjoys the peaceful seclusion of her beautiful home in Connecticut.[20]

Remarkable enough is the record of her deeds, which for a woman have seldom been equaled and in one instance never excelled. Almost unbelievable are the authentic reports of the many mad bulls she has wrestled with, finally throwing the powerful animals to the earth. But for Anna Mathilda Winger, a lass from Norway and later a New York hairdresser, her achievements, embracing stunts too much for girls, natives of the Golden West are as yet unsurpassed.

But the West claims Tillie Baldwin as its own. And the West has a good claim for it was there that Tillie became a cowgirl, and it was in the land of the cattle and trails that she won her spurs. The West is the land she loves and there is no disputing that she is a real rider of the West.[21]

Her home is typical of the West. It resembles a ranch house in appearance with a circular driveway in back. Many valuable saddles, weapons, Indian trinkets, a beaded vest, bridles, broad brimmed hats, and boots adorn the wall of the Slate residence. Often, Mrs. Slate becomes Tillie Baldwin for the time, and she may be seen dashing about the country on her pony, of which she is maintaining several at present.

Almost daily she passed with the throng in a nearby city. There is no semblance of the cowgirl in this tall and finely dressed woman. A lone medal attached to a ribbon, which she generally wears, is the only way one might learn that Mrs. Slate is Tillie Baldwin, broncho buster, buckaroo, and trick rider of note.[22]

When Tillie retired from the professional rodeo world, she took a job managing the ranch of musical comedy actor Fred Stone in East Lyme, Connecticut. Then when Stone sold his interest in the ranch in 1931 and the land was taken over by the government, Tillie stayed on as caretaker. It is said that Tillie would not tolerate rough stuff from the cowhands around the ranch. In an article in the August 18, 1957, edition of the *Hartford Courant*, Tillie laughingly recalled a couple of "boys," Mike and Ike, who always raised Cain when they drank too much. "One day they got on my nerves," she explained, "and I picked them up and heaved them bodily out of the bunk house. You never saw two more sheepish and surprised fellows in your life."[23]

In 1932, Tillie opened her own riding school in South Lyme. She owned more than thirty horses and enjoyed teaching aspiring equestrians the art of trick roping and good horsemanship.[24]

When Will Rogers died on August 15, 1935, Connecticut newspaper reporters who knew of Tillie's onetime professional relationship with him sought her out for an interview. She was quite distressed about his passing. Tillie explained to reporters that the reason she won the world championship at Pendleton, Oregon, in 1912, was because of Rogers's training. "I can't believe he's gone," she remarked. "Rogers was a frequent visitor at the ranch, and we always enjoyed his company."[25]

Tillie made the news again in August 1936 when she applied for a job as the first and only policewoman in New London, Connecticut. The former cowgirl assured the police chief that since she could handle a wild steer, she ought to be able to throw any ordinary roughneck. "There's no doubt that I am fitted for the job," she told reporters for the *Daily News*. "In show business a girl meets a certain number of men who are not so gentlemanly. She has got to learn to handle herself. I always managed to do so. I never had to ask anyone to fight my battles for me. A capable and fearless woman can handle any situation as well as a man, if she has training."[26]

Her application was ultimately denied.

Tillie returned to the rodeo arena for a special presentation in September 1946. She appeared at Madison Square Garden along with Frank Biron, the men's world champion trick rider.[27]

Tillie spent her later years painting and hosting exhibits of her work. The rodeo star died on October 23, 1958. She had suffered from a heart ailment and passed away at the New London hospital. She was seventy years old.[28]

Allene Ray

Miss Allene Ray, who won a motion picture contest in 1920, has just come West to enter pictures.

—*The Los Angeles Times*, August 27, 1922

When silent film producer Harry Myers arrived in San Antonio, Texas, in the summer of 1919 to photograph the landscape for the Western he was working on, he announced to the community that he needed a woman who could ride well. A general store owner told him about nineteen-year-old Allene Ray Burch. Myers found the beautiful blonde woman at her father's ranch near Divine, Texas. She was working alongside her brother and some of the other hired hands, rounding up cattle on a massive, open range.[1]

Allene had a style he'd never seen before. She had a strong seat in the saddle and was confident in her ability. Harry introduced himself to Allene, asking if he could take pictures of her riding as she gathered strays and pushed them back to the herd. She agreed. Shortly after the filmmaker viewed the footage, he hired her to star in his movie. "I wasn't even thinking about a career in pictures," she recalled later in her life, "but he liked me and signed me up to make Westerns."[2]

While making Myers's film, Allene's sister entered a photo of her in a beauty contest sponsored by the publishers of such well-known magazines as *Photoplay* and *Movie Monthly*. Allene won the Fame and Fortune Contest. A Hollywood agency quickly signed her to a long-term contract, and the magazine editors predicted she would be a star. Her

Allene Ray in the film *The Indians Are Coming* AUTHOR'S COLLECTION

representatives committed her to make two Westerns near the Texas home where she was born in 1901, billing her simply as Allene Ray.[3]

It was her ability to ride a horse that got Allene her first job in pictures. She began riding at the age of three. By the time she was discovered, she was an accomplished equestrienne who would use her talent numerous times during her screen career.[4]

Her first film, *Honeymoon Ranch*, was released in October 1920. That was followed by *West of the Rio Grande* and *Partners of the Sunset*. Not only did she act in the pictures, she performed her own stunts.[5]

Her talent as an all-around athlete was evident in each film. Directors were surprised that she was such a daredevil. Her delicate features and wealth of golden hair fooled them into thinking she was too fragile for such demanding work. No matter how severe the stunt, it was said, she always carried through with it.[6]

In early 1922, critics boasted of the dramatic range Allene demonstrated in *Partners of the Sunset*. Promoted as a film that "possessed miraculous feats of horsemanship," she was singled out for delivering a quality performance. "*In Partners of the Sunset*, fate tosses her from the society whirl of Newport to an unmanageable ranch in Texas," the July 19, 1922, edition of the *Herald Statesman* read, "and she rendered a better account for herself than she did in her two previous successes." Another review noted, "There is nothing about this story that is not true to life; it's naturalness is borne out of Miss Ray on horseback."[7]

In 1923, Metro-Goldwyn-Mayer bought out the contract Allene had with her agents. That same year she signed a five-year deal with the French film company Pathé. They were looking for a woman to do stunts. After watching Allene work, they wanted her to be their next serial heroine. She was to follow in the celluloid footsteps of actress Pearl White and Ruth Rowland, both of whom starred in action-adventure series for the studio. White's serial *The Perils of Pauline* was particularly popular.[8]

Allene's first project without her agents was *The Way of a Man*, an adaptation of Emerson Hough's famous novel of frontier days. She was selected for the lead because of her exquisite beauty, her acting talent, and her skill in the saddle. Pathé executives called her "the best wild west girl rider they had ever seen." *The Way of Man* was a ten-part serial, and audiences returned to cinemas everywhere for their weekly dose of thrill and adventure.[9]

The trademarks of the serial-queen melodramas were the dangerous situations that heroines found themselves in and how often they were rescued by their prospective husbands. Allene was imprisoned and placed in chains in an Egyptian tomb in the series *The Fortieth Door*, thrown in front of a team of racehorses and battled thieves trying to steal her land in *Galloping Hoofs*, and dodged fiery arrows in *The Green Archer*. Each of the nine episodes ended with Allene being in some kind of life-threatening situation.[10]

When *The Green Archer* premiered in October 1925, Pathé hosted a party to celebrate Allene's contribution to the young film industry. It was a gala affair with several hundred guests in attendance, including motion picture critics of the daily, trade, and fan press, as well as literary celebrities and executives from Pathé.[11]

According to the October 24, 1925, edition of the magazine *Moving Picture World*:

> *the guests were transported from New York in a fleet of deluxe motor buses and arriving at the studio they found themselves cast into an air of mystery. Following green arrows and green lights they ascended the stairway and stepped into the baronial dining hall of Bellamy Castle. Here Miss Ray received and poured tea.*[12]
>
> *Those who met Miss Ray for the first time found her to be an exceptionally charming young lady; a splendid hostess and genuinely idolized by all of her associates. . . .*
>
> *While half of the party were dancing others wended their way to the archery gallery in the studio annex. All of the archers had a good line on the bow and came within a few circles of the bull's eye.*
>
> *The crowning event of the party was the coronation of Miss Allene Ray as "Queen of the Serials."*[13]

Sunken Silver, filmed in Florida and released in 1925, was the fifth Pathé serial Allene starred in. She played the love interest of a Secret Service agent, seeking information regarding a cache of stolen silver. The couple travel to a remote location where hostile natives have buried the treasure deep in the Everglades. Allene's character is captured by a pair of outlaws who subject their victim to a potential shark attack, being boiled alive in water, and hungry alligators. The actress again performed all her own stunts.

"The studio preferred not to use stunt doubles," Allene recalled later in her life. According to Pathé executives, if the actor and stunt double were the same person it was an advantage for the cameraman because he could get close-ups of the performer doing her own dangerous moves. With a few rare exceptions, Allene never used a substitute to cross a rickety bridge or to scale a high wall.[14]

The next outdoor mystery serial Allene costarred in was set in the high Sierras and titled *Snowed In*. She portrayed the sister of an airmail pilot forced into an emergency landing in the middle of a forest, teaming with timber thieves and game poachers. Allene's character treks into the dense woods with a handsome forest ranger. Their goal is to find her brother, and the government bonds he was transporting, before the villains do. Allene endured the flames of a wildfire, was pursued by corrupt airmail pilots, chased by a bear, and buried in a snowslide.[15]

Between filming the serials, Allene decided to get married. In mid-July of 1925, she and motion picture producer Larry Wheeler exchanged vows. The bride was twenty-four, and the groom was ten years older.[16]

From 1927 to 1929, the Queen of the Serial, or chapter plays as they were also called, made six different serials. *Hawk of the Hills* and *Melting Millions* were released in 1927. *The Terrible People*, *The Yellow Cameo*, and the *Man Without a Face* came out in 1928. The *Black Book* released in 1929. Each series was more popular than the one before.[17]

The Indians Are Coming was the first talking picture in which Allene appeared. The Western, produced by Universal Pictures, costarred popular cowboy actor Tim McCoy. The twelve-part pictorial record of Buffalo Bill Cody's life was the first film to have a Broadway opening. It was released in both silent and sound versions. McCoy played a gentleman who traveled from Gold Creek, California, to a midwestern town with a message from a prospector to his brother and niece. The message announced that he'd struck gold and invited his family to join him. Allene played the part of the niece. Much of the action involved driving wagons and riding horses across the prairie, so she was able to make her equestrian skills shine.[18]

"*The Indians Are Coming* is filled with drama, suspense, thrills, and a charming romance," the *Los Angeles Times* noted in September 1930. "This chapter play is like none other. It depicts the winning of the Old West by daring frontiersmen and is packed with incidents and events of the most stirring nature."[19]

The Indians Are Coming was a critical and financial success. It reportedly cost $160,000 to make and grossed over $1 million within a year.[20]

Allene's next picture was another Western, this one called *Westward Bound*. She had yet another chance to show off her riding skills, holding her own against a band of cattle rustlers led by Hollywood's most respected stuntman, Yakima Canutt. She made two more films before retiring from the business in 1949. During Allene's twenty-five-plus years in the industry she had the privilege to work alongside such film legends as Mervyn LeRoy and Gloria Swanson.[21]

Allene and Larry left the movie industry in the early 1950s and moved to a ranch in Temple City, California, where he became a successful real estate broker. For a time, Allene worked at a high fashion department store as a seamstress and fitter. "Then my husband developed cancer, so I attended real estate school and passed my test as a broker, so I could help him in his business," she shared with a reporter for the *Monrovian News Post* in 1978. "I used to go out and do the measuring and drawing of plans while he stayed in the office and did the desk work. Although he was ill."[22]

The silent film actress and stunt woman died of cancer on May 5, 1979, at the age of eighty-four.[23]

Bonnie Gray

Bonnie is an exponent of modernism and proves that the Victorian era is quite in oblivion and that the woman of today is a true athlete. Bonnie is one of the most popular cowgirls in the business and one of the most unique characters in the frontier arena.

—*The Woodburn Independent*, June 27, 1929

Trick rider Bonnie Gray bolted across the rodeo arena like a flaming comet, balanced securely atop her cream-colored Palamino, King Tut. In the near distance, directly in their path, sat a Ford Model A convertible filled with people. If all went well, King Tut, known as one of the greatest jumpers of the track or sawdust arenas, would leap over the car and passengers with ease. There was one time when Bonne and King Tut performed a similar feat, jumping into the sun. Both the horse and rider were blinded, and the animal misjudged the distance, clipping the door of the vehicle with his hoof as he went over. But he recovered, maintained his footing, and stuck the landing.[1]

The conditions at the grounds of the Stampede Rodeo in Monte Vista, Colorado, on July 31, 1929, were perfect. The sun was behind Bonnie and King Tut. There was nothing to interfere with the successful execution of the stunt. The passengers in the vehicle ducked as the horse and rider sailed over them. When the pair landed safely on the other side of the car, the anxious audience broke into applause and cheered. Bonnie patted King Tut's neck and waved her hand at the plaudits of the crowd.

Bonnie's peers called her the "nerviest girl that ever sat a horse." It was her daring and fearlessness that made her a natural stunt woman.

Bonnie Gray on her horse, King Tut WYOMING STATE ARCHIVES

She not only doubled for Hollywood actresses such as Helen Ferguson and Carlotti Monti but for the cowboy stars Tom Mix, Tim McCoy, and Ken Maynard.[2]

She had been born Verna Grace Gray Smith on December 15, 1891, in Grant, Iowa, and her life took many turns before she entirely devoted herself to being a cowgirl. "I was raised on a ranch in Kettle Falls [in Washington] and took my first ride when I was six years old," she told a reporter in 1927. "I have never been without a horse since. I wanted to become a circus rider, but my mother protested."[3]

In addition to being a natural athlete, she was also a gifted musician. An accomplished pianist, she attended the University of Idaho, where she majored in music and participated in a variety of sports, including track and tennis. She won the scholastic high-jump record for girls, and afterward she held the girls' all-around athletic honors for the institution.[4]

Bonnie received her Bachelor of Arts degree just before the United States entered World War I. Wanting to do her part for the country, she returned to school to study nursing. After graduating, she became an army nurse at Camp Lewis, south of Tacoma, Washington.[5] While in nursing school, she met and married Dr. Harry Greenwald. The doctor enlisted in the army shortly after they exchanged vows on May 29, 1917. When the war ended and Harry returned home, the pair traveled around with his practice, finally settling in the Los Angeles area. It was there Bonnie decided to pursue a rodeo career.[6]

"I quit music and nursing and followed my natural instinct that had been with me since childhood that of riding wild horses and doing trick riding," she shared with a *Salt Lake Tribune* reporter in September 1927. "In it I hoped to attain the fame I sought and the excitement I enjoy. It is the life I feel I am best fitted."[7]

One of the first newspaper accounts about Bonnie's entry into the profession is from May 6, 1921. She competed in the cowgirl relay race at the Newhall Rodeo in Newhall, California, and placed second behind Vera McGinnis. Two months later she took part in the Frontier Days Festival in Cheyenne, Wyoming. There, any mention of her riding skills was lost in the scandal buzzing around a cowboy and his wife in attendance. Wild West performer Ed Wright and Bonnie had arrived at the event together, but they were nothing more than friends and competitors. However, Wright's wife, a bronc busting champion, believed there was more to their relationship and that her husband planned to give Bonnie the saddle and trophy she'd won at a previous contest. She attempted suicide over the perceived betrayal.[8]

After Cheyenne, Bonnie entered the cowgirl trick riding contest at the annual rodeo roundup in Okmulgee, Oklahoma, and came in second behind Ruth Roach.[9] She finished her first year in the trade at rodeos in Buckeye, Arizona and El Paso, Texas.[10]

At the Arizona event, she was billed as the "Champion Lady Wild Steer and Trick Rider" and appeared on the same bill as Ed Wright. According to the December 29, 1921, edition of the *El Paso Herald*, Bonnie was one of four "western girls" who entered the rodeo. "She is not only a rider of wild broncos and steers," the article read, "but holds several enviable athletic records, among them the women's tennis championship of the University of Idaho. Miss Gray also holds a record for having hiked the Bright Angel Trail at the Grand Canyon in six hours, twenty-five minutes, and it is believed that this feat will never be equaled by another woman."[11]

As Bonnie's reputation on the rodeo circuit grew, so did the contracts for her services. She was signed to give riding exhibitions from Madison Square Garden in New York to the fairgrounds in Las Cruces, New Mexico. Between events, Bonnie practiced new routines and tricks, including a stunt called "under the belly crawl." The maneuver was daring and risky. While riding her fast-moving horse, she would drop down on the nearside of the animal, feed herself headfirst between its galloping legs, reach through, haul herself up the off side, and jump back into the saddle again. Audiences were astonished by the skill it took to execute the death-defying move.[12]

Inside the rodeo arena, Bonnie regularly competed against some of the best cowgirls in the field. Bonnie McCarroll, Donna Glover, Fox Hastings, and Prairie Rose Henderson were among the top contenders. It wasn't until August 1922 that Bonnie became the new queen of trick riding. She captured the title from Mabel Strickland, a talented rider she'd faced many times but had never beaten. Encouraged by the win, Bonnie entered the world series of Western sports at Madison Square Garden two months later. Many of the other women involved in the contest were the same cowgirl rivals, including Strickland. The women had to prove themselves as the best in bronc and trick and fancy riding. The prize was $25,000. Bonnie McCarroll was the winner.[13]

As if riding competitions on solid ground wasn't difficult enough, Bonnie also participated in cowgirl swimming events. On July 19, 1923, she was one of eleven other contestants to swim Lake Terry near Cheyenne. Hundreds of automobiles lined the shore to watch as the women and their mounts took off into the water. Several of the horses bucked and pitched as they struggled to swim. A few failed to make it across but stuck to the shallow water, wading the distance to the other side. Bonnie finished in the middle of the pack.[14]

In late summer 1923, Bonnie acquired a horse that would become as well-known for his work in rodeo and film as she. While in New York, she purchased King Tut from a Georgia rancher for $275. He was two years old at the time of the purchase, suffering from "shipping fever," and was not eating well. But, under Bonnie's expert care, the horse's health was restored.[15]

Not long after she transported King Tut to her stable in Southern California, she discovered that he enjoyed jumping—he had escaped from his enclosure by leaping over it. It was apparent to Bonnie that the horse would be perfect to train for stunts. King was a fast learner and responded easily to her instructions.

It was suggested by Bonnie's close friends, who had witnessed King Tut's talent, that she train the animal to jump a car. The idea intrigued her, and the pair went to work. It would become their most famous stunt. "When I once win the confidence of a horse it will do almost anything I want it to," she shared with a reporter in 1928. "The rider must remember that a horse is just as sensitive as a human being and should be treated accordingly."[16]

In between rodeos, Bonnie would return to California where, in time, she and her husband purchased property in the Burbank area. The sprawling acreage that included their house and horse stalls was known as Bonnie Gray Ranch. The Los Angeles County neighborhood was delighted that the accomplished cowgirl chose to call the area home.[17]

An article appeared in the January 22, 1924, edition of the *Burbank Pathfinder* regarding Bonnie's decision to spend her off time there and noting that she was well-known and respected.

> *This is the third winter which the famous rider has spent in Burbank, and she likes it very much. We're happy she's here and although we could boast of her varied achievements, we thought we'd ask her which ones most pleased her.*[18]
>
> *Bonnie Jean Gray is the extremely proud possessor of two valuable cups. One presented her by Spencer Penrose, prominent citizen and millionaire of Colorado, and national politician, at the time of the rodeo at Colorado Springs last fall. It is made of copper and brass and was made in the 13th century. It bears the coat of arms of the Hapsburgs and was taken to Paris in the loot of the Napoleon army about in 1809 and bought by Mr. Penrose, in Paris in 1909.*
>
> *It is said it was won and lost thirty times on the Versailles racetrack. The other cup which the rider greatly prizes is silver and was presented by the Argonne Association of America, for championship in*

woman's trick riding and cowboy contest in Madison Square Garden. Both of them have intrinsic value of several hundred dollars.[19]

Bonnie's equestrian skills and King Tut's fearlessness caught the attention of Los Angeles film producers. Westerns were the most popular genre of motion pictures being made in the mid-1920s. Bronco Bill Anderson, Barbara Bedford, Jacques Jaccard, Buck Jones, and Hoot Gibson were a few of the top Western actors, starring in as many as seven films a year. The number of Westerns produced by busy studios brought on a demand for capable stuntpeople. In one of the first moving pictures Bonnie was hired for, she was to double for an actress in *Spook Ranch*. Released in September 1925 by Universal Pictures, the film starred Hoot Gibson as a cowboy who finds himself stranded and penniless in a little desert town. He is arrested for knocking out the owner of a restaurant for refusing to serve him and placed in jail. He is promised his freedom if he solves the mystery of a nearby haunted ranch that no one will go near. Bonnie stunted for actress Helen Ferguson, who portrayed the daughter of the ranch owner.[20]

Movie studios kept Bonnie busy after her work in *Spook Ranch*. Although often uncredited, she and King Tut appeared in a variety of films, mostly Westerns, riding and jumping over fences, busted stagecoaches, and narrow chasms. King Tut doubled for prized horses who costarred with Will Rogers, Tom Mix, and William Hart. A gifted makeup department transformed the stunt horse, using wearable paint to look exactly like the lead actor's ride.[21]

In one film (Bonnie's writings don't identify which one), Bonnie and King Tut were paid more than the average stunter to jump over a stand of scrub brush and down a steep embankment. Most of the time, both rider and horse executed the stunts without incident. That was not the case this time. Tut lost his footing and fell backward, injuring Bonnie. She was pleased they survived the feat but vowed never to attempt anything like it again, regardless of the pay.[22]

Like most cowgirls moonlighting as stunt women, Bonnie was torn between film work and her love of the rodeo. Every season she was drawn back to the road to compete. Considered by many in the business to be the world's champion trick rider, she traveled to various events with no fewer than ten of her horses. Each horse had a specific use, and Bonnie believed in being prepared for every contest she entered. Ginger was her relay horse. King Tut, of course, was the jumper of the herd, along with Domino. Timbuck was ridden for bronc busting, and Black Beauty was a trick riding horse. Each of Bonnie's horses helped her win competitions from Pendleton, Oregon to Prescott, Arizona.[23]

Bonnie experienced her fair share of injuries on the rodeo circuit, some more serious than others. On May 31, 1926, at the fairgrounds in Riverside, California, she had a brush with death. An enraged steer crashed through the railing onto the track in front of the cowgirl riders who were racing in the open one-quarter mile. Bonnie was crushed beneath her horse as the animal catapulted. She was rushed to the hospital, where the doctors determined she suffered a slight concussion. But she was unconscious for more than two weeks.[24]

By August she was in Colorado competing in the Pike's Peak Rodeo and telling a newspaper reporter:

> *The doctors all gave me up. They said I was going to die. I had a fractured skull and for eighteen days knew nothing. . . . I was riding with five other girls in a relay race. Some Brahma steer got loose and two of them ran across the track.*[25]
>
> *My horse turned two complete somersaults when he struck one of those steers. The steer was knocked down and rolled over and over and the horn of the saddle was smashed. The last thing I knew was when I was struck. Many days afterward, I came to in a hospital. They all thought I was going to die. And here I am back in the game again, in the life that I like so well.*[26]

Patrons in attendance at the Pike's Peak Rodeo in Colorado Springs who watched Bonnie and King Tut leap over an automobile filled with people had no idea that less than three months earlier she'd been lying in a hospital bed in critical condition.[27]

Bonnie had no intention of allowing an injury to sideline her for a long period of time and keep her from realizing all she could in her chosen profession. "Getting to this point wasn't easy," she commented in a magazine interview in 1927 regarding her health. "Success doesn't come all at once . . . and then you have to fight to keep it no matter what is ailing you. It's just like a battle with the elements." It was her dogged determination and strength of will that helped her get beyond the brush with death and fulfill the contracts she signed with rodeo promoters.[28]

From August 1926 to the winter of 1928, Bonnie was a favorite with crowds wherever she performed, adding to her trick riding and relay racing wins.

Heartbreak was around the bend, though. In May 1929, Bonnie's husband of twelve years passed away. That loss was another battle in life that she had to fight.[29]

Bonnie's first big outing after becoming a widow was the Molalla Buckaroo Rodeo in Molalla, Oregon. The local paper announced the tenacious cowgirl's participation in glowing terms. "This year's roster of talent is quite impressive," the June 9, 1929, edition of the *Statesman Journal* read. "For shear grace and marvelous riding Bonnie Gray leads them all. She has twelve beautiful trophy cups and honors all attained through hazardous struggle, all webbed about with lady-like manners, accomplishments, and education, backed by diplomacy always grounded on absolute fairness."[30]

For a while, Bonnie was content to travel alone, from one rodeo to another, with just King Tut and the rest of her horses for company. However, after meeting fellow rodeo performer and rancher Donald W. Harris in late 1929, she decided she wanted more. They married June 19, 1930 in a lavish ceremony on the range at the Lasky Ranch near Griffith Park. The bridal party and more than one hundred guests attending the event on horseback. Adorned in a white riding costume, Bonnie paraded down a flower-strewn aisle atop King Tut.[31] Reverend Earl W. Dorrance performed the nuptials astride his horse, Lovey. Shortly after the couple exchanged vows, Bonnie christened the happy occasion by riding King Tut as he jumped over an open car with her new husband and maid of honor inside.[32]

There wasn't much time for a honeymoon. Bonnie was scheduled to give a trick riding exhibition at the annual Onion Day and Harvest

Festival in Payson, Utah; compete in a jumping exhibition at the rodeo in Pomona, California; and participate in the Garrett and Wright Rodeo at the Orange County Fair in Anaheim, California. She was a highly sought after talent and enjoyed the notoriety.[33]

Preferring not to turn down work, Bonnie continued to lend her talents to film productions as well. She and King Tut had added jumping over the tail end of airplanes to their repertoire, and moviemakers were eager to hire the daring duo to execute more on-camera stunts. Bonnie had proven herself to be such a capable stunt double that executives at Hooper Connell Productions offered her a chance at a starring role in a Western called *Flying Lariats*.[34]

Filmed in Northern California, the movie featured Sam Garrett, six-time World Champion Fancy Roper at the Cheyenne Frontier Days. Others in the cast included cowboy stars Wally Wales and Fred Church. The story involved a pair of brothers, played by Garrett and Wales, who both fall in love with Bonnie Gray's character. Their dispute over who should marry Bonnie is interrupted when the pair have to go after a con man who has cheated the bank out of $5,000. Released in August 1931, *Flying Lariats* aptly showcased Bonnie's on-screen appeal.[35]

The trick rider and actress's personal life wasn't as successful off-screen or away from the rodeo arena. Bonnie and Donald's marriage was a volatile one. He was physically abusive, and she filed for divorce.[36] According to the August 27, 1932, edition of the *Spokesman Review*, Bonnie "charged that he came to a rodeo where she was performing in December of 1930 and kicked her with a booted foot so hard her face was discolored and swollen for day." On another occasion, she told the court Harris had whipped her with a bridle. The Harrises' divorce was finalized by September 1932.[37]

Bonnie fully turned her attention to her horses and making personal appearances with King Tut. The pair gave jumping and trick riding exhibitions throughout the West and Canada from 1933 until 1936. After this, rider and horse eventually retired from rodeo performing. King Tut spent the bulk of his days on Bonnie's ranch, enjoying time out of the spotlight. He occasionally appeared at special events where he thrilled audiences jumping over touring cars and wagons.[38]

At forty-four, Bonnie shifted her focus primarily to film. She was fascinated with the moviemaking process and was eager to attempt the stunts necessary to add to the picture's realism. Paramount Pictures hired her in the summer of 1936 to make sure the stunts that Bing Crosby's character was supposed to perform in the film *Rhythm on the Range* looked real. In the Western musical, Crosby played a cowboy who competed in a rodeo, trying to earn money so he could start a ranch of his own. Bonnie was his stunt double in the rodeo arena.[39]

At twenty-nine years old, Bonnie's famous stunt Palamino made the front page of the *San Fernando Valley Times* when he had the honor of receiving the first horse's license issued by the city treasurer in 1946. The January 10, article reminded readers of King Tut's career[40] and his stunt woman owner:

> *King Tut is the horse that has been pictured throughout the world as the one that jumps over fully loaded automobiles. He's done the stunt for the movies, performed before three U. S. Presidents—Harding, Coolidge, Hoover. . . . General of the Armies, John J. Pershing, the Prince of Wales now Duke of Windsor, have all marveled at King Tut, including thousands of boys and girls in every state in the union.*
>
> *King Tut developed into a world known figure for his ability as a jumper, winning twelve trophy cups and numerous prizes and awards.*
>
> *King Tut has saved the life of his mistress five times. Once in a lake. Bonnie Gray is the only woman to have ridden fighting bulls in Mexico—was champion horsewoman of the world.*
>
> *Weighing around 1,200 pounds at present, the Palomino's diet consists of alfalfa, ground oats and barley, mashed bran, and carrots. He goes for apples in a big way and sugar. He gets his apples now and then but no sugar. He always got sugar after his high jumps in performances—that's why he never refused to make his historic leaps into space.*[41]

By 1956, Bonnie was no longer involved with stunt work or giving riding exhibitions. The sixty-five-year-old cowgirl was employed at Gladden

Productions Corp. as a machine operator. Gladden manufactured aircraft parts during World War II and later automobile parts.[42]

Bonnie might have been out of the limelight, but the public had not forgotten her. She was the subject of a handful of articles reflecting on her career. "My yesterdays encompass a lifetime of thrills and danger interlaced with a hope that the show would be successful and that I would live to be in the next one," she shared with a reporter in November 1959.[43]

Bonnie's motion picture career spanned the eras of the silent films and talkies. "Pictures in the early days were all two-reel Westerns, and my job was to double in stunts for cowboy actors such as William Hart, Tom Mix and Helen Twelve Trees," she noted.

In 1981, Bonnie was inducted into the National Cowgirl Hall of Fame. "The profession you follow, the work you do or the life you lead is between yourself and God," she wrote in her memoir. "I follow the life I am leading because I love it. A girl does not need to sacrifice the real things in life to become a professional rider."[44]

Bonnie Gray passed away on April 28, 1908, at her Burbank home, from congestive heart failure. She was ninety-seven years old.[45]

Mildred Douglas

Four women gave some fine exhibitions of sticking in the saddle, but the last one to appear was given first place. It was Mildred Douglas, on Hair Trigger, who was selected for the purse, and her riding warranted the selection.

—*El Paso Times*, March 8, 1917

One-half mile from town, a buckboard wagon idled by the side of the tree-lined road leading westward. Actress Wanda Petit sat on its wide seat, quietly listening to the rhythmic beat of the approaching horse's hooves. When the sound swelled, with a muffled metallic echo, she turned her head and looked behind her. She caught a glimpse of the horseman and smiled when she saw it was cowboy actor Tom Mix. He looked up and touched the brim of his hat as he pulled alongside her. It was February 1918, and both were acting in a scene from the Western film *Six-Shooter Andy*.[1]

Before the two said a word of dialogue, a sheriff's posse appeared on the dusty road, riding fast toward them. Tom Mix quickly turned his horse around and hurried away. Hoping to outrun the lawmen, he spurred his steed up a steep embankment. The officers gave chase. Some fell backward down the hill when their horses lost their footing. Tom's stunt double continued on until they reached the top of the precipice.

The frantic rider looked back at the posse members—they were gaining on him. He studied the rushing river below and made a quick decision. Choosing to take the plunge, the rider dismounted and coaxed his horse to make the leap. He watched the animal plummet forty feet into

Champion Lady Bronco Buster Mildred Douglas WYOMING STATE ARCHIVES the water. The dazed and slightly confused horse emerged unhurt from the death-defying jump. It swam to the riverbank, stumbling over rocks until he got his footing, where he stood shaking from the experience. The stunt double leaped from the precipice minutes later. The stunter hit the water hard and finally popped to the surface. The director overseeing the filming of this harrowing stunt shouted to the cameraman to stop rolling.

Mildred Douglas, dressed as Tom Mix's character, had actually performed the daring feat that would be attributed to the famous actor.[2]

Six-Shooter Andy was one of a handful of silent films Mildred appeared in as a stunt double. Not only did she stand in for Mix in the movie, she also doubled for his leading lady. She made the work look effortless and didn't shy away from attempting any stunt directors suggested. In the 1922 Tom Mix film *Up and Going*, Mildred tumbled off a rocky slope into a pool of water several feet below, and in *Oh, You Tony*, released in 1924, she leapt off the back of a galloping horse onto a fast-moving stagecoach.[3]

Born in Philadelphia on August 21, 1895, to Hugh and Emma McConnell, Mildred knew at the age of seven what she wanted to be when she grew up, and it had nothing to do with working in motion pictures. Her parents had taken her to the Barnum & Bailey Circus at Franklin Field in Pennsylvania. Mildred sat on the end row where she could look over the canvas and see the animals and performers coming in. She just knew she had to be a part of such a show and wanted to work with every kind of animal. The road to achieving that goal had many twists and turns.[4]

After completing her primary education, Mildred traveled east, attending an exclusive school in New England. During her time away from home she decided to see a performance of the Miller Brothers 101 Ranch Wild West Show. She was so taken by the various acts she decided to leave school and seek employment with the troupe. Mildred spent years touring the country in rodeos, circuses, and other popular western shows in addition to the 101 Ranch.[5]

Sometime during this period, Mildred married a cowboy named Tom Douglas. The relationship was short-lived.[6]

Mildred became an expert equestrian. She competed in rodeos from Cheyenne, Wyoming, to Kansas City, Missouri, routinely finishing in the top five women riders in bucking horse contests.[7]

In 1917, at the age of twenty-two, Mildred won the title of World Champion Girl Bronc Rider at the Pendleton Roundup. At the same event, she gave trick riding and shooting exhibitions, further demonstrating her overall cowgirl skills. And it was those skills that helped her win five riding championships in 1917 and 1918.[8]

"I'd rather sit in the saddle on a bucking horse than in a rocking chair," she told a reporter at the *News Tribune*. The reporter continued:

> *It's all in a day's business for her to crawl gingerly from the back of one horse into the saddle forced by camouflage onto a rearing, plunging "killer." She knows all the outlaw's tricks and devilish cunning. She knows how to keep him away from the fence, how to elude him when he throws himself backward to crush her beneath him. She can stick on, without "pulling leather," and she has the grim determination that holds out until the outlaw's heart is broken and he meekly submits himself to her guiding hand upon the reins.*[9]
>
> *The bump, bump, bump of a bucking animal beneath her is a most natural feeling to Mildred. She learned to hang on in spite of the jars, so many years ago that she can't remember. She always rode, she said, and from the time she was a fat little overalled urchin of four when she took her daily exercise by climbing from the corral fence of her father's ranch to the back of an indignant and protesting calf, she has always taken the keenest joy in straddling some humping, jumping creature (if she can't get a horse a steer will do) and subduing it to her will.*

"Yes, I've broken a few bones myself," Mrs. Douglas confessed. "My hip and my foot and other less important members. All Wild West business is a matter of life and death. We get to be fatalists I suppose, but I never have the least fear, no matter how ugly the horse I am riding. I'm sure it would spoil my chances of success if I were afraid."[10]

Stunt woman Mildred Douglas Chrisman on the set of the film *Stage Coach Race*
MUSEUM OF THE GREAT PLAINS

Mildred wasn't satisfied riding only wild broncos, and in the summer of 1919, she decided to try her hand at riding steers. The momentous event marked the first time a woman in Garden City, Kansas, ever rode a steer in competition. Afterward, she vowed to demonstrate each day that she is a "permanent fixture on the bareback of any bovine that ever bounced."[11]

Between rodeo contests, Mildred committed to supplying her riding ability to motion picture executives producing Tom Mix Westerns. Her second husband, Ora "Pat" Chrisman, whom she met working for the 101 Ranch, was a horse trainer for the film star. He was also an actor who appeared in several of Mix's movies. Chrisman suggested his wife be hired as a stunt double, and the filmmakers happily agreed. She proved to be exceptional.[12]

Although the work had challenging moments, Mildred found making movies lacked the nonstop action she loved. In addition to her on-screen duties, she was training and working with horses, lions, leopards, and other animals scheduled to appear in various motion pictures being produced.[13]

A gifted seamstress, Mildred also made the costumes she wore on film. The leather divided skirt and bolero with fringe and beaded trim that she created for the film *Six-Shooter Andy* sold for a substantial amount to a Hollywood costume designer after the production.[14]

In 1935, Mildred and Pat settled in Lawton, Oklahoma, where they were both involved in raising Dalmatians. They also served on the board of the Kennel Club. The pair gave exhibitions, featuring their five trained Rocky Mountain Angora goats, billed as the "Aristocratic Goats." One of the goats was trained to walk a tightrope.[15]

Pat passed away in 1953. Not long after, Mildred decided to pursue another dream she had, that of becoming a nurse. At the age of fifty-nine, she officially entered the profession and took a position at the Comanche County Memorial Hospital in Lawton. In 1954, she traded her fringed leather riding outfits for a white uniform and a starched nurse's cap.

Her life as a Wild West performer was never far from mind, however. She often brought her scrapbooks to the hospital and showed photographs from her other life to interested coworkers and patients. She always spoke fondly of the animals she had trained and the audiences she entertained. Mildred eventually donated those scrapbooks, saddles, movie photos, rawhide ropes, and other memorabilia to the Muscum of the Great Plains in Lawton, Oklahoma.[16]

Mildred Douglas Chrisman died in January 1982 at the age of eighty-seven.[17]

Lorena Trickey

The worse they buck, the better Miss Lorena Trickey of Cheyenne, Wyoming, likes to ride 'em. No wonder she's the world's champion horsewoman. She won the title at the Cheyenne Frontier Days celebration against the best women riders of the west.

—*The Grand Rapids Press*, July 13, 1921

On a warm spring day in 1921, more than two thousand women gathered at the Fox Hollywood Studio to film the all-female chariot race for the silent picture *Queen of Sheba*. Because the story centered around the ill-fated romance of Solomon, King of Israel, and the Queen of Sheba, the majority of the cast were dressed in biblical-era garb. The women who were to drive the chariots were adorned in colorful tunics, leather helmets, and tall, period-style boots. Each was focused on the four-horse team fastened to a yoke and attached to the chariots.[1]

Western cowboy actor and director Tom Mix belted out instructions to the camera crew, telling them to stand by to begin filming. Then he prompted the drivers to take their places. Among the skilled chariot drivers was World Champion All-Around Horsewoman Lorena Trickey. Trickey caught the attention of studio head William Fox during preproduction talks for the picture. He'd read an article about the twenty-eight-year-old's talent in the saddle and believed she would be a perfect stunt woman. In addition to setting records in relay racing, she was also an accomplished Roman-style racer. Before the shoot was over, Mix would call on Lorena to give a demonstration for the cameras.[2]

Lorena Trickey CENTRAL NEVADA MUSEUM, CENTRAL NEVADA HISTORICAL SOCIETY

Not long after filming completed on the *Queen of Sheba*, the rodeo star lent her expertise to a picture with Mary Pickford, *Through the Back Door*. Pickford played a young woman who had moved to America from Belgium just before World War I in search of her mother. Trickey performed most of the horseback riding stunts in the film.[3]

Growing up in northwest Oregon, Lorena couldn't foresee that her skill with horses and riding would lead to her opportunity to work with film pioneers Mix and Pickford. Born in Palmer Hills, Oregon, on February 14, 1893, to Edward and Lucy Trickey, it was assumed she'd become a farmer's wife, living her life working the land with her husband and children. The course of her life changed when Lorena's mother passed away eight months after giving birth to a son. Lorena was just four years old. Raised on her father's ranch with two brothers, Lloyd and Arthur, she learned how to ride at a young age.[4]

Lorena's father encouraged her love for horses, and in September 1910 took his daughter to the first Pendleton Roundup in Pendleton, Oregon. Lorena was thrilled to attend the festivities with thousands of others who had come to see the rodeo. Among the amazing acts she saw was Goldie St. Clair, the Champion Woman Bronc Buster of the World. Lorena was inspired! Goldie had only been competing for a short while before being named the Lady Bucking Horse Rider of the World in 1907.[5]

A year after returning from the Roundup, Lorena married a logger named Howard Udey. Unfortunately, Udey would leave for work and be gone for weeks at a time. By 1917, the marriage was all but over. Lorena filed for divorce, citing desertion.[6]

During her husband's long absences, Lorena continued to hone her horseback riding skills and help her father with his livestock. When she wasn't working at the Trickey homestead, she was perfecting her equestrianism in Clarence Adams Wild West Show. Adams, a saddle bronc rider, hired the most entertaining Pendleton Roundup participants to travel with him to various locations in the Pacific Northwest. They also gave riding exhibitions. Lorena learned a great deal working with the gifted horsemen and women in the show.[7]

Seven years after watching Goldie St. Claire ride at Pendleton, Lorena decided to enter the Roundup herself. She competed against Dorothy Morrell, Cheyenne Frontier Days Rodeo Women's World Champion Bucking Horse Rider, in the bronc riding event and in the cowgirl relay race.[8]

In July 1918, Lorena took part in the Great Stampede Rodeo in Missoula, Montana. Again, she participated in the cowgirl relay race and the bucking horse exhibition. The other women in the contest were experienced equestrians. Dorothy Mullins, Peggy Warren, and Kitty Cannutt had been riding in rodeos much longer than Lorena, and they had earned titles and money along the way. But Lorena gave a respectable showing in the events and received encouraging words from the veteran competitors. Two months later, she made her second appearance in the Pendleton Roundup. Her father was in the stands, cheering her on to her win in the relay race.[9]

Rodeo fans enjoyed watching Lorena's unique riding style. She created a technique that she called "let 'er fly." The term referred to the way she transferred from one horse to another in a relay race, wherein a contestant switched horses three times. Usually, contestants stopped their horses, jumped off, and jumped onto the next one. Lorena found a way to reduce the time by jumping from the back of one horse directly to the back of the next during the race.[10]

Newspaper articles about Lorena and her "let 'er fly" method called her the "pluckiest cowgirl in the world." Reporters covered her first prize wins in bucking contests and Roman riding races. "When you see her standing up on horses' backs rushing them around the arena you will be ready to vote that she is plucky," a column in the October 8, 1918, edition of the *Idaho Republican* read. "She is a brunette with a curl or two playing hide and seek about her shoulders. You are going to cheer her when you see her on the racecourse."[11]

At the heart of the rodeo season in 1919, Lorena agreed to take part in the Kansas Roundup held at the state fairgrounds in Hutchinson. There she competed alongside accomplished Western women, from bronc rider Prairie Rose Henderson to bulldogger Fox Hastings. At the conclusion of the three-day program, Lorena was crowned World's Champion All-Around Cowgirl.[12]

In addition to the awards Lorena was starting to accumulate, she was also collecting injuries. While competing in Cheyenne in late July 1919, she rode an unbroken horse that ran into a high board fence, seriously injuring one of Lorena's legs. After the event, Lorena was taken to the hospital, where doctors removed a six-inch splinter and stitched her thigh.[13]

The tenacious cowgirl refused to let the wound keep her from participating in the Pendleton Roundup. She took home the first-place prize in Roman riding, cowgirls' bronc riding, and the cowgirl relay race, beating out Vera McGinnis in the latter event. McGinnis, like Lorena, became a Hollywood stunt woman.[14]

From October 1919 to March 1920, Lorena repeated wins in the three categories in which she regularly excelled and was a part of rodeos in Washington, Idaho, and Utah. Between rodeo seasons, she continued to appear in various Wild West Shows. Billed as the Pendleton Roundup Champion, Lorena gave Roman riding demonstrations, portraying a Pony Express agent in one of the program's historical reenactments.[15]

Throughout the early 1920s, Lorena dominated both relay racing and bronc riding in the rodeo arena, winning a trophy for each three times at Cheyenne Frontier Days. The press was enamored with the rider and gushed over her abilities in newspaper articles throughout the West.[16]

The *Kansas City Star* reported this on July 13, 1921, when Lorena was twenty-eight:

> *Slim, weighing a scant 100 pounds, and barely turned 21, little Miss Lorena Trickey looks anything but the champion horsewoman of the world. It is harder still to believe that she is known as one of the best "cowboys" on her home range, and yet for several years she rode with her brothers, handling lariat and branding iron with the best of them, and she has "bossed her own roundup," no mean accomplishment for one small maid. . . .*[17]
>
> *Last year before the gathered thousands at Frontier Days, she electrified the big rodeo. She won the cowgirl relay race and conquered the worst outlaw broncos that a combing of the ranges of many states could produce. She started other riders with new trick feats while her pony was dashing at breakneck speed. She rode in the Roman standing races against men contestants, and overcame a wild steer, riding with but a surcingle by which to hold on.*
>
> *No lengthy deliberation on the part of the judges was needed. Little Miss Lorena Trickey was announced the champion horsewoman of the world, and the gold, silver, and diamond McAlpin Trophy became hers. A modern Cinderella had come into her own.*
>
> *But that was not all, she was taken to New York to receive the plaque emblematic of her championship and in her first view of the big cities of the East, this little Cinderella was truly entertained as a princess. Maids and motors were at her call. Millionaires and society*

folks lionized her. Boxes at the opera and the horse shows were hers, and theater invitations poured in until toward the end of her stay she had shyly to beg off.[18]

Newspaper reporters covered Lorena's lows as well as her highs. In July 1922, while competing in the women's relay race at Cheyenne Frontier Days, Lorena was seriously hurt when she was crushed between two horses, and she was unable to continue in the contest. With her arm in a sling, she stood by the rail, wistfully watching cowgirls Mabel Strickland, Mary Harsh, and Vera McGinnis battle for first place.[19]

A year later, Lorena had another accident while riding in an event in Spokane, Washington. "In attempting a trick stunt, she was thrown from her horse who turned and kicked her in the shoulder," the July 4, 1923, edition of the *Spokane Review* noted. A big cowboy ran out from the chute and lifted her up with both arms. He had gone no more than ten steps before the woman rider feebly indicated with one hand that she wanted to get down. Cowboys poured water on Lorena's face, and she dusted herself off. She shook the numbness from her head, got back on the horse, and did the trick over again.[20]

According to Lorena's family, the injuries she incurred during her rodeo years included a skull fracture, a broken jaw, a cracked ankle, and dislocated ribs.[21]

Toward the latter part of the 1920s, Lorena's occasional struggles weren't limited to events inside the rodeo arena. The woman that the press had deemed "Little Cinderella" became romantically involved with a cowboy named J. P. "Slim" Harris in early 1927. By the fall of that same year, the authorities arrested her for his murder.[22]

The crime occurred while the pair were driving from the stables outside Lakeview, Oregon. Initial reports claimed that Slim had been stabbed by an unknown male assailant who leapt on the running board of his car, plunging a knife into the victim's chest. Lorena told investigators that the incident happened so fast she couldn't identify the strange man. She said he fled into the darkness as soon as the car ran into an embankment. She later told authorities that the murderer had been a passenger in the car with them who had suddenly lost his mind, reached out, and stabbed Harris.[23]

After questioning the rodeo star for a few hours, the Lake County District Attorney discovered she had made many conflicting statements. He decided to place Lorena under arrest pending an inquest. In addition to Lorena, bulldogger Robert Brown was taken into custody.

The rumor was that Robert and Lorena were having an affair, and Slim had vowed to kill the couple over their betrayal. Robert killed Slim before the jealous lover had a chance to attack him. Lorena later admitted to investigators that the knife in question belonged to her. That important detail prompted speculation that the crime had been planned. Lorena was formally charged with the murder of Slim Harris on September 13, 1927. Jealousy was alleged to have been the motive, but it wasn't actually the scenario most had speculated.[24]

Authorities claimed Slim was the one having an affair and that Lorena killed him over his unfaithfulness. During the preliminary hearing, the prosecuting attorney presented four witnesses. One of those witnesses was a hardware store employee who testified that Lorena had purchased a long-bladed knife several days before Slim was stabbed to death. Investigators were unable to find the murder weapon at the scene. When Lorena was asked on the stand if she knew what happened to the knife, she told the grand jury she hadn't seen it since it had been stolen from their barn.[25]

Enough evidence was presented that jurors felt they had no choice but to hold Lorena over for trial. The charge was first-degree murder. Bail was denied. The September 14, 1927, edition of the *Klamath News* reported that Lorena was so sullen and despondent she threatened to kill herself if she had the chance.[26]

When the trial began on November 7, 1927, the courtroom was packed. It was reported that Lorena looked sickly as she was escorted there from her cell. She sat beside her lawyer in silence, unable to make eye contact with anyone around her, as the state and defense questioned members of the jury panel.[27]

The special prosecutor hired by Slim Harris's family prompted jeers from the spectators in the galley when he accused a local jeweler of "arousing prejudice in the community in favor of Miss Trickey." The jeweler had placed all the cups and trophies Lorena won in various riding competitions on display in his store's front window. The prosecutor wanted the court to order the jeweler to remove the display, but the judge denied his request.[28]

Lorena's voice was barely audible when she was asked to enter her plea. She pleaded self-defense. When she took the stand, she burst into tears and confessed. She told the jury:

> *I'd die for the man I love. And I loved Slim. At times I want to scream out and talk and talk and talk. To me it's all a dream. I am so weary of it. I cannot sleep.*[29]
>
> *I pull the blankets of the jail cot about me and stare into the darkness and always I see the face of Slim peering down at me, and he is always smiling. . . .*
>
> *Have you ever really loved? If so, you will understand. I loved Slim and he told me he was through; that when the Lakeview Roundup was over, he would put the horse in the barn and ride over the hills. I couldn't let him leave me. I didn't mean to kill him, so help me God. I didn't.*[30]
>
> *Slim was drunk. The automobile he drove zig-zagged at precarious angels down the road. And when I suggested that I drive he flared up. He cursed him and then struck me. I screamed. He stopped the car, and I jumped out and ran. He pursued him with a wrench. He struck at me but fell in the process. When he got to his feet he renewed his insane attack.*
>
> *I drew a dagger from my belt. I didn't mean to kill him. I didn't. I didn't.*[31]

Sobbing, Lorena buried her face in her hands, unable to continue. Her attorney called numerous witnesses to testify to the abuse and beatings she had suffered at the hands of Slim. They explained to the jury that she was being subjected to another beating the day Slim was killed and that she acted in self-defense against the violence.[32]

Despite the district attorney's claim that the slaying was deliberate and that Lorena, with calculating and cunning, tried to throw suspicion from herself by saying the victim was abusive, the jury believed her testimony. After deliberating for twenty minutes, they found Lorena not guilty.[33]

"I'm flat broke," Lorena told reporters as she left the courthouse, "but I'm not worrying. I've been up against it before and have come out of it."[34]

Cowboys and cowgirls who attended the proceedings and gathered outside the justice building afterward cheered the beleaguered rodeo star on as she walked away from the approving crowd.[35]

But life after the trial proved to be difficult for Lorena. Not everyone was as supportive as the encouraging men and women who attended the trial. A woman's organization in Portland, Oregon, protested an appearance she was scheduled to make there. They disagreed with the "not guilty" verdict and believed she should be punished for the crime. Members of the organization took the matter to the city council, asking them to intervene and prevent Lorena from performing. The women's group was unsuccessful in their attempt. "There's no law to prevent Miss Trickey from appearing here," Mayor George Baker stated regarding the women's request.[36]

Long after the trial had ended Lorena's career, her relationship with Slim Harris and his subsequent murder, continued to be the subject of many newspaper articles. It wasn't until May 1928 that the acquitted woman felt as though she might be able to move on from the tragedy. Organizers of the Railroad Jubilee and Roundup scheduled to take place in September in Lakeview, Oregon, invited Lorena to ride in the event. She happily accepted.[37]

Shortly after agreeing to perform at the Jubilee and Roundup, Lorena signed a contract to participate in the La Pine Roundup, held in Bend, Oregon, in July. According to advertisements, she would ride the wildest broncs on the circuit. Days after the La Pine event, Lorena ran afoul of the law again. She was ordered to pay a $10 fine for violating the city ordinance against riding a horse across any sidewalk within the city of Kalispell.[38]

"In true old western style, she rode her horse into the lobby of the National Hotel, where a cabaret program was in progress," the July 12, 1928, edition of the *Billings Gazette* reported. "She hadn't reckoned with the ordinance made by the city dads of long ago. The revelers were delighted, and the proprietress of the hotel offered no objection, but the law stood, and policemen notified the equestrienne to appear in court."[39]

Lorena made news again in August when it was announced that the rodeo queen had married a rancher named Magnus Peterson of Prineville, Oregon, on the 22nd. The couple honeymooned in Montana, where Lorena had contracts to ride in a number of rodeos and races. Between September 1928 and September 1929, the tenacious cowgirl won several races on Thoroughbreds she purchased, including races in Tijuana, Vancouver, British Columbia, and the first running of the Hillsborough Town Plate, a race exclusively for women. Her last professional ride was on Labor Day 1929 at Klamath Falls, Oregon. Lorena Trickey Peterson retired undefeated as the World's All-Around Champion Cowgirl.[40]

By early 1930, the Petersons had moved to Nevada. For a while, they continued to raise and train Thoroughbreds. They traveled the state, showing their horses at county fairs and carnivals. In 1934, Lorena was seriously injured while giving a trick riding demonstration at the Five Mile Station, forty miles east of Tonopah. She was thrown from the saddle, and her foot was caught in the stirrup. She was dragged a quarter of a mile across the desert before fellow riders caught the spooked horse.[41]

In addition to raising Thoroughbreds, Lorena and Magnus bred and sold cattle and milk goats. Their livestock received several blue ribbons at the Nye County Fair. The Petersons' goats were a highly prized commodity in the United States and aboard. The Agricultural Bank of Greece arranged loans for businesses in the country to have the animals shipped to them. According to the June 14, 1946, edition of the *Reno Gazette Journal*, the request from Greek consumers was the first time in the history of Nevada that a foreign government had sought to purchase goats bred in the Nevada desert.[42]

Lorena's business interests extended beyond ranching into prospecting and mining. The mines around Tonopah had produced more than $700,000 in gold and silver since 1901, and the former cowgirl was convinced she could find a rich vein that would yield millions. She was so serious about the endeavor she enrolled in the Tonopah School of Mining and Engineering for three years. After graduating with a degree in minerology and assaying, she and Magnus began scouting the region for a big discovery. They began prospecting a claim called the

Longstreet Mine located sixty miles east of Tonopah. Several months later they abandoned the dig there and started a search for the Lost Mexican Mines. It wasn't until 1938, when Lorena was prospecting in an area around Horse Thief Springs, that she happened onto promising ore. Horse Thief Springs was named for Chief Colorow Ignacio Ouray Walkara of the Timpanogos Band of Ute. It was there she made her first claim, calling it the Old Cowgirl Mine.[43]

Lorena and Magnus would go on to stake out additional claims and make news doing so. In the fall of 1948, they took over operation of the Smith Quick Silver Mine, forty-five miles northeast of Tonopah in Stone Cabin Valley. At one time the mine produced more than $70,000 in quicksilver. In January 1951, Lorena announced that they were mining the property for antimony, a semimetal used to make medicine, cosmetics, and bullets. That particular find was located sixty miles north of Tonopah. The find yielded a considerable tonnage of high-grade antimony and made Lorena a substantial profit.[44]

In late 1959, Lorena struck gold in a volcanic mountain range called the Hot Creek Range in central Nevada. The May 19, 1951, edition of the *Nevada State Journal* reported that several tons of ore had been extracted from the property in the first shipment, valued at $93.70 per ton.[45]

"The original strike of the rich ore was made by Mrs. Peterson, who found pieces of the ore at the foot of a small hill and which was subsequently traced to the vein," the *Nevada State Journal* article read. "Development work done since by the Petersons has disclosed a strong north-south vein that has steadily increased in width as depth has been gained. Selected samples from the vein have assayed as high as $300 per ton in gold with a small amount of silver."[46]

During the more than twenty-five years that had passed since Lorena had retired from trick and stunt riding, she'd built a successful career for herself far from the rodeo arena. The high honors she'd won in bronc riding and relay racing had not been forgotten, however. The Pendleton Roundup staff decided to recognize her contribution to the sport at the event in 1956. It was fitting that Lorena's appearance at the Roundup was sponsored by the Hamley Saddle Company. She had won two Hamley saddles at Pendleton in 1919 and 1921. She was the only woman rider to have won such a prize up to that time.[47]

Reminiscing with fans after the Pendleton celebration, Lorena relived her days Roman riding on the set of the film *Queen of Sheba*. At the director's request, all eyes were on her when she leaped onto two horses, placed one foot on top of each horse, and slowly led the animals into a trot. After a few moments she urged them into a run. The cast and crew erupted in applause as she guided the horses around the enormous outdoor set. Tom Mix smiled approvingly at Lorena as she rode by him. The faith he'd had in her talent had not been misplaced.[48]

When asked about her time as a champion all-around cowgirl, she recalled the days with mixed emotion. "It was a rough game, rodeoing in the early days," she shared with the Pendleton Roundup patrons. "The old-time riders are becoming few in number and scattered thin over a wide range. On occasion we gals would compete against men and we sometimes beat them. I've got saddles and a table full of trophies and a lot of memories, some good, some not so good."[49]

Lorena Trickey Peterson passed away on November 15, 1961, after emergency surgery on perforated ulcers. She was sixty-eight years old. On October 22, 2000, the woman the press referred to as the Queen of the Riders was inducted into the National Cowboy and Western Hall of Fame.[50]

STUNTING IN THE TALKIES

An article on the front page of the June 22, 1926, edition of the *New York Times* announced that talking pictures were the primary topic of conversation in every corner of the nation. "Few things prior to the invention, except perhaps a great war, or a worldwide epidemic, had attracted so much attention this century," the piece read.

The advancement of silent pictures to "talkies" would touch the lives of people around the world. Elections, books, and sporting events had all excited interest over time, but they paled in comparison to the excitement of talking pictures.[1]

For more than twenty-five years, movies had been a universal source of amusement and had more audiences than any other entertainment in the world. The fame of film actors and actresses exceeded the fame of politicians, generals, ministers, and artists. But it had, until 1925, been a faraway sort of fame. Silent filmgoers paid tribute to those stars in the same way Roman citizens paid tribute to their gods. Silent film stars flitted across the screen, and they were gone. Sounds were never heard, and the characters seemed to belong to another world. The stars appeared before mesmerized audiences, beautiful and voiceless, and their words were interpreted by means of writing.

This illusion was dispelled by the talkies. Movie performers became humanized when they spoke.

Talkies were introduced in August 1926 when Warner Brothers Studio presented the first practical sound film, using a process known as Vitaphone to record musical accompaniments and brief passages of dialogue. In 1927, Fox Studios launched a similar program. Its Movietone

News created considerable excitement with its camera and microphone recording of the triumphal return from Europe of the American aviator Charles A. Lindbergh after his solo flight to France. In October 1927, Warner Brothers presented its first talking film, *The Jazz Singer*, featuring the American actor and singer Al Jolson. The immediate success of that film signaled the end of the silent era.[2]

The popularity of Westerns in the final years of the silent cinema had fallen dramatically. Critics blamed focusing on saintly and celibate characters as the reason, noting they were out of step with the liberated twenties. Fading from the scene was the time moviegoers stomped, whistled, and cheered when the names of their favorite Western stars flashed on the screen, usually on Saturday matinees, which was serial time. Hoot Gibson, Harry Carey, William S. Hart, and Ken Maynard were serial kings, defying outlaws and saving the day every week. But it wasn't enough to sustain the genre. The only chance for revitalizing the Western was talkies.[3]

Two films emerged in the late 1920s that altered the future of the Westerns and Western stars. Those films, both of which were made in 1928, were *In Old Arizona* and *Overland Bound. In Old Arizona* was the first major sound Western production. Directed by Raoul Walsh, it starred Warner Baxter as the Cisco Kid—a colorful character of the Old West who outran the law sent to arrest him. The movie was hailed as the "covered wagon of talking pictures." One of the film's most notable features was its use of outdoor sound. Walsh's recordings of hoofbeats, gunshots, and the sound of bacon cooking in a pan helped persuade leaders in the film industry that sound, as well as speech, could be of great advantage to the Western. *In Old Arizona* represented a distinct step forward in talking pictures.[4]

Overland Bound was the second sound Western and the first independently produced. The story centered on a railroad agent out to defraud a rancher of their land. The film's success led to other independent studios saturating the market with similar, low budget, quickly produced Westerns known as "B movies." With the revitalization of the Western, new screen heroes became a colorful spot in movie lovers' hearts. William "Hopalong Cassidy" Boyd, Gene Autry, Roy Rogers, and John Wayne were a few of the talking and singing cowboys who became stars.[5]

The 1928 film *In Old Arizona* was the first major sound Western. AUTHOR'S COLLECTION

Overland Bound, released in 1929, is considered the first all-talking B Western.
AUTHOR'S COLLECTION

Just as they had in the Wild West Shows and silent pictures, cowgirl stunt women generated a fan base that returned to the theater time after time to see them save the day. Betty Miles, Nell O'Day, Polly Burson, and Olive Fuller Golden were a few of the women who dared to put themselves in harm's way for the sake of entertainment.

Nell O'Day, a stunning, athletic talent, appeared in thirteen Johnny Mack Brown Westerns in the early 1940s. She was a skilled horsewoman who prided herself on performing all her own stunts. Born Mildred Nell Roach on September 22, 1909, in Prairie Hill, Texas, she had a fascinating family background. Her mother, Mildred, was a descendant of Elder John Parker, a minister who was killed at the massacre at Fort Parker, Texas. Elder Park's granddaughter Cynthia Ann Parker was captured, raised with the Comanche Indians, and became the mother of Quanah Parker, last chief of the Comanche Indians.[6]

Nell's parents moved to Southern California in 1912. While attending primary school in Los Angeles, she got involved with local theatrical productions, performing as a dancer and singer in a few programs. Her exceptional talent as a singer and dancer led to her first big break. At age eighteen, she was touring with the Tommy Atkins Sextet. While playing West Coast variety houses, the act was hired to appear in a number of feature pictures. Critics hailed Nell as the most promising ingenue of the season in 1931.[7]

Nell O'Day appeared opposite cowboy film star Johnny Mack Brown in thirteen films. AUTHOR'S COLLECTION

In 1932, Warner Brothers and Fox Studios signed Nell to lucrative contracts for performing in a variety of musicals, as well as other films. Her first starring role was in the Western *Smoked Lightning* with George O'Brien. Based on Zane Grey's book *Canyon Walls*, *Smoked Lightning* was a thrilling picture of hard riding, with the hero finally winning several battles with the crooked sheriff. Nell played O'Brien's love interest. She went on to appear in more than forty films, mostly Westerns, starring opposite Johnny Mack Brown. Between acting and stunting in various pictures, she also sang songs to the popular cowboy stars.[8]

In 1938, Nell began pursuing a Broadway career and traveled the country from New York to San Francisco performing in musicals. She changed careers again in 1943, focusing on writing stage plays, screenplays, and teleplays. She retired from show business in the early 1960s and became the editor of a publishing company. She lived to be seventy-nine.[9]

When producer-director Robert Tansey signed actress and stunt woman Betty Miles to a multi-movie deal with Monogram Pictures in 1941, he was hiring the reigning Champion Cowgirl of California. At thirty-one, Betty had been riding horses for more than twenty years. She was an expert.[10]

Betty was born in Santa Monica, California, in January 1910, and her parents were ranchers who taught her to ride and to rope. Betty's venture into motion pictures came about after she graduated from the University of Southern California with a degree in speech. She made her first screen appearance on horseback in the United Artist film *Nothing Sacred*. Although her part was small, Betty enjoyed the work and decided to pursue a career in the entertainment industry. Oddly enough, she chose to focus on writing rather than being in front of the camera. From 1937 to 1940, she was a regular contributor to a radio series about American history.[11]

In mid-1940, Betty left her typewriter to double for Linda Darnell in the film *Chad Hanna*, starring Henry Fonda and Dorothy Lamour. Based on a book of the same title, *Chad Hanna* was the story of a young man who joined the circus and fell in love with the show's popular equestrian performer—an ambitious bareback rider threatening to get top billing. While stunting for Darnell—who was allergic to horses—Betty handled not only difficult bareback riding but some of the more mundane tasks with the animals.[12]

Once the filming on *Chad Hanna* was complete, Betty was sent to Monogram Pictures to do stunt work on a string of Tex Ritter Westerns produced at the Monogram Ranch in Newhall, California. According

Stunt woman Betty Miles alongside cowboy film star Bob Steele AUTHOR'S COLLECTION

to the studio's press material, Betty caught the series director's attention when she volunteered to double for an actress who was unable to control her horse and execute the stunt. Betty performed the difficult feat in a single take. From there, she became a regular cast member in cowboy pictures featuring Tom Keene and Billy Elliot. Her colleagues complimented her skills, noting that "she was very professional, very talented, loved horses, and doing her own stunts."[13]

The daring stunts she tackled included Roman riding a wagon team in the film *The Driftin' Kid*, racing her horse Sonny along a narrow mountain path to escape a gang of mounted outlaws in *Riding the Sunset Trail*, and jumping from an out-of-control buggy in *Sonora Stagecoach*.[14]

Betty left the motion picture world behind in 1946. She wanted to teach school and was employed as an educator for more than thirty years in Fresno and Turlock, California. She lived to be eighty-two.[15]

Polly Burson was one of ten ladies referred to by film historians as the "Queen of Western Stunt women." Born in Western Oregon in 1919, she learned to ride at the age of six. Seven years later she was giving riding exhibitions at rodeos and performing in Wild West Shows across the country.[16]

Between 1941 and 1944, Polly appeared regularly in rodeos at Madison Square Garden in New York. Newspapers often wrote about her equestrian skills, noting that when she rode in a show she was rarely in the saddle. Once around the arena, riding upside down and holding only to the saddle horn, served as a warm-up for the specialty tricks to come. The ride that most impressed the crowd was the Russian drag. While her horse Duke sprinted around the arena, Polly would hang by one foot from the saddle horn, her head just skimming the ground and missing Duke's churning hoofs by inches.[17]

Polly's expertise in the saddle was sought after in Hollywood. In 1944, Republic Pictures President Herbert Yates hired her as a stunt woman. She made her debut in a serial called the *Purple Monster Strikes*. Polly doubled for one of the series' female leads, doing everything from falling off a horse to jumping off a twenty-five-foot cliff.[18]

Polly was a stunt double for many of Republic Pictures' star actresses, including Dale Evans, Vera Ralston, and Anne Jeffries. Other studios hired

Stunt woman Polly Burson in costume for the film *Sword of Monte Cristo* AUTHOR'S COLLECTION

her to double for their key players, too. While working for Paramount, she doubled for Yvonne De Carlo in *Frontier Gal* and for Betty Hutton in *The Perils of Pauline*. During the filming of the Hutton picture, Polly was required to leap from a galloping horse onto a moving train. Universal Pictures had her double for Shelly Winters in *Winchester 73*, 20th Century

Fox hired her to double for Marilyn Monroe in *Niagara*, and she was also in MGM's film *How the West Was Won*, doubling for Debbie Reynolds.[19]

Over her forty-year career, Polly stunted in more than fifty films. Her peers said that she was a "brave woman who would risk anything to put on a good show for moviegoers everywhere." She was inducted into the Stunt woman's Hall of Fame in 1986 and the Cowgirl Hall of Fame in 2002.[20] She lived to be eighty-seven.[21]

The influence stunt women had on the early, ever-evolving, motion picture industry was significant. Many of the brave souls received no credit line for their work and little or no recognition for their accomplishments. Few stunt women got rich or famous or were sought after for autographs. They did get bruised and battered and occasionally hospitalized, performing stunts ranging from riding a horse through a plate glass window, over a precipice, down a steep and rocky embankment, or a thousand other death-defying acts. Their work has been seen by millions of filmgoers who seldom consider the amazing feats of daring that were performed by women other than the names on movie posters.

Vera McGinnis

Vera McGinnis, champion equestrian jumps right into the limelight as she hops over horse and man putting her mount, Blondy, over a double hazard. The stunt is a daring one, which few of the roughriders of Hollywood would attempt.

—*The Oakland Post Enquirer*, September 15, 1928

Five thousand motion picture stuntpeople and extras dressed in pioneer costumes gathered at the Quinn Ranch outside Los Angeles to take part in the filming of the Western movie *Cimarron*. Based on the novel by Edna Ferber, the story is about the opening of the Oklahoma Territory and its fight for statehood, told through the lives of a newspaper editor and his wife.[1]

Director Wesley Ruggles maneuvered back and forth in front of the cast, shouting instructions in preparation for the shoot. Crowds of people taking his direction perfectly mimicked the torrent of humanity waiting to pour onto Oklahoma soil in 1889 in order to claim homesteads. Thousands of extras sat aboard a fleet of prairie schooners, horses, stagecoaches, and handcarts, and a few sat on bicycles.

Twenty-eight cameramen, a host of camera assistants, and photographers positioned at various spots around the setting made last-minute adjustments to their equipment. One of the cameras was trained on thirty-eight-year-old Vera McGinnis. The cowgirl-turned-stunter sat atop a horse named Blackie, anxious to get moving. While listening to what the director had to say about the filming, she tried to calm her ride, struggling to stand still in the lineup.

Cimarron was the first film stunt woman Vera McGinnis appeared in.
AUTHOR'S COLLECTION

Vera glanced at the riders on either side of her. She knew many extras had told the employment agency who hired them that they were fine equestrians, but she could tell by the way they sat their horses they were far from experts. She hoped she could successfully lead Blackie through any mishap that might occur as a result of inexperienced riders.[2]

Vera was the stunt double for actress Estelle Taylor, who portrayed a "soiled dove" hoping to secure a section of land for herself in the soon-to-be opened territory. Vera had the unique position of being the only woman to run in the race. The other extras in the scene, dressed in women's clothing, were actually men. With the exception of Vera, the director believed the ambitious undertaking was too dangerous for the average female extra to take on. Ruggles was familiar with Vera's daring and talent, and he was confident she would get through unscathed.

When the signal was given for the action to start, a great wave of cheering arose, and the assemblage moved en masse as fast as they could toward the appointed destination. Vera held Blackie back, waiting for the wagons and schooners to move ahead and provide space for the horse to run without interference. Blackie didn't take long to narrow the gap between himself and Vera and the teams of horses pulling buggies. The novice drivers guiding those animals crossed in front of Vera and her ride, almost hitting them. More than once, the cameras were rolling as horse and rider continued on their way with the rest of the cast.

Just when it seemed the scene would end without injury, the great fleet of extras, stuntpeople, and their vehicles traveled over what appeared to be a level plain. It was anything but. The ground was littered with prairie dog holes, some two feet across and others in clusters. Before filming began the production company sent a crew out to fill in gaping trenches with dirt. The work was only done on the area that would be used in the shot, and the ground wasn't touched beyond that. Vera skillfully guided Blackie through the potentially hazardous section of prairie. He cleared the holes with big strides and didn't stop until they were out of harm's way.[3]

The action of the mad scramble translated well on the big screen. Critics hailed *Cimarron* as a "magnificent film production" and boasted that it was "in the class of the never-to-be-forgotten productions." It would go on to win the Academy Award for the best film, best adaptation, and best set design. Vera McGinnis would go on to be one of the most admired and respected cowgirl stunt women in the business.[4]

Vera McGinnis was born on November 12, 1892, in East Lynne, Missouri. Her father, Robert, was a physician and her mother, Melissa, took care of the family home and watched after Vera and her older brother Owen. The McGinnis family soon moved to New Mexico, near the Cimarron River. It was there the toddler learned to ride. In 1897, Robert moved his family back to Missouri. He had been employed as a surgeon for the Union Pacific Railroad, and his own health suffered because of the

Vera McGinnis AUTHOR'S COLLECTION

long hours and distance he had to travel to see patients. He established his own practice in Warrensburg, Missouri. However, less than two years after going into business himself, Dr. McGinnis died as a result of a heart attack on February 22, 1899. Six-year-old Vera was devastated.[5]

Vera's uncle Harold McGinnis came to the family's aid. He was also a physician and in love with his brother's wife. Vera's mother and uncle married and, just as the family had done before, moved around to accommodate the doctor's medical practice. Vera was fond of her uncle, and he recognized how she struggled as she went from one school after another. To help her along, he purchased a mustang for her named Cricket. The pair were inseparable. Vera perfected her riding technique on her gray and white horse. In her mind, this solidified the notion that she was destined to be an accomplished equestrian.[6]

In late September 1905, Vera competed in the first of many races that would come. The McGinnis family was living in Norborne, Missouri, where Dr. Harold McGinnis served on the board of directors for the annual street fair. One of the fair events was a contest for best lady rider, and Vera managed to convince her mother and stepfather to allow her to enter.[7]

Melissa made the riding habit for Vera, required for her to take part in the event. Both Dr. McGinnis and Melissa let Vera know her competition was steep. The majority of the ladies who had entered were older and more seasoned. The teenager was nervous but not discouraged when the contestants were asked to take their places.[8] Vera recalled later in life:

> *With weak and shaking knees I mounted Cricket, who was suddenly as skittish as a yearling.*
>
> *It must have been my getup that disturbed her, for I generally rode her bareback dressed in calico. Mincingly she stepped out into the street with her ears cocked and her muscles quivering. To me she felt as if her feet could hardly reach the ground.*[9]
>
> *The judges had us walk, trot, and canter around the ring. Then they asked us to "figure eight." By now the tension had eased for Cricket, and me, too, so we really made the figure-eighting snappy.*
>
> *After all the ladies put their horses through their paces, we lined up to wait for the judges' decision. Standing thus, beside tall saddle horses and grown girls, with my head coming level with their waists, I suddenly knew what mama had meant. I not only felt foolish, I felt so insignificant. Then my name was called and, pocketing my emotions, I raced Cricket toward the stand and slip to a stop with an unnecessary flourish.*

The judges saw past Vera's anxiety and concentrated on her talent in the saddle. She was elated when the announcement was made that she had won first place. She thought of that first win often as she went through school and graduated from Nevada High School in Nevada, Missouri. After graduation, she attended business college and took a job as a stenographer in Kansas City. In February 1912, she married J. S. Himes. But, by March 1913, she was single and living in Salt Lake City, Utah.[10]

Few things in her short life had given her the same pleasure as horseback riding had. She decided to abandon everything to pursue her ambition of riding for a living. A chance meeting with Western motion picture and rodeo star Art Acord in June 1913 gave her hope that such a dream was possible. In addition to producing and performing on camera and in the arena, Acord was a promoter for the Salt Lake Fourth of July Rodeo celebration. When Vera shared her love of riding, he invited her to train for the upcoming event, using his horses. She happily accepted his offer. Vera participated in the two-mile relay race, coming in third behind Rose Wenger (aka stunt woman Helen Gibson) and Ruth Wiseman.[11]

From Utah, Vera traveled to Oregon to compete in the Pendleton Roundup. In mid-September she again entered the cowgirl relay race. This time she competed against top riders Bertha Blanchett and Ollie Osborn. Vera placed second behind the veterans.[12]

During her time at the Pendleton rodeo grounds, Vera became acquainted with a champion bronc rider named Earl Simpson. Simpson was fearless inside the rodeo arena but shy and reserved when it came to the opposite sex. He and cowboy Hoot Gibson worked with Vera to hone her relay racing skills. Barney Sherry, a Native American from Oregon, offered to lend her his string of relay horses for use in future rodeos.[13]

In August 1913, Vera joined Barney and his rodeo team on an exhibition through Winnipeg, Canada. Among the other cowgirls on the excursion were Blanche McGaughy and Rose Wenger. Vera spent a great deal of time with the expert riders, learning how to be one of the best in the sport. Barney's riders earned a percentage of the prize money they'd won. Hoot Gibson and Earl Simpson were also a part of the Winnipeg team and the top moneymakers. The education Vera gained watching the pair work was priceless.[14]

In her autobiography, Vera credited Barney with providing her the animals needed to prove herself in the arena and for encouraging her to pursue Earl, with whom she had developed more than a passing interest.[15]

After her time in Canada, Vera took part in a number of rodeos from Tulsa, Oklahoma, and Abilene, Texas. Between competitions, she returned to Missouri to visit her mother living in Warrensburg. Somewhere during her travels, she received a letter from Earl Simpson inviting her to come to Los Angeles where he was staying. He explained that they could go on the "rodeo road" together when the spring shows opened in California.[16]

"No one else would have called it a love letter or a proposal," Vera wrote in her memoir years later. "But, knowing Earl, I fancied I could read between the lines." Vera hurried to meet him in California. They were married in April 1914 at the home of the people Earl was living with. The ceremony was simple—only immediate family and close friends were present. The newlyweds planned to look for a small ranch they could buy and work most of the year. Their summers would be reserved for the rodeo.[17]

Less than a week after they exchanged vows, the Simpsons were riding in the Bakersfield Rodeo. Vera took home top prize in the trick riding category. Almost from the start, the Simpsons had a different idea of what married life involved. Although Vera was fiercely independent, she wanted a permanent home they could return to after events. Earl didn't want to rush into anything. Vera recalled in her memoir that her husband wanted to be married but not tied down. One example of him wanting to be unencumbered came immediately following the Bakersfield event. Vera traveled next to a rodeo in Stockton, and her husband left to do a show in Klamath Falls, Oregon.[18]

Vera wasn't satisfied simply performing the same routines over and over. She'd mastered relay racing, and in Stockton she decided to study Roman riding. Well-known cowgirl Hazel Hoxie taught her how to ride Roman style, stressing the importance of good balance—the trick involved standing with one foot on the back of each of two horses, side by side. It didn't take Vera long to catch on. She drove herself until she mastered the style. She didn't want merely to know how to ride but to do it well enough to make money. Vera excelled at Roman riding, winning her first major competition at the Wizard's Roundup in Salt Lake and at Pendleton in the fall of 1914.[19]

Vera and Earl spent their first winter together as man and wife in Jackson Hole, Wyoming. She persuaded him to purchase a homestead in the area and settled on a rustic cabin near Antelope Flat. For a while, the Simpsons were content with their homelife. They'd vowed to put down roots in one place and to become faithful Wyoming citizens. But the lure of the rodeo was strong, convincing them to abandon such notions.

They had almost depleted their earnings from the previous rodeo season, and a lack of funds prompted them to accept a $500 offer to appear at the Los Angeles Rodeo in May 1915. Vera and Earl were reunited with many friends at the event. Art Acord, Hoot Gibson, Rose Wenger, and Hazel Hoxie were just a few of the regular circuit riders to take part in the exhibition.[20]

The quality performances the Simpsons gave at the rodeo led to offers for appearances at additional shows. Both did well competing in various events, earning their share of financial rewards as well as injuries. Earl was hurt bulldogging at rodeos in Billings, Montana, and Cody, Wyoming, in July 1915. The couple took time to heal and rest at their homestead between programs, and then it was off again to the next rodeo. Vera excelled in relay racing, bronc riding, trick riding, Roman racing, and bull riding. Rodeo announcers often referred to her as an all-around champion cowgirl. It was Vera's reputation for being a well-rounded rider that led to the producers of the stage show *The Passing of the West* to offer her a job.[21]

The idea behind *The Passing of the West* was to bring a glimpse of the great Old West to rodeo arenas throughout Montana during the summer of 1916. Produced by Charles L. Harris, one of the leading attorneys in the state, the focus would be on entertaining and educating audiences who attended the Stampede in Sheridan and the Roundup at Miles City, Billings, Butte, Helena, and Great Falls. Various attractions, cowboys and cowgirls, exponents of pioneer western life, horses and cattle, plus stagecoaches would travel the *Passing of the West* circuit. Earl was contracted to join the cast as well.[22]

Although *The Passing of the West* attracted big crowds at each showing, Charles L. Harris proved to be an unscrupulous businessman. He not only stopped providing transportation for the troupe after the fourth program, he also stopped paying them. The show ended abruptly with cowgirls and cowboys scrambling to get to the nearest rodeo to register to compete. Vera and Earl made their way to Cheyenne, Wyoming, to ride in the Frontier Days Rodeo.[23]

Every rodeo the Simpsons participated in, and every mile they put between themselves and their homestead, pushed their dream of living and working together farther away. Their relationship was troubled. When Vera broached the subject of having a family someday, Earl let her know he had no interest in being a father. Neither choose to address the problems in their marriage. They hoped the distraction of the rodeo would eventually lead to a resolution, one way or another.[24]

In the summer of 1916, Vera and Earl ventured into the Thoroughbred horse business. Vera had to learn another form of riding, because they raced the stock they purchased. She didn't care about being a jockey; she only wanted to be a cowgirl. Simpson assured her that she'd be able to return to the arena, and that when she did the other "race ridin' gals better look out." Vera wasn't as sure of the outcome as her husband, and she worried that they might have overextended themselves.

Her concerns proved to be well founded. A mishap at the Southern Arizona Fair in Tucson, Arizona, in late October 1916, resulted in the death of competitors' horses and a spinal injury for Vera's mount when several horses collided on the track. Vera suffered several cuts and bruises and a torn ligament in her knee. For the remainder of her riding career, she had to bandage the knee tightly to keep it from popping out of the socket.[25]

From Tucson, the couple traveled to Phoenix, where they met up with cowgirl Prairie Rose Henderson and her cowboy husband Johnny Judd. The four of them decided to produce a Christmas rodeo to be held in the Arizona towns of Miami and Globe. The crowds were unruly, and a fight broke out among the spectators and performers. Vera held her own against a drunken cowhand who tried to put his hand up her skirt.[26]

Between 1917 and 1918, Vera appeared in rodeos from Fort Worth, Texas, to San Francisco, California. The majority of the time she made the trips alone. She won numerous titles, including World's Champion Trick Rider and The Cowgirl Relay Race Champion. Her marriage was severely strained when Earl was drafted for World War I in September 1918 and sent overseas to fight. At a loss about what her next move should be, Vera contacted Winnie Browne, a friend she'd met while riding the rodeo circuit. Winnie lived in Los Angeles and was working as an extra in silent films. She helped Vera get work at the same studio that employed her.[27]

"I started doing stunts for pictures that winter [1918], which was hard and at that time a poorly paid profession," Vera recalled later in her life. "I remember doubling for a star on the Beverly Hills bridle path one day and doing five falls off a cantering horse for ten bucks a fall. But I was glad to get the work. My only complaint was that there wasn't enough of it."[28]

Vera graduated from stunt work to acting in the summer of 1919, appearing in the Paramount film *Nobody's Home*. Starring Dorothy Gish, sister of the famous actress Lillian Gish, *Nobody's Home* was about a fortune teller and fortune hunter, hoping to ruin the budding romance that her superstitious character had with two different men. Vera portrayed Gish's good friend Molly, who helped her elope with the love of her life. But the cowgirl-turned-stunt woman-turned-actress didn't care much for acting. She preferred stunt work, specifically stunts where she could ride a horse.[29]

Letters from Earl during this time were few and far between. In his absence, Vera learned to provide for herself, combining what she earned working as an extra, stunt doubling, and riding in rodeos. According to the June 30, 1919, edition of the *Reno Gazette Journal*, Vera was the highest salaried artist, in her line of work, in the world. Referred to as the "Blonde Dare-Devil," articles about her stunt work appeared in newspapers throughout the West.[30]

In Bend, Oregon, an August 21, 1919, report in *The Bulletin* read:

> *You wouldn't think to see her risk it that Vera would give a nickel for her life! But as has been remarked in these columns before, you never can tell from where you're sitting. And she does. She's perfectly crazy about life and living and everything.*[31]
>
> *She gets more joy out of five minutes than most people do out of five months. That's just the kind of girl she is. You ought to see her. But come to think about it, I guess you have seen her, but you didn't know it.*
>
> *This paragon of joy is Vera McGinnis. Vera McGinnis is a little, slim, but very wiry, blonde. And by profession she's the last thing on earth you'd expect from the looks of her. She's a wild west cowgirl, a*

rider of bucking broncos, a performer of dare-devil stunts on horses. In fact, she doesn't care what she does just so it's on horseback.

She it is who seemingly throws her life away every day or so, only she doesn't look at it from that angle. Says she: "Why there's nothing dangerous about that stunt. It's just as easy to stand on your head on horseback as it is to sit in a saddle. That is, if you're used to it."

And now I'll tell you where you've seen her. . . . Vera is the girl who does all the hair-raising stunts in the movies like snatching up the wounded hero from the ground just before he is bitten by a rattlesnake, in place of the well-known and famous actresses when they appear in wild west pictures and don't know how to ride. Poor Vera. She gets none of the applause or credit for any of it.[32]

When Earl returned from overseas, he and Vera struggled to keep their marriage together. They divorced in 1921.[33]

The following year Vera signed a contract to ride in the Elk's Wild West Carnival in Hawaii. Cowgirl Gail Claire and a host of other trick riders, bronc busters, and bulldoggers were part of the exhibition that took place in February 1922 in Honolulu. Before Vera set sail for the islands, she had one last stunting job to complete that winter. Not all went as planned with the stunt and she was seriously injured.[34] As she explored in her memoir:

It happened while I was doubling for one of Hoot Gibson's leading ladies. According to the script, I was to drive a runaway team hitched to a buckboard. The horses were to swerve from the road and run wild across a plowed field. When Hoot gallantly dashed to the fair maiden's rescue, I was to jump into his waiting arms. Instead, my foot slipped on the iron railing of the bouncing rig and draped my body over the front axle. My feet and legs remained on the buckboard. The team raced on, with the lines dangling, and the spokes of the front wheel played a tattoo on my ribs, piercing the skin in places with slivers.[35]

Vera sought medical attention. After being treated for her injuries (including cracked ribs), she boarded a ship with other members of the Wild West Show. The voyage was a rocky one for her, but once she reached Hawaii her health improved. The trip proved to be one of the best experiences of her life. She fell in love with Hawaii and the people. She was billed as a champion rodeo rider, and fans came from every part of the island to see her demonstrate equestrian skills. Vera entertained the audiences with a smile on her face, never letting on for a moment that she was experiencing pain in her damaged ribs.[36]

Back on the mainland, Vera signed contracts to appear in rodeos across the country. She bought a new horse named Cowboy, and the pair made their debut at the Santa Clara Centennial Celebration in May 1922. She finished the rodeo season with a number of new trophies and winnings—enough to get her through the winter. Vera celebrated her seventeenth year as a professional rider in September. Although she was pleased with all she'd accomplished, she wasn't entirely satisfied. Traveling from one rodeo to the next had become tiresome, and she longed for stability. She found it when she was hired by the Ringling Bros. and Barnum & Bailey Circus.[37]

Vera's first appearance with the show was in late March 1923. Not only was she a trick rider in the show, she was also a background character in a variety of other equestrian acts. She wore elaborate costumes and rode a magnificent Palamino horse. When her contract ended with Ringling Brothers at the close of the season, she returned to the rodeo. "Working in the circus was more or less routine," Vera wrote of her experience, "without the challenge and hazards of rodeo life. It seemed a fairy land to me."[38]

After more than five years with no single location to call home, Vera purchased a house for herself in the San Fernando Valley. She called the piece of land with vineyards and a stable Pleasant View. Whether she was participating in the Southern California Fair Rodeo in Riverside, working with stuntman Yakima Canutt, or trick riding at the Ambassador Horse Show in Ventura with cowboy humorist Will Rogers, Vera had a place of her own to return to when the job was done.[39]

It wasn't until a friend persuaded her to join rodeo promoter Tex Austin's troupe, bound for England to take part in the British Empire Exhibition, that she considered being away from her new home for an extended period of time. The ocean journey took thirteen days, but the reception the entertainers received more than made up for the tedious trip.[40]

"When we docked, the wharf was lined with eager faces. London was out enmasse," Vera noted in her memoir. "Our shipload of cowboys and cowgirls must have presented a colorful picture—all of us were in full western regalia, some were even mounted and waiting to gallop down the gangplank. Once ashore, we were loaded into all sorts of vehicles and paraded by devious routes to our hotels. Without doubt, we were a thrilling sight to those Londoners who had never been any closer to our great west and its inhabitants than the motion picture screen."[41]

Vera's trek through Europe was successful and educational. She amassed numerous awards in relay racing and trick riding, participating in several prestigious rodeos such as the Wembley held at the London Coliseum. From England, the riders traveled to Ireland, where they gave exhibitions at Croke Park in Dublin. Vera competed in bull riding events there, having had her fill of bronc busting in previous contests. France and Belgium were also on the tour. Tex Austin's troupe attracted thousands interested in seeing the uniquely dressed cowboys and cowgirls perform. Vera learned the customs and history of the various locations she visited, acquiring a particular appreciation for English teatime.[42]

When the tour concluded in late 1924, the award-winning equestrian returned to Pleasant View. Vera's time at home was brief, however. The Wild West Show promoter who recruited her to be a part of the program in Hawaii was organizing a show headed to the Far East. Forty-nine performers, in addition to Vera, agreed to make the journey. Indians, dancing girls, steer wrestlers, calf ropers, bronco riders, and Russian Cossacks sailed out of San Francisco on the Japanese ship the *Siberia Mane* on March 31, 1925. The cast was scheduled to be on tour for two years.[43]

Vera was grateful for the chance to visit Japan but was not overly impressed. Parts of the country had been ravaged by earthquakes and the constant rain was wearisome. Tent living left a lot to be desired. "I have to defend myself from the elements," she wrote in the diary she kept during that time. "Intense heat or cold or torrents of rain. One of the three for sure. There seems to be no temperate point.[44]

Vera found the Japanese people to be warm and generous, as was the Sultan of Johor, ruler of Malaysia. He interceded on behalf of Vera and the others with the show's management to pay the performers what they'd earned during their time abroad. The cast had routinely gone without pay and that added to Vera's overall unhappiness with the excursion. She counted the days until their arrival back in San Francisco.[45]

Home again in May 1926, Vera joined a rodeo show organized by a pair of respected promoters. She was eager to be on the circuit again and to try to reclaim the riding titles she'd lost while overseas. She competed against award-winning cowgirls Mabel Strickland and Ethel Barry in the relay race at the Southern California Rodeo in Riverside on May 31, 1926, as well as Bonnie Gray at the Alameda County Rodeo in Stockton in July 1926. She finished first and second in the contests. She did well at Cheyenne Frontier Days and was expected to win trophies at Pikes Peak Rodeo, but the horse she rode at the Colorado Springs event made that prospect impossible. The horse threw Vera, breaking her collarbone and dislocating her shoulder. She was hospitalized and out of the saddle for several weeks. But by September, she was riding relay in the Pendleton Roundup, and she won all four days that she competed.[46]

"There was a lot of work in 1927," Vera recalled in her memoir. "It seemed I spent most of my time driving up and down the highways from north to south and back again. Trick riding had become an exhibition event, and I tried to juggle my trick riding contracts to fit with good relay strings, which didn't always work out. In '28, back to the old rat race in California. Rodeos, long drives, and more rodeos."[47]

Vera's life was much the same in 1929 and 1930. In 1931, she moved to Palm Springs to work for Norman Livery, becoming a bookkeeper and horseback riding instructor. It was a much-needed change of pace for her, and she thoroughly enjoyed the job. The business was owned by brothers Norman and Homer Farra. Homer was in charge of the daily operations of the livery. As such, he and Vera were constantly together, discussing the accounting and the stables. In a short time, their working relationship blossomed into romance. The two were married on March 24, 1931. Homer left the livery profession and moved to Pleasant View with his bride. There the pair decided to join Hoot

Gibson's Rodeo Ranch. Times were tough for the Farras as it was for everyone during the Depression. But they managed to eke out a living and had a wonderful time traveling together.[48]

Any plans Vera and Homer had to continue riding the circuit were dashed on June 10, 1934. Vera suffered another serious accident in the arena. It happened while participating in the women's relay race before twenty thousand spectators at the rodeo in Livermore, California. She was hurled from her horse when forced against the rail on the back stretch. As she pitched forward, her hip struck a post, causing her to roll over the ground for thirty feet.[49]

According to the June 11, 1934, edition of the *Oakland Tribune*, "Three other riders were abreast of her horse when the accident occurred." Vera was rushed to the Alameda County Emergency Hospital by ambulance. X-rays showed she had a fractured right leg and injuries to her right hip, chest, and back along with a collapsed lung. Her condition was listed as critical. Doctors informed Vera and her husband that they didn't expect her to live. And, if she did live, she would be an invalid. Although it was hard for her to talk, she managed to inform the physician that he was wrong on both accounts. "I won't die, and I won't be a cripple either," she said.[50]

Encouraged by her determination, the hospital staff rallied round their patient, resetting her hips and exercising her legs. After more than five weeks, Vera left the hospital. Homer took her home to Pleasant View, where she spent the rest of the year recuperating. When Vera had fully recovered, she and her husband sold their house and moved to Van Nuys. There they raised Thoroughbred horses. In time, they relocated to a small home in the Sierra Foothills.[51]

Stalwart Vera McGinnis Farrar briefly returned to the rodeo arena in 1940. Her body was too fragile to compete, but she was able to sit on her horse and wave to the fans who recognized her as the onetime woman relay riding champion.[52]

Vera passed away on October 24, 1990. She was ninety-seven years old.[53]

Marie Walcamp

Miss Walcamp is a spectacular talent, unafraid of danger. She is the heroine most admired by moviegoers everywhere.

—*Press of Atlantic City*, March 11, 1915

The passengers onboard the train leaving the depot in Dennison, Ohio, in the summer of 1903, gazed out the window at the tree-lined hills on either side of the tracks. The scenery gave way to open plains as the train moved steadily on its way. In the near distance, nine-year-old Marie Walcamp emerged from the forest, riding a black-and-white Appaloosa. She and the horse hurried toward the train. When the pair caught up with the locomotive, they rode along beside it as if in a race. Marie giggled happily and offered the travelers a wave. Horse and rider dashed over the grasses and over the tufts and mounds, bound together in excitement.

The train gained speed and pulled away from the pair. Marie bent slightly, held the animal close and steady, her hands buried in the flying mane, firm on the stout muscles of his neck. Unable to keep pace with the train, she sat straight on the horse's back and the animal slowed. Still laughing from the sense of wild exhilarating freedom, Marie waved enthusiastically at the passengers. Some pressed their faces against the glass and watched as the girl and her horse faded from view.

Apart from the rides Marie took through the countryside on her favorite horse, Jed, in Tuscarawas County, little is known about the early life of the Ohio native who grew up to be one of the bravest women in the film world.

Marie was born on July 27, 1894, to Arnold and Mary Walcamp. Her father was a locomotive driver for the Pittsburgh, Cincinnati, and St. Louis Railway. When Marie was six years old, her father fell from the control room of the engine and died from head injuries. In 1904, Mary remarried and Marie moved with the newlyweds to West Virginia. When she was fourteen, Marie left home and headed to New York, where she worked as a manicurist in Buffalo. It wasn't until she met a few cowgirl performers with the Miller Brothers 101 Ranch that her profession changed.[1]

In May 1909, cast members from the 101 Ranch Wild West Show were in town to entertain. After watching the troupe parade through town, Marie followed them to the fairgrounds where the program would be held. She introduced herself. Impressed by her boldness and ability to ride a horse well, Zack Miller, one of the show's organizers, invited her to join them.[2]

During the Buffalo trip, the Miller Brothers formed a partnership with the Bison Film Company. The set of a Western town and an Indian village were built on the family's Oklahoma ranch—this is where their motion pictures would be made. Contracts were signed and sealed with cowboy actors Tom Mix, Buck Jones, Hoot Gibson, and Will Rogers to star in Western films for the company. Members of the Wild West Show were employed to appear in silent pictures as well. Marie was among those employees.[3]

Marie was a capable horseback rider and a fair actress. For a while, she was content to be a background character in the pictures. However, as time went on, Marie wanted to learn more about the craft. She decided to pursue a stage career to get the experience she needed to secure a job as the lead in a Bison Film. The seventeen-year-old traveled to San Francisco. She was quickly hired to appear in musical comedy productions, backed by vaudeville stars Clarence Kolb and Max Dill.[4]

Marie made her stage debut in the summer of 1912 with Kolb and Dill in the play *Peck O Pickles*. The show was regarded by critics as "one of the funniest musical comedies of the year." Her role in the play brought rave reviews and a fair amount of publicity. California newspapers from Fresno to San Diego printed Marie's picture along with articles about how she dressed, the jewelry she loved, and the time she spent with fellow actors giving food and clothing to children in need.[5]

An article in the February 17, 1913, edition of the *Los Angeles Evening Express* focused on her position regarding flirting:

> *Is it a sin to flirt? No, not always. At least that is the opinion of Miss Marie Walcamp, one of the statuesque show girls who adds color and beauty to Kolb and Dill's production of Victor Herbert's "Algeria," in which the German fun makers are appearing at the Majestic theater this week.*[6]
>
> *Miss Walcamp declares she was a born flirt. She couldn't help it any more than she could help the shape of her nose or the color of her eyes. Youthful training, however, and a habit of keen observation, early persuaded her that the flirt who flirts too flirtatiously is pretty pat to get herself into trouble sooner or later. Therefore, she studied repression and ultimately hit on an amazingly satisfactory safety valve.*
>
> *Today Miss Walcamp does her flirting vicariously, so to speak. This is to say, Miss Marie Walcamp doesn't flirt at all as Marie Walcamp, but as somebody else on the stage and she flirts outrageously with everyone in the whole audience.*
>
> *And this particularly young woman declares that is the function of every young woman of the chorus, and that if any girl would succeed even in the chorus, she must at all times flirt with her audience. That's why some bright producer thought of a chorus—not only for the voices, but to make things merry and lively.*
>
> *Away from the stage Miss Walcamp declines coldly even to discuss the subject of flirting. She doesn't approve of it even as a topic of conversation. She's a blonde, but she couldn't help that either, which probably isn't true of all blondes.*[7]

Marie's publicized thoughts on flirting prompted movie producer Patrick Powers to cast her in one of her first films, *The Blacksmith's Daughter*. The plot of the single-reel Western was this: A rider who stops at a blacksmith shop to get a new shoe for his horse strikes up a relationship with the shop owner, and she flirts with him. Marie played the part of the blacksmith's daughter.[8]

The budding actress's next film, *The Girl Ranchers*, produced by the Nestor Film Company, provided Marie an opportunity to perform a few stunts. She had to outrun a herd of cattle without being tossed from an out-of-control wagon. The breezy Western comedy was about an Eastern widow and her five beautiful daughters who inherit a ranch. They're forced to run it themselves when the working cowpunchers go on strike. The film received rave reviews.[9]

Marie's compelling on-screen presence and willingness to put herself in harm's way for the sake of capturing a realistic shot attracted directors. She was Bison Film Company's top choice when it came to casting the eighteen-minute motion picture *The Werewolf*. Film historians claim that the two-reel short was the first werewolf movie ever made.[10]

The Werewolf, released in 1913, was about a Navajo woman who believed she'd been abandoned by her husband, who had been killed, and became a warlock. As her daughter (played by Marie) grows up, her mother teaches her to hate all White men and seek revenge by turning into a werewolf. Critics called the film a "distinctively novel feature" and singled out Marie's performance as "haunting." The part required her to leap from building to building and hang from high mountain ledges—all of which she did, to the great satisfaction of the movie's director.[11]

According to the March 2, 1914, edition of the *Los Angeles Evening Express*, the success of *The Werewolf* prompted Henry McRae, head of Bison Film Company, to choose Marie to travel to Hawaii. She appeared in more than a dozen dramas set on the island. "We must have her for our leading woman," McRae told newspaper reporters. "We can make her up to look like a Hawaiian maiden, and we know she's game for any stunt we have in mind." His statement about her willingness to perform stunts proved accurate. By the end of the shooting schedule, Marie was recognized by the studio as the "Daredevil Girl of the Movies."[12]

She was handpicked to star in the dramas because there were no hazards she couldn't and wouldn't face. Not every stunt went as planned, however. The crowning test of her nerve was when she was attacked and severely wounded by an African lion and a rebellious leopard while filming. A story about the dangerous encounter in the December 28, 1914, edition of the *Santa Cruz Evening News* read:

> *The jungle creatures were restless in their pens. In the wilderness it was roving time. Wild geese were winging south. The beasts used for scenes that included wildlife felt the mystic stir of the season. They stretched and whined and snapped their tails ceaselessly.*[13]
>
> *Miss Walcamp studied them closely, with that sixth sense she has developed to register animal moods. What she saw alarmed her, but did not deter her from going ahead with production. This morning, however, it was different. There was something new in the wind.*
>
> *Miss Walcamp prepared for the first scene where an African lion was supposed to leap over her head and to encourage the beast to make the plunge, a chunk of raw meat was held out tantalizingly through a screen of heavy wire by an attendant. When the director yelled "action" she advanced toward the lion within the enclosure. He crouched immobile. Only his tail flicked slightly.*
>
> *Suddenly as she moved within the range, the lion catapulted straight at her throat. He struck her a stunning blow on the neck and shoulders, knocking her to the ground. Fighting desperately, although dazed by the unexpected attack, Miss Walcamp managed to keep the fangs from her throat. Armed with pitchforks, the attendants rushed to her rescue, and she was finally pulled to safety.*
>
> *It was now that Miss Walcamp demonstrated her real mettle. Still quivering with the shock of her narrow escape, swathed in bandages, but with her amazing fighting pluck at white heat, she insisted on going ahead with her part of the drama. This required that she face another enraged mankiller—a leopard.*
>
> *Waving aside all objection and warnings, she again entered the arena. This time she was to cross a rickety foot bridge while from offshore the jungle leopard menaced her. That was the way it was supposed to be in the production. But the second beast had become infected with the lion's rebellion. Suddenly when the bridge on which she was*

Marie Walcamp in *The Lion's Claw* ACADEMY OF MOTION PICTURE ARTS AND SCIENCES

crossing accidentally collapsed, throwing her in the water, the beast leaped upon her where she was struggling in the stream.

The leopard misgauged his spring by an inch or two, but his claws ripped her forehead and shoulders, wounding her far more seriously than had the lion. Again, the helpless and unarmed woman fought for her life with the animal clawing and tearing at her. It was only the fact that this struggle took place in waist deep water which saved Miss Walcamp's life.

Again, the attendants rescued her in the nick of time, and she consented to call it a day. She was taken to the hospital to recover.[14]

Stunts that didn't go as planned weren't relegated only to wild animals. Marie explained in an interview with *Motion Picture Magazine* in March 1915:

I was being held captive by savages on the Isle of Abandoned Hope for one of the film company's thrillers. It was in the Hawaiian Islands. I was supposed to have found a means of escaping my aboriginal captors. By the time we got ready to film the scene, the tide was running strong. My stunt was to swim across a little rockbound bay or pocket in the cliffs. I did not like the looks of it, but if I didn't do it then we would have to wait for low tide, a matter of six hours.[15]

Thinking I might be able to wade part of the way, I started in. A breaker almost immediately flung me with stunning force against a rock. Regaining my feet, I had gone on but a few yards when another breaker equally violent, caught and flung me. And then I made the trip, battered from rock to rock. How I ever got through that scene I don't know. Those who watched me from shore did not appreciate my peril, I am sure. I couldn't cry out. All of my energy was required in fighting for my life.

With each outrushing wave I would be strongly sucked toward the open sea with its powerful undertow. Bruised from head to foot, full of salt water and weighted with seaweed, I finally managed to drag myself out. And then disappointment of disappointments! They did not even have a decent picture of me to salve my bruised feelings.[16]

By 1919, when Marie was cast in one of her most popular action-adventure series, the *Tempest Cody* serial, she had made more than ninety films. Produced by Universal Pictures, the serial was about a horse-loving female agent of the government stationed out West. The action in each

Stunt woman Marie Walcamp was the star of the popular *Tempest Cody* serial. AUTHOR'S COLLECTION story centered on the courageous acts of the main character in cowboy country.[17]

Between motion pictures, Marie participated in rodeos across the West. A production crew followed her wherever she competed and filmed her riding wild broncos and roping steers. They planned to use the footage in future projects. The first film in the series was titled *Tempest Cody Hits the Back Trail.* Footage shot of Marie riding in a rodeo in Sonora, California, was featured in the picture.[18]

Released in September 1919, audiences rushed to theaters to watch the thrilling Western filled with daredevil stunts. *Tempest Cody Flirts with Death* and *Tempest Cody Rides Wild* were the second and third installments of the chapter play. In total, Marie made nine *Tempest Cody* films. Each earned praise from ticket buyers and a substantial profit for studio executives. "The Tempest Cody half-hour masterpiece is popular chiefly because they are not artificial," one reviewer wrote, "but instead are little bits of real life with plenty of chucklesome humor mixed in with the galloping.[19]

There wasn't a stunt in the *Tempest Cody* series that Marie didn't perform herself. Producers nicknamed her the "Daredevil of the Films" because she wasn't afraid to try dangerous feats. The majority of the films Marie starred in were shot in two days. She thrived on her work despite the predictability of the scripts. "Of course, it's always the same old thing," she commented in a magazine interview in 1920. "I get chased, abused, nearly killed, rescued in the nick of time, loved, hated, and finally the forever after."[20]

After completing the filming of the *Tempest Cody* serial, the actress and stunt woman flew to Japan to begin work on a groundbreaking series called *The Dragon's Net.* It was the first and only serial Universal filmed in Asia. Marie played a woman who knew no fear—she learned of a set of golden lotus leaves that held the secret of eternal life. When she was tricked out of one of the lotus leaves, she hired an adventurer to help track down the entire set. Critics called *The Dragon's Net* "a scenic travelogue" and a "fast-paced action thriller."[21]

Before leaving Japan, Marie accepted the marriage proposal of her costar in the series, Harlan Tucker. The two were wed by the American

Consulate General in Yokohama, Japan, on October 3, 1919. She told newspaper reporters:

> *We decided to get married when we were five days out of Yokohama. We confided our wishes to a dear old Scotch minister on the boat and found him very sympathetic. But we couldn't get a license. When we landed in Yokohama there was a big delegation of local celebrities and moving picture people to welcome us. They wanted some sort of celebration and a lot of news reels, but we told them to wait a few minutes as we had to see the American consul first. He issued us a license and married us.*[22]

Seven months later, Marie and Harlan returned to Los Angeles. She agreed to appear in a film produced by Lois Weber, one of the most prolific film directors of the silent era. The picture called *The Blot* was about an underpaid teacher. It depicts the poverty he is forced to endure with his wife and daughter. His wife, desperate and in need of food and clothes for their sick daughter, is on the verge of becoming a thief. The film was well received and reviewers made note of how well Marie did with the small but important part she had.[23]

Not long after *The Blot* was released, Marie decided to take a break from filmmaking to consider a return to the stage. "I like motion picture work very much," she told newspaper reporters in May 1922. "It is not as interesting in some respects as the legitimate stage and the requirements are not as exacting. Working with a stock company is a frightful strain. For a long time, I was with a road company and toured the South, playing the juvenile lead in *Fair and Warmer*. That was interesting work, but it got to be drudgery after a while. Working on a moving picture lot gives one an opportunity for home life. Still, I miss the theater."[24]

Marie did return to the stage in 1922, performing at the Egan Theater in Los Angeles in a play with her husband called *The Hummingbird*. She also signed a contract with the Stewart Motion Picture Company to star in an eighteen-episode action-adventure serial.[25]

In 1924, Marie starred in the feature Western film *A Desperate Adventure*. She played the daughter of a notorious outlaw, named the Wasp, who was on the run from the law. Marie hoped she'd be able to perform stunts as she had previously, but the roles didn't call for any daring feats.[26]

At the age of thirty-one, Marie was offered fewer and fewer parts, and those parts required her to do little else but bat her eyes. She made her last film, a talkie, in 1925. Based on a novel by Laura Jean Libbey, the romantic comedy *A Moment of Temptation* followed the adventures of a woman storekeeper wrongly accused of theft, and imprisoned through the maneuvers of a jealous woman.[27]

From 1928 to 1932, Marie acted onstage in a variety of plays and in vaudeville working alongside her husband and rising star Jack Benny.[28]

Desperate to revitalize her career and regain the title of "serial queen," which she held in 1915, Marie made a screen test, hoping to land the lead in a remake of the series *The Perils of Pauline*. The chapter play thrilled fans in 1914 during the silent era, and Universal Pictures looked to gain a new audience with a talkie of the famous serial. She didn't get the part.[29]

Not only was Marie struggling professionally, but her marriage was experiencing difficulties. Although the Tuckers continued to live in the same apartment on Mulholland Drive in Los Angeles, they separated in March 1934.[30]

She was unable to get work on-screen or onstage, was low on funds, and was disappointed over the dwindling newspaper attention. Wondering if news readers remembered her, she speculated about why she wasn't able to successfully transition from silent films to talkies. Marie, thoroughly despondent, committed suicide. Her husband, who had been out of town on a business trip, discovered her body at home in a gas-filled room. Marie was forty-two years old when she died on November 17, 1936.[31]

According to her will, she wanted to be cremated, her ashes scattered from the top of a hill on the back lot of Universal Pictures. A few forlorn friends gathered with her husband for a small ceremony. There they scattered the remains of an actress-stunt woman who never gave a second thought about being able to handle any situation. They said good-bye on the very ground where she made a name that lasted and a fortune that did not.[32]

Mary Wiggins

Miss Wiggins of late has been one of the most sought-after doubles in the movie colony of Hollywood. Sensational jumps from high cliffs, motorcycle spills, dives from ships at sea are all part of the day's work for her while doubling for movie stars.

—*Auburn Journal*, August 1, 1929

Mary Wiggins's head bobbed beneath the icy, choppy waters of the Nooksack River near Mt. Baker, Washington. She struggled to rise up to the sun-flecked surface. When she broke through, she quickly gulped the winter air and then, with barely a splash, went under again. The camera crew, standing safely on the riverbank, watched in rapt silence as they filmed the stunt woman's realistic drowning scene.

Mary was one of the best stunt women in the business, having perfected the art of portraying a distressed victim fighting a river's strong current. Until the former award-winning diver arrived in Hollywood in 1927, drowning scenes were played in a broad, melodramatic way. They were loud and splashy, the stunt double would yell, and then frantically wave their arms. They would dip below the waves screaming and come up in a dramatic fashion. Those on the shore scrambled to rescue them.

Mary's technique was much more subdued but nonetheless effective. The temperature of the water was fifteen below zero, and she was adorned in thick wool trousers, a large coat, and heavy boots. She held herself under the water as long as possible. Her hair rose upward like seaweed, rippling in the current, and then with superhuman effort she emerged

Mary Wiggins appeared in numerous advertisements promoting her stunt work.
AUTHOR'S COLLECTION

completely out of the water. Director William Wellman shouted "cut" and the technicians working on the 1935 film *Call of the Wild* hurried to help Mary out of the freezing river. Her part was so seamlessly woven into 20th Century Picture's adaptation of Jack London's popular novel, audiences couldn't tell her apart from Loretta Young, the star she was doubling for.[1]

Born on November 8, 1910, in Plant City, Florida, Mary soon developed a daring nature. Her mother, Nellie, told movie magazine columnists that her daughter was a "tomboy growing up" and was more at home "climbing and jumping out of trees than playing with dolls." Mary attended Hillsborough High School, where she was part of the swim team and became an expert diver. In July 1927, she traveled to New York, and there she established a new world's highest diving record in Ocean Park. She also caught the attention of Max Sennett, producer and president of Keystone Studios.[2]

Sennett hired Mary to be one of his "Bathing Beauties." The bathing costume–clad beauties were featured in several comedy shorts. Several of those women went on to became film stars—Mabel Normand, Gloria Swanson, and Carole Lombard, to name a few. May preferred standing in for stars when a qualified stunt woman was needed. During the first year after Sennett hired her, she dove out of a car tumbling off a pier in Santa Monica, jumped from one moving vehicle to another, and leaped off high cliffs into the ocean. By the end of 1928, Mary was one of the most sought-after doubles in Hollywood.[3]

During the summer of 1929, between filming Sennett pictures, Mary was the featured attraction at the California Diamond Jubilee State Fair and Western Exposition in Sacramento. She performed the death-defying fire dive. Dressed in a special suit, Mary took her place on an extremely high platform, enveloped herself in flames, and dove eighty-six feet into a tank of water that was five feet deep and fifteen feet in diameter.[4]

Between 1930 and 1931, Mary appeared in a handful of Western films starring Ken Maynard, a champion rodeo rider and a trick rider with the Buffalo Bill Wild West Show as well as an actor. Mary helped Maynard choregraph and executed stunts for the women in movies that included falling off galloping horses and runaway wagons and leaping out a window to escape the villain. The last Mack Sennett film Mary made with the Bathing Beauties was released in 1931 and titled *Movie-Town*. In addition to being one of the beauties who spent time at a swimming pool in a glitzy Hollywood setting, she could be seen in the water portraying a water polo player.[5]

After learning how much stunt fliers could earn, May added aviatrix to her resume in 1932. Not only did she obtain her pilot's license after several months of extensive training, she also learned how to jump from an aircraft. Using a parachute, Mary mastered the art of pulling the ripcord at the last possible moment. She planned to use the technique, known as chute dropping, to heighten the drama during aviation pictures she had been contracted to work on.[6]

Shortly after acquiring her flying certification, Mary became a member of Club 99. The organization, made up of ninety-nine women pilots (out of the 285 licensed women pilots in the United States at the time) was formed in 1929. The mission of the group was to support one another as they navigated their way through the aviation industry. Among the members of the club Mary met with regularly were journalist and broadcaster Faye Gillis Well, film star Ruth Elder, and the first female pilot to circumnavigate the globe, Amelia Earhart.[7]

On April 30, 1932, Mary and more than twenty of her fellow club members were the featured performers at the American Legion Air Circus held at the Kern County, California airport. The women performed a series of air races, the winner returning in the shortest time and stunting by the group's noted acrobatic flyers. Mary gave a number of parachute jumping exhibitions.[8]

Throughout 1932, Mary participated in several air circuses. As a high-altitude parachute jumper, she performed solo on the same bill as plane and glider pilot Frank Terns.

Her time spent entertaining at various air shows served as preparation for the stunt work she was hired to do in the film *Central Airport*. The plot of the picture involved a disgraced commercial pilot and his brother who were not only daredevil flyers but rivals competing for the love of a beautiful parachutist.[9]

Director William Wellman recruited Mary to be the stunt double for leading lady, Sally Eilers. Mary made all the parachute jumps that Eiler's character, Jill Collins, was to make. Not everything went as planned for Mary or the other stunt flyers in the film. One of the stuntmen crashed his plane practicing one of the maneuvers. He managed to walk away from the incident with only a broken shoulder. A passenger plane, carrying the pictures' two male leads, miscalculated a landing and struck a telephone pole. No one was seriously injured, but they were badly bruised and shaken. Another plane, unoccupied, went up in smoke when a mechanic applied a blowtorch to one of the instruments which was stuck. And Mary stepped in front of a whirling airplane propeller, with her parachute strapped to her shoulders, and was blown across the field. She too was shaken, but no bones were broken.[10]

According to the April 22, 1933, edition of the *Tucson Daily Citizen*, "the nearest to a very serious calamity came when a twelve-foot lighting machine, which blows fire into the air to light the sky, fell into the studio lake, aiming directly at a float on which were stationed director William

Wellman, his assistant, and several cameramen. Had it not been for the quick action of a prop man in pushing the falling column of fire sideways as it fell, changing the direction of its landing, Wellman and his crew would have been blown into the lake by a blast of fire."[11]

Central Airport did well at the box office. Critics praised the "nerve wracking adventure for its realistic and thrilling action scenes."[12]

After her work in *Central Airport*, Mary signed on to be the stunt double for Claudette Colbert in Frank Capra's film *It Happened One Night*. At the beginning of the picture, Colbert's character dives off a yacht to get away from her father. Mary stood in for the award-winning actress, plunging into the water and quickly swimming from the ship's crew who were ordered to hurry after her.[13]

Mary followed her part in *It Happened One Night* with work on three other popular films. In *Journal of a Crime*, she threw herself in front of a truck while doubling for actress Ruth Chatterton. In *Lost Lady*, Mary tumbled off a cliff, doubling for Barbara Stanwyck, and in *Looking for Trouble*, she was buried under a falling wall as the stunt woman for Judith Woods.[14]

By the fall of 1934, Mary had become one of the most noted daredevils in Hollywood. Since she had become a part of the business, she'd appeared in more than fifty pictures. She had doubled for leading stars in scenes that not only called for parachute jumps and high dives but automobile collisions, train wrecks, free-for-all fights, and horseback riding stunts. Her success led to being featured in several print advertisements, including Camel Cigarettes—they referred to her as "America's Greatest Stunt Girl."[15]

Mary was also the focus of newspaper articles. Reporters were fascinated with the woman behind the risky maneuvers they saw her tackle on screen. In October 1935, Fred Moon, a journalist for the *Atlanta Journal*, wrote how Mary first caught his attention and why he was inspired to pen an article about her.[16] Moon noted:

> Atlanta *made the acquaintance of Miss Wiggins during the recent Southeastern Fair, at which she participated in the convention of B. Ward Beam's International Congress of Daredevils. She was*

the only woman competitor in this grand event which featured the world's leading stuntmen, and she performed a feat no man had ever attempted. It was a feat that Mary herself had never attempted before.

Two board walls, solidly built of planks and scantlings, each wall measuring three inches thick, were set up fifty yards apart on the racetrack. Mary, riding as fast as her stock-model motorcycle would clip, sped down the track. Crash! She went through the first wall in a shower of splinters. Crash! She went through the second wall. Fragments of the demolished barriers were still whizzing through the air when she stopped her machine. She was uninjured, calm, and grinning happily because she had found a brand-new way to risk her neck.[17]

Motion picture industry leaders agreed that what made Mary exceptional was that she wasn't limited to one particular stunt. Most of the stunt women specialized in riding, falling, or fighting, but Mary was good at all of them. Consequently, she was in high demand. Mary was also attractive and the same size as the majority of starlets, making her the ideal double for many of the leading ladies.[18] She told an *Atlanta Journal* reporter:

I'm always on the lookout for a new thrill, and for that reason I prefer real stunt work to routine scenes in which I have nothing to do but save the star a black eye or a bruised shin. For example, I had never had an opportunity to swing a freight until Wild Boys of the Road *was filmed, and that gave me lots of fun. I felt that the director cheated Dorothy Coonan when he put me in to double for her in all the train scenes and fights.*

I dearly love to fight—in make believe battles, I mean. I think one of the nicest fights I was ever in was in Springtime for Henry. *I was doubling for Nancy Carroll, and the director put me in a mission with five men extras and ordered us to fight until we wrecked the place. Boy, what a grand fight that was!*[19]

One of the next pictures Mary was hired to appear in required that she once again show off her swimming talent. *Hell Ship Morgan*, written by Harold Shumate and directed by D. Ross Lederman, was a romantic drama set on the Pacific Ocean. It centered around a boat captain's bride who falls in love with the first mate. George Bancraft portrayed the ship's captain, Victor Jory played the first mate, and Ann Sothern played the bride. Mary doubled for Sothern and spent a great deal of time in the water. When the ship was overcome by a storm and Sothern's character was tossed into the waves, Mary was the one seen fighting to stay afloat.[20]

Like all stuntpeople, Mary was susceptible to serious injury, regardless of the precautions taken and safety measures in place. Prior to filming *Hell Ship Morgan*, she miscalculated a jump in another film, fell, and broke her back. While recuperating in the hospital, several of her stuntmen and women friends came to visit her, including well-known stuntman Harvey Parry. Like Mary, Harvey got his start in films working for Mack Sennett. He doubled for Harold Lloyd, Humphrey Bogart, and George Raft. A month after Mary was released from the hospital, Harvey chipped two vertebrae during a fight scene, and he ended up in the same hospital and room Mary had been in. As Harvey had done with her, she paid him regular visits.[21]

Both Mary and Harvey had healed by June, and they agreed to take part in a film project for Paramount Pictures. Stuntman Gordon Carveth and stunt woman Loretta Rush joined the cast as well. For *And Sudden Death*, the stunters were hired to drive cars that they would ultimately crash, showing the public how the deaths from reckless driving were on the rise. The educational picture was produced with the cooperation of the California Highway Patrol, the city of Los Angeles, and the Automobile Club of Southern California. It starred Randolph Scott and Frances Drake. Twenty-two automobiles were sacrificed in the making of the film. Miraculously, none of the stunt drivers were seriously hurt. They suffered only superficial cuts and bruises.[22]

In July 1936, Mary had the privilege of working with a stuntman she'd long admired, Yakima Canutt. The champion rodeo rider and actor had developed many stunts for films plus the techniques and technology to protect stuntpeople while performing. Mary and Yakima were featured acts at the Filmland Field Show in Los Angeles. Mary gave a high diving exhibition, and Yakima gave a runaway stagecoach demonstration.[23]

Mary was able to use some of what she learned watching Yakima in her next film. *Mountain Justice* was the story of a stalwart Appalachian woman who finds romance while struggling to better herself and her people amid prejudice and familial abuse. The film starred George Brent, Margaret Hamilton, and Josephine Hutchinson. Mary was the stunt double for Hutchinson, and the job turned out to be more difficult than she expected.[24]

In one of the opening scenes, Hutchinson's character is being pursued by an actor, with a mule whip, who portrayed her father. Hutchinson, who was on the receiving end of the whip's blows, worked only in the actual takes. During rehearsals, Mary took her place. The stuntman standing in for the actor playing Hutchinson's father was well-trained in using the whip. He promised Mary he would do his best to wield the weapon in a way that looked realistic but would spare her real pain.[25]

For the most part, the whip cracked around the furniture and did not touch Mary. Bad timing ruined one of the run-throughs when the whip missed the furniture and caught Mary around the torso. The stunt was rehearsed four times, and each time the whip managed to hit her. The stuntman sincerely apologized, explaining that the tip kept getting away from him. While helping Mary off the floor where she was supposed to have fallen, he asked her if she was all right. She smiled at him and lifted her shirt, revealing four welts on her back.[26]

The finished scene was convincing, and director Michael Curtiz was pleased with the stunt work. Mary later admitted she'd rather "fall off a dozen horses and walk on the wings of a dozen planes before encountering the business end of a whip again."[27]

When Mary wasn't working on a film, she presented aquatic exhibitions for various organizations such as the American Legion and the Institute of Family Services. She also organized a group of stunt women who would perform for audiences throughout the country. The Hollywood daredevil demonstrated a number of dangerous stunts to thrill seekers at county fairs and carnivals, including bronc roping and fancy motorcycle riding.[28]

Mary made news in February 1938 when she was hired to be the stunt double for Lola Lane in the *Torcy Blane* film series. The Torcy

Blane character was a reporter and amateur detective. A crime was committed in each picture, and Torcy was tasked with getting the story behind the incident and, along the way, cracking the case. Some of the death-defying stunts Mary was to perform were jumping out of a malfunctioning plane, parachuting into the ocean, sliding down the side of an ocean liner on a rope, and falling out of a window backward into a horse trough filled with water.[29]

According to an interview Mary gave on February 8, 1938, to a Hollywood reporter about her upcoming job in *Torcy Blane in Panama*, stunting wasn't work to her. She considered it a game to master. "I'm always studying how to make my body do things without getting hurt," Mary remarked. "Keeping fit is my slogan. A trained body is the best safeguard against injury in stunt work."[30]

Insurance companies, such as Lloyd's of London, were encouraged to learn the steps Mary and other stunt women and men took to protect themselves from getting hurt. In May 1938, the famous firm agreed to accept stunt performers as good risks. It was a positive move for the profession. When stunt people had the option to insure themselves, it lowered the risk to the studios, many of which were cutting out difficult stunts because of insurance costs.[31]

It took several months to investigate every stuntman and woman in the motion picture industry. In the end, Lloyd's decided to cover twenty-five stunters, offering them yearly insurance against death and dismemberment during the course of their work. Mary was among those twenty-five offered policies, along with fellow stunt women Betty Danko and Ione Reed. With only three independently insured women, it meant Mary's talent would be in even higher demand.[32]

One month after Lloyd's policy had been issued, Mary was hired by 20th Century Fox to perform a tremendous stunt for the film *Suez*, starring Tyrone Power and Loretta Young. The studio paid Mary and four other stunt women $150 each for the hazardous duty. The five were transported to a fake desert scene, complete with sand, in the back lot of the company. They were positioned in front of twenty-four giant wind machines. When turned on, the machines were meant to simulate a massive sandstorm. The sandy gales reached seventy-five miles per hour.

Mary and the others were knocked off their feet and swept off the set. They left work with sand-cut faces and bloodshot eyes.[33]

Hollywood newspaper reporters were fascinated with female daredevils. They always wanted to know from Mary, who they considered the "greatest feminine daredevil," if she'd ever been frightened. She told the Wilkes-Barre *Times Leader*:

> *Only twice in my life. Once was when someone had shifted my diving platform out of line with the five-foot tub of water eighty-six feet below me, and I had to twist in the air in order to hit the water. I scraped the tub as I splashed into the water, but I made it.*[34]
>
> *The other time was the most recent when I was given some dialogue by director Allan Dwan to scream during the filming of a desert scene in* Suez. *Dialogue always frightened me, but to scream your lines while you are literally being blown off your feet by huge wind machines is a terrifying experience.*
>
> *While I shouted, "Save me! Save me!" the speed of the wind machines was increased until the desert sand forced me to shut my mouth while the force swept me off my feet and I was blown through the air into a big net just out of camera range.*[35]

The next film Mary signed on to appear in was a Western titled *Union Pacific*. Directed by Cecil B. DeMille and starring Barbara Stanwyck, Joel McCrea, and Brian Donlevy, the story was about the battle between the Central Pacific and Union Pacific Railroads competition for rail lines to California. McCrea was the overseer on the job of building the first transcontinental railroad, and Donlevy was the gambler trying to stop him. Stanwyck was the athletic heroine, leaping on and off boxcars with the best of them. Mary was Stanwyck's stunt double.[36]

Production began in November 1938, ten miles west of Cedar City, Utah. Mary had the unique distinction of being the only stunt woman on the set in a troupe of 350 men. A scene with Mary and stuntman Ted Mapes, who was stunting for Joel McCrea, was the first to be filmed. Ted was driving a buckboard, pulled by two horses, to get help for the railroad crew who were about to be overtaken by Indians. He had just urged the horses into a fast trot when Mary ran toward the wagon. She was to leap onto the back of the buckboard and climb up on the seat next to Ted. All cameras were trained on Mary. Her timing had to be perfect. One misstep and she would land under the wheels of the moving vehicle. When she successfully executed the stunt, the director yelled, "Cut!" The cast and crew offered a round of applause for the job both she and Ted did. It would be one of the many they performed in the picture.[37]

In early 1939, Hollywood trade papers reported that Mary Wiggins was the "biggest money-maker" in the stunting profession.[38] Between April 1939 and 1941, she took on such stunts as being struck by a truck going twenty-five miles an hour, diving off a jagged cliff and the back of a galloping horse, and walking on the wing of an airplane before falling hundreds of feet to the earth. For curious moviegoers who wanted to know how the various stunts were executed, Mary gave a demonstration in the short film *Spills for Thrills*. Her friend, stuntman Harvey Parry, starred in the picture with her.[39]

Mary took a beating in the 1942 film *The Black Swan*, starring Tyrone Power and Maureen O'Hara. As O'Hara's stunt double, she earned $100 every time Power punched her in the chin, and $50 extra when he dropped her down a stairway. He punched her seven times in the pirate picture. Mary had worked with Power several times in the past, and in previous films he'd dumped her off a ship, dropped her in a mud puddle, threw her out of a rowboat, and smacked her in the face.[40]

As soon as Mary completed filming *The Black Swan*, she was hired to stunt again for Claudette Colbert. The film, *No Time for Love*, also starred Fred MacMurray and Yvonne De Carlo. Colbert portrayed a newspaper photographer who falls in love with MacMurray's character, a construction worker building the Holland Tunnel. Mary's hazardous duty included crawling through the muddy, confined spaces of a faux tunnel as it collapsed on top of her.[41]

During World War II, Mary, like many others in the entertainment profession, wanted to participate in the war effort. In 1943, she took what she hoped would be a brief departure from stunting, becoming a Women's Airforce Service Pilot (WASP) trainee at Avenger Field in Sweetwater, Texas. The licensed female civilian pilots were trained to fly military aircraft, ferrying them from factory to shipping point, and on occasion flying damaged planes back for repair.[42]

Mary graduated in mid-August 1943, after more than twenty-two weeks of instruction. As a commanding officer in the Women's Airforce Reserve, she served as a noncombat flyer for the nation-straddling network of the Army Air Forces' Command. Her fellow pilots came from all parts of the country and from many walks of life. One of the WASPs had been a professional golfer, another a Broadway stage manager. All were ferry pilots, flying aircraft from where they were made to various eastern ports.[43]

Officer Wiggins was not content to ferry planes from one point to another. She wanted to do more. Toward that end, she continued her education, completing several intensive courses in instrument flying with different aircraft. But any hope Mary had of moving ahead with her career in the Reserves was dashed when the Army Air Force disbanded the WASP program in December 1944. Like the other female flyers, Mary returned to civilian life—without veterans' benefits.[44]

Other stunt women had emerged during Mary's absence and her talent wasn't in demand as it once had been. The previously in high demand daredevil had difficulties finding work again in motion pictures. In November 1945, after fulfilling the one job offer she received stunting for actress Claudia Drake in the horror picture *The Face of Marble*, Mary opened a furniture store with a friend who was a carpenter. The business venture did not turn out well, and she lost a substantial amount of money.[45]

On December 20, 1945, Mary's mother drove to her daughter's home in North Hollywood to visit her. She knew Mary hadn't been herself and was feeling alone and despondent. But she didn't expect to find Mary in the backyard in a kneeling position in front of a chair. Mary had shot herself in the head. Her mother told reporters that she wasn't sure why she would have taken her own life. "She was starting a business with a paint refinishing man a month ago and that fell through, but she had plenty of money left," she insisted. "I guess she was just disappointed in everything."[46]

News of Mary's suicide shocked her peers, the actors, and the directors she had worked with. "She was just like any other discharged veteran," said stuntman Harvey Parry. "After she came out of the service everybody had forgotten how great she was. She couldn't get a job around town anymore. Add all that together and you get a broken heart. That's why she killed herself."[47]

Mary Wiggins was laid to rest at Forest Lawn Memorial Park in Glendale, California. She was thirty-six years old.

In 1977, Congress granted veterans' benefits to the 850 remaining WASPs. In 2009, Mary, as well as the other women who served in the Women's Air Force during World War II, were awarded the Congressional Gold Medal.[48]

Texas Guinan

Before becoming a nightclub hostess, Texas was a cowgirl, a torch singer, a dancer, and a movie actress. She made scores of Western thrillers, and she didn't use a double. She did all the stunts herself.

—*The News Journal*, November 6, 1933

A young woman wearing a buckskin dress and leggings rode her white horse fast into a thick forest. Branches slapped her, but the sound of hoofbeats ahead kept her going. It was imperative that she catch up with the rider she was chasing. She urged her horse to go faster, and the animal complied. They broke through the other side of the trees, emerging behind a rickety set of fence posts. The woman leaned forward in the saddle as the horse made a spectacular jump over the barbed wire strung between the posts. Horse and rider gained on the bad guy they were pursuing. The leathery-faced villain, dressed in rough cow-country garb, dared to look back to see how much his lead had shrunk. The woman was bearing down on him now. She was close, determined.[1]

Rising out of her saddle with her horse in full gallop, she placed the reins in her teeth, then put one foot behind the pommel and the other in front of the cantle. Now standing, she leapt off the back of the horse onto the man she was after. The pair tumbled hard onto the ground. The man tried to get to his feet, but the woman got up first, hurried to him, and hit him over the head with the butt of a pistol. They wrestled a bit until finally the woman cracked him on the head with her gun again. Exhausted, she stared down at the unconscious outlaw contemplating her next move.[2]

The actress and stunt woman playing the part of the Indian maiden in the 1920 silent film *The White Squaw,* directed by D. W. Griffith, was Texas Guinan. Agile and daring, the vivacious talent insisted on performing her own stunts in numerous motion pictures filmed between 1917 and 1933.[3]

Born Mary Louise on January 12, 1884, to Michael and Cecillia Guinan on a ranch in Waco, Texas, she showed talents for riding and theatrics at an early age. Her family relocated to Denver when she was in grade school, and they stayed in Colorado during her high school years. Upon graduating, she was awarded a scholarship to the Chicago Conservatory of Music. Deciding to use the first name Texas rather than Mary, she embarked on a stage career after leaving the conservatory. She bounced from productions in New York in vaudeville to performing in the Miller Brothers 101 Ranch Wild West Shows.[4]

In 1910, Texas made her first Los Angeles theater appearance, starring in *The Gay Musician.* "Prior to that role I had mostly been relegated to the chorus," she told a newspaper reporter in 1923. "I was so far back in the chorus they had to take a brick out of the wall to find me."[5]

Texas received rave reviews portraying a struggling singer. This led to an invitation to join the Fisher Stock Company and an opportunity to take on the lead in a comedic play titled *The Kissing Girl.* From there, she worked with such stars as May Boley and Lon Chaney at the Lyceum. Her alluring stage presence and infectious personality charmed the film executives who attended her performances, and she was offered studio contracts to appear in motion pictures. The film that launched her career in Westerns was *The Gun Woman*, released in 1918. She played the part of a saloon owner who loaned money to her lover so that he could buy a house for them in anticipation of their marriage. Instead, he uses the money to buy a saloon in another town.[6]

Critiques praised Texas's performance as one "possessing a gripping force filled with intense power." Her tough, no nonsense, gun-wielding portrayal of a wronged soiled dove prompted moviegoers and producers to refer to her as the "female William S. Hart." Hart was the foremost Western star of the silent era. Texas was flattered by the comparison and also to be billed as the "two-gun tigress" by those who believed she was the equal of any "tobacco-chewin' cowpoke."[7]

Texas Guinan LIBRARY OF CONGRESS

Texas starred in several two-reel Westerns with titles such as *The Hell Cat*, *Two Gun Girl*, and *The She Wolf*. She was tough as nails in each and unafraid to engage in on-screen fistfights with her costars, jump off roofs onto the back of her horse, square off against wild animals, or any other stunt that film directors asked of her.[8]

In 1921, she formed her own film company, Texas Guinan Productions, and produced and starred in a number of Western shorts. "I had twelve real cowboys, a scenario writer [Mildred Sledge], a cameraman, a carload of cartridges, my horse 'Waco' from Texas, and went to work. We made a picture a week," she remembered years later. "We never changed plots, only horses."[9]

Three years after creating her own production company and doing her own stunts in more than two hundred pictures, Texas left Hollywood for New York to establish one of the first modern nightclubs. When asked why she decided to abandon acting and stunt work for such a venture, she replied, "It's good business. Besides, it has always been the West that has made the East wild." To finance her dream of providing theatergoers with a place to meet when the curtain closed, she turned to a bootlegger and labor promoter named Larry Fey. Within a year, her Three Hundred Club on West Forty-Eighth Street was in its heyday. Texas cherished the

Stunt woman Texas Guinan LIBRARY OF CONGRESS

job of midnight hostess and, according to the August 31, 1924, edition of the *Buffalo Times*, she was brilliant at it.[10]

The article read:

> *She is a hostess sufficiently gifted with charm and tack and inventiveness to do that sort of thing. Imagine a universe where sociability is shrouded in the sad songs of the saxophones; where gold and silver slippers slide along the shining floor while the waiters come in softly with soup or salad; a universe filled with all sorts of people—millionaires from Wall Street, wage earners with pay envelopes in their pockets, amused foreigners with or without titles or monocles, thrilled debutantes and their boyish escorts who think they are having a wild night, wives and mothers and grandmothers who will need a good day's sleep to recuperate from all this excitement, metropolitan sophisticates entertaining friends from the "sticks," actresses and actors, singers from the Metropolitan Opera and stars of the movies.*[11]
>
> *In the center of this universe Texas Guinan moves about, keeping her bright eyes on the children of the night who do not want to go home, making sure that they are being amused and that they are being properly fed while the gay, gold-ceilinged room throbs with music and talk and movement, and the waiters, dressed in artists' smocks, plunk down plates of food.*[12]

Texas greeted most customers with an enthusiastic "Hello, Sucker!" and introduced her patrons to celebrities and the girls who worked for her to big spenders. She boasted to newspaper reporters that she made ten thousand dollars per week.[13]

"I like the noise, rhinestone heels, customers, plenty of attention and red velvet bathing suits," an article in the November 6, 1933, edition of the *St. Louis Globe-Democrat* read. "I smoke like a five-alarm fire; I eat an aspirin every night before I go to bed; I call every man I don't know Fred and they love it; I have six uncles; I sleep on my right side, and I like carrots. I eat a dozen oranges every day, and I once took off thirty-five pounds in two weeks. I guess that settles my personality."[14]

The nightclub Texas ran was raided several times by police who'd heard liquor was being served at the establishment. She was arrested a handful of times and spent a few hours in jail while her attorney arranged for bail.[15]

In April 1929, she was acquitted in federal court of charges of maintaining a nuisance and selling alcohol. The trial was a sensation. One prohibition agent said that he took his wife a dozen times to the nightclub, paid $20 a quart for liquor, $25 for champagne, and saw waiters slipping bottles wrapped in napkins into the laps of patrons, some of whom had to be helped to the street. None of the agents, however, linked Miss Guinan directly to any liquor selling. From the witness stand, she told the court she never drank liquor nor sold it, and the jury believed her.[16]

Having lost a great deal of money trying to open new nightclubs and fighting law enforcement to keep them from shutting her business down, Texas returned to California. She decided to take advantage of her fame, signing with Warner Brothers for an astronomical amount to make a movie based loosely on her life. The picture was called *Queen of the Night Clubs*. According to the August 4, 1929, edition of the *Los Angeles Times*, "In the studio's latest talkie, Guinan is an environment that fits her like a proverbial glove. As a matter of fact, she is shown in her own fashionable club and the story woven into and around it takes on a tragic turn when a pistol shot proclaims a murder within its brilliantly hued confines."[17]

The next talkie in which Texas appeared, and for which she received a sizeable amount of money, was *Broadway Through a Keyhole* by 20th Century Pictures. It was the story of a Broadway entertainer, beloved by a gangster, and a nightclub crooner who was not afraid of his rival's gunmen. Because of the nightclub background of the story, the picture was filmed as a musical with a large dancing chorus and many musical comedy and vaudeville stars performing in it. Texas was among the talented individuals who entertained the patrons flocking to the nightclub.[18]

Before the release of *Broadway Through a Keyhole*, Texas traveled to Canada and to the birthplace of her father. She made the trip with her troupe to present a special show for the citizens of Vancouver. While there, she became ill and was hospitalized with ulcerated colitis. Doctors operated on the actress to correct a perforation of her bowels, but to no avail.[19]

Her friends and physician shared that before the surgery she was in a bright and cheerful mood. But, she told those with her that if she were to die, she would be willing to do to experience relief from the pain she suffered. She assured the physician and nurses she knew they were doing all they could, and would never forget them. She passed away on November 5, 1933. "When I go," she once told a friend, "I want my funeral to be the speediest ever given with a cop on a motorcycle ahead, a wake for me in a nightclub, and a bunch of college boys singing college songs loud as they can while they lower my coffin."[20]

The cowgirl stunt woman was laid to rest at the Calvary Cemetery in Queens County, New York. She was forty-nine years old.[21]

Ruth Roland

She was a Hollywood social leader, respected for her business capacity and a general favorite because of her buoyant spirit, generous nature, and sparkling humor.

—*The Kansas City Star*, September 17, 1937

Ruth Roland struggled to break out of the locked miner's shack in which she was trapped. She pounded on the heavy wooden door and cried for help, but no one was around to hear her. A fire was set among the picks, shovels, and barrels of explosives, and the flames inched closer to her. She scanned the small room, looking for a way of escape. Spying a trapdoor in the floor, she dropped to her knees to wedge it open. A swift current of water running through a sturdy and long sluice box below was her only chance of survival. Without hesitation, Ruth lowered herself into the water. She was quickly carried away from the building just moments before it exploded in a blaze. Free from the burning rubble, she found herself in the grip of a new danger. The fast-moving water hurtled her along the sluiceway toward a massive, rapidly spinning waterwheel.[1]

Audiences watching the actress were on the edge of their seats as she scrambled to find something to grab on to that would keep her from devastating harm or death. The suspense moviegoers experienced, worrying about the plucky protagonist's fate, was a terrific ordeal and not to be taken lightly. In the stuffy darkness of the theater, a piano player pounded out a suspenseful tune that accompanied the frantic action. The spine-tingling silent film *Ruth of the Rockies* was one of more than two hundred motions pictures the equestrian stunt woman Ruth Roland appeared in during her twenty-two-year career.[2]

Known as the "queen of the early movie serials," Ruth made her mark on the industry as the replacement for Pearl White, the initial star of the popular series *The Perils of Pauline*. Produced by William Randolph Hearst, the chapter drama's title character was an ambitious young heiress with an independent nature and a desire for adventure. Ruth, a twenty-five-year-old skilled equestrian, took over the role when Pearl deserted Hollywood to live in Europe just before World War I.[3]

Whether in chaps or an elegant gown, Ruth was always just a hair's breadth away from the most appalling situations in her pictures. Her director, with an astute comprehension of how to build suspense, would leave her tied to a railroad track with the express thundering around the bend or leaping on horseback from the edge of a cliff to escape a fate worse than death.

Ruth Roland performing a stunt for the film *The Timber Queen* AUTHOR'S COLLECTION

Ruth's screen career began in 1910. "I reached Los Angeles on April Fool's Day," she related to a reporter at the *Kansas City Star* in September 1937, "and stepped out at once and got a job. I fixed up a stage sketch and it was booked in Los Angeles and dozens of nearby towns." Kalem Film Company signed her to a film contract on Independence Day. For four years she was with Kalem, earning a top salary of $115 a week.[4]

Her first picture was an action-adventure Western, *The Last Shot*. Most of the filming was done in the mountains around Santa Monica. Whooping Indians chased Ruth, dashing cowboys rescued her, and tough hombres threatened her virtue. "Even though I was an experienced rider, they had to lift me from the saddle after riding a horse forty miles the first day of shooting," Ruth later recalled.[5]

Ruth Roland between takes of a Western film she appeared in AUTHOR'S COLLECTION

After watching her perform, Balboa Films offered Ruth $150 a week to work for them. Kalem refused to meet the increase in pay. With Balboa, Ruth quickly became one of the nation's screen idols in such heart-stirrers as *Hands Up*, *Tiger's Trail*, *Neglected Wife*, *Price of Folly*, and *Fringe of Society*. The stories highlighted the versatility of the vivid young star, demonstrating that she could act as well as do stunts. But the Balboa contract lasted only two years. Ruth got into a quarrel with the film company executives and left them in 1917. They demanded $50,000 for alleged breach of contract and made it difficult for her to get another job.[6]

In 1927, Ruth decided to produce her own serial under the banner of Pathé Exchange Films, ran by the company's president, Paul Brunet. Brunet didn't think he was taking much of a chance in agreeing with Ruth in the sales value of her name—and Ruth Roland Serials, Inc., was organized. Ruth Roland, actress, rented herself, as she expressed it later in her career, to Ruth Roland the producer. And, as it turned out, both Ruths were happy with the arrangement. After Ruth the actress had pawned all her jewelry, Liberty bonds, house, cars, and some land she had bought in Los Angeles, Ruth the producer acquired a bank loan and was able to start shooting.[7]

From the Ruth Roland Serials Inc., came *Adventures of Ruth*, *The Avenging Arrow*, *White Eagle*, *Ruth on the Range*, and several other Western adventures of the William S. Hart type—lots of fast shooting and riding.[8]

The name of the horse Ruth rode during those adventures was Prince Belvedere. He was a beautiful stallion she had trained to do all kinds of tricks. Interviewers enjoyed talking with Ruth as she sat on Prince Belvedere. One of the reporters once asked her about her narrowest escape.[9]

"There wasn't any narrowest," she told them. "They were all narrow; coming close to breaking your neck was just the same regardless of the system or the time it happened. And I didn't have a double. I did my own stunts. Taking chances was my job. The only time I had a double was when the director was afraid I might 'get mine' and stop the pictures. But I prefer to do my own stunts. I liked it. Give me danger and speed."[10]

The speed Ruth so longed for eventually caught up with her in late 1927 while working on the film *Where the Worst Begins*. She was thrown

A poster for the film *White Eagle* featuring Ruth Roland AUTHOR'S COLLECTION

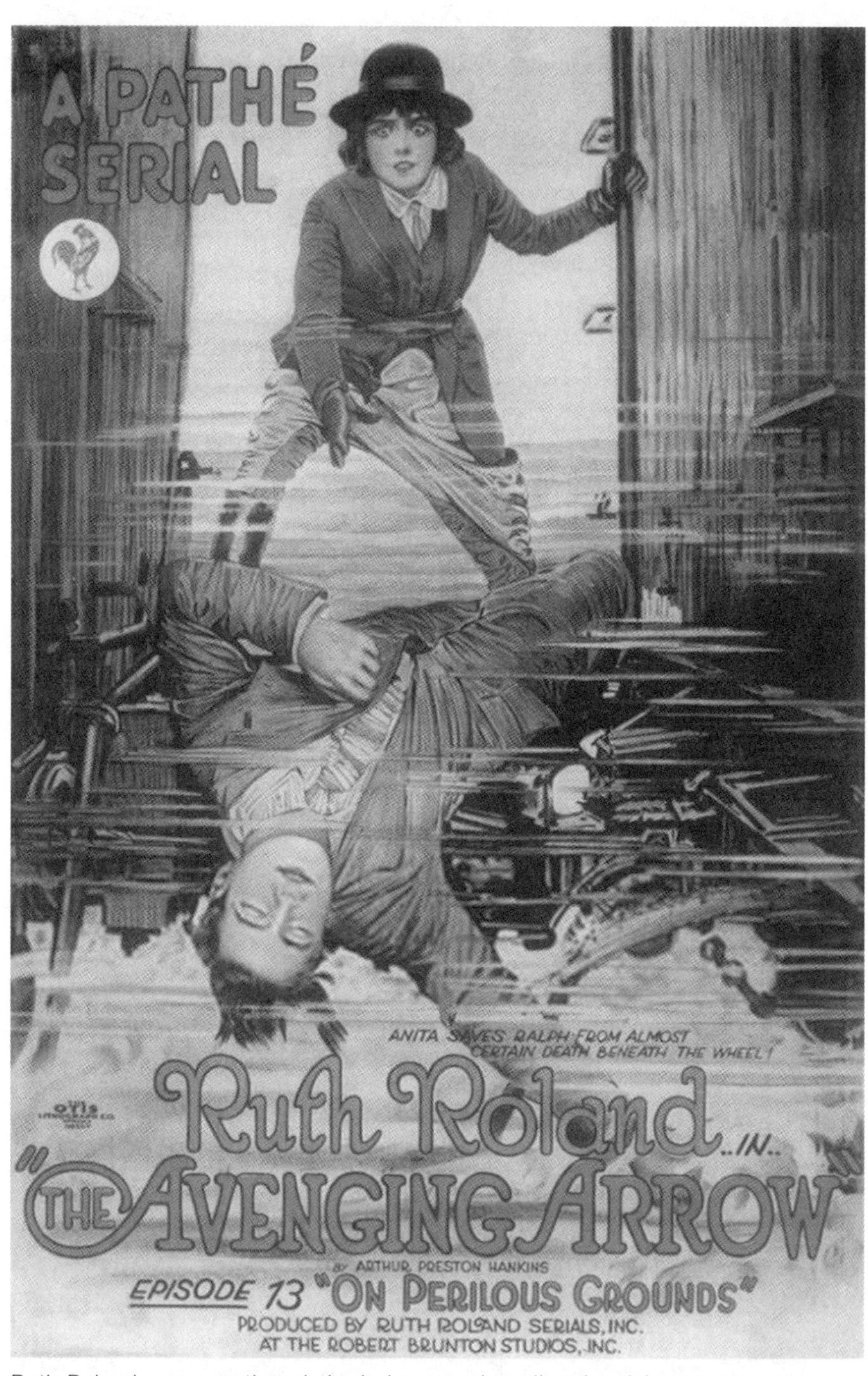

Ruth Roland saves another victim in her popular railroad serial. AUTHOR'S COLLECTION from a fast-moving horse, and the accident injured her spine. She was in constant pain for the rest of her life.[11]

In the heyday of her serial films' popularity, Ruth traveled around the country making personal appearances, collecting for one cause or another, and attending rodeo events. She enjoyed meeting new people and discovering new business ventures.[12]

Early in her movie career, some Los Angeles landsharks, thinking her an easy mark, unloaded a few miles of vacant lots on Ruth. Years later she recalled feeling as if she were the most naive individual in the world. "I was fascinated with business and too eager," she remembered to newspaper reporters in late 1937. "I thought I'd made the worst mistake ever, buying the land, but when the property turned out to be the choicest lots in Beverly Hills, I realized how wrong I was."

Ruth traded in moviemaking to go into real estate.[13]

"I gambled that I could make more money in Los Angeles real estate and in other investments than in in the movies. I found a wheat field containing ninety-seven acres at $3,500 an acre. I tried to get three or four movie stars to go in with me. They promised eagerly to put up the money, and when the time came they either failed to show up at all or came moaning that they were broke. I couldn't handle it alone, so I decided on sixty-one acres of the ninety-seven."[14]

She decided to purchase the land one day when she was in the Mojave Desert with some cowboys, filming a scene. She telephoned her broker from a small store on the edge of the location. "My hand trembled as I waited for the connection. 'Hello. Hello there, Ruth,' came my manager's voice. 'Well, do you take it or leave it?' Quick as a pistol shot, I answered, 'I'll take it,' and hung up. I staggered out of the booth and cried to the waiting cowboys, 'Well, you desert dudes, I bought it.'[15]

"I named the sixty-one acres Roland Square, and I had to move some of it quickly or go completely broke. I subdivided and syndicated thirty acres at one end into twenty units, sold them for $5,000 each, and used the proceeds to improve the whole thing. That left me with thirty-one acres, which gave me control of the development. How much am I worth? Well, I don't believe I want to say, but the talk around town is that if I don't clean up ten million dollars before 1935, it'll be because I don't want to."[16]

By 1928, Ruth's income was running far into six figures, and she was rated the wealthiest movie star. In the following year, when Ben Bard, famous movie villain of the silent screen, married her she was reported to be worth several million. Her wedding was the largest ever held in the film colony up until that time. An amazing display of orange blossoms, white satin, and lace adorned the church where their vows were exchanged.[17]

Following her marriage, Ruth made one unique return venture in films—a two-reeler in color. The story ran along to a vital point and then the projector was turned off. Then, Ruth would appear on the stage in front of the screen and ask the audience to mail in suggestions for the finish. There weren't many suggestions, and of those received, none were acceptable. The innovation flopped.[18]

In early 1937, Ruth was diagnosed with cancer. She died on September 22 of that same year. One of her final requests was that she be buried in her wedding dress. She was thirty-nine-years old when she passed away.[19]

Alice Van Springsteen

Trick riding by Alice Van of Los Angeles, who was one of the sensations of the Salinas rodeo, thrilled crowds at the state fair show last night.

—*The Register*, September 8, 1934

A well-used buckboard pulled along by four sturdy horses traveled lazily along a rugged, dusty road. A blustery wind swept across the rocky mountainous landscape, looming over the vehicle and its six passengers. Cowgirl actress Dale Evans, adorned in a stylish, mid-1940s business suit, sat next to actor-musician Pat Brady, who was driving the team. Members of the singing group the Sons of the Pioneers rode in the back of the wagon, laughing, talking and playing various instruments—a fiddle, harmonica, and a guitar.

Accomplished director William Whitney led the cast of the film *Bells of San Angelo* through the opening scenes, introducing Dale's character. All seemed peaceful and uneventful, until suddenly a lone rider spurred his horse out from behind a rock toward the buckboard. It wasn't until the rider fired several shots in the direction of the people that the driver urged the team into a gallop. The horses willingly complied. The fast-moving rider behind them aimed his pistol, firing another volley of shots.[1]

Panicked, the passengers ducked down in their seats. Dale crawled into the back of the buckboard with the others as bullets flew past her head. When the driver let go of the team to take cover, the conveyance bounced along, out of control. The horses sped up, and the buckboard wheels vaulted off massive boulders, fishtailing from side to side. Dale and the others were tossed about like rag dolls, in danger of being thrown out of the buckboard.

The masked, gun-wielding bandit continued in pursuit of the vehicle. When he caught up, and recognized there was no driver, he jumped from his ride onto the team rushing toward the danger. Bringing the animals to a stop was a struggle, but the feat was managed. The bandit climbed off the back of horses and hurried to the buckboard. He leveled his gun at the disheveled and dazed passengers inside, ordering everyone out. All complied with the exception of Dale—he didn't know she was lying face down on the floor of the vehicle covered by a sheet of canvas. After forcing the Sons of the Pioneers to remove their cowboy boots and tossing them into the vehicle, the armed man hopped onto his horse and led the team and buckboard away.

The bandit left the crude roadway and guided his horse onto the open range. The buckboard hobbled recklessly over rocks and sagebrush. While being thrown from one side of the vehicle to the other, Dale cried out in pain. The rider pulled back on his horses' reins, slowed the animals' gait, and rode to the buckboard to inspect. "Come out of there," the armed man demanded. Dale slowly emerged from under the canvas sheet. Her fashionable hat was slightly askew, but apart from that she looked lovely.

The stunt double who actually endured the uncomfortable ride on the buckboard, and who indeed looked like the ride had been a rough one, was Alice Van Springsteen. Alice was an accomplished stunt woman who, during the course of her years stunting, doubled for such stars as Doris Day, Barbara Stanwyck, and Ingrid Bergman. She was happy to double wherever she was needed but served as Dale Evans's stunt double throughout most of her film career.[2]

Born to Dutch parents Peter and Jennie Van Der Veen on July 12, 1918, in Denver, Colorado, Alice enjoyed being outdoors and helping care for the animals on her father's farm in Hynes, California. By the age of twelve, Alice was an expert horseback rider, having learned how to sit in a saddle from her older sister, Tilly. The pair performed in various rodeos throughout the state giving trick riding exhibitions. Alice made her solo public riding debut at the opening ceremony of the Olympics on July 30, 1932. The following year, she competed in

Alice Van Springsteen NATIONAL COWGIRL MUSEUM AND HALL OF FAME

the Ventura County rodeo, where she won the title of Champion Lady Trick Rider of California.[3]

Audiences were particularly enthused about Alice's equestrian skills. They marveled at the girl's ability, and newspaper reports noted that "the diminutive blonde drew all eyes with her daredevil stunts on the back of a racing horse."[4]

Her time appearing with her sister at events throughout the state ended abruptly in April 1934—Tilly passed away at the age of nineteen. The loss had a profound effect on Alice. Though despondent, she found some relief by continuing to ride in rodeos. She excelled in fancy tricks, including standing on her head on a prancing horse's back, riding two horses at once, and performing other extraordinary feats. By September

1934, Alice had earned the reputation as "the most thrilling act of any horse show."[5]

The September 8, 1934, edition of the *Sacramento Union* covered the well-received exhibition she gave at the state fair. "Clad in a becoming costume of slacks and a white shirt, Alice Van (she shortened her name for publicity purposes) of Los Angeles carries out trick riding acts that would make a circus performer envious and does all this to honor her sister whom she credits with teaching her how to ride," the article read. "What she does requires nerves of steel and a copious amount of skill."[6]

Between 1935 and 1936, Alice participated in rodeos outside her home state of California, including events at Cheyenne Frontier Days and Madison Square Garden. Her strong showing at both prestigious venues captured the attention of executives at 20th Century Fox. They hired her to be the stunt double for actress Dorothy Wilson in the Will Rogers picture *In Old Kentucky*. Set in the heart of the Blue Grass region, the story revolved around horse-loving people, their feuds, wrangles, romance, and the drama in their lives.[7]

In the film, Wilson's character has to take the place of a jockey in a major race, and Alice demonstrated her ability to handle a fast-moving horse in the climactic scene that ended with her winning the contest. Her stellar performance led to work with other major studios such as Warner Brothers and Republic Pictures.[8]

In May 1937, the Queen of England invited the nineteen-year-old world champion, woman trick rider to travel to Sydney, Australia, to ride in a grand Easter pageant. Alice gladly accepted and left from the port of San Pedro on the ship *Monterey*. When Alice returned to the States after a month abroad, she signed up to take part in the California Rodeo held in Salinas in July. She came in first in the cowgirl race and the trick and fancy riding competition.[9]

In September, Alice repeated wins in both those events at the Vallejo Rodeo. Shortly after accepting trophies for her performance, Alice was hired by Warner Brothers to be actress Olivia de Havilland's stunt double in the film *The Adventures of Robin Hood*, also starring Errol Flynn. When the swashbuckling action picture opened in May 1938, audiences witnessed Alice at her best, riding a horse named

Golden Cloud. Golden Cloud would later be renamed Trigger and ride to fame with his owner Roy Rogers.[10]

The Adventures of Robin Hood was one of seven films in which Alice appeared between 1937 and 1938. She did the stunts for the lead actresses in a series of Dick Foran Westerns, including *Land Beyond the Law*, *Cherokee Strip*, *Blazing Sixes*, *Empty Holsters*, *The Devil's Saddle Legion*, and *Prairie Thunder*. The steady work and her eagerness to attempt daring feats solidified her place in the industry. In addition to her reliability and flair for making the most difficult stunts look easy, she was attractive and could act. Executives at Warner Brothers recognized her talent and, in anticipation of offering her the role of Annie Oakley in a movie about the sharpshooter's life, they sent Alice to the studio's drama school. Along with acting and voice lessons, she was required to take classes in fencing and firearms. Her time as a student was cut short, however, when her fencing instructor made unwanted advances toward her. She was expelled from the class after slapping his face.[11]

Alice decided to abandon her acting aspirations and focus on stunt work and rodeo riding. In August 1938, she signed up to compete in bareback riding and trick riding contests at the National Championship Rodeo and Cowboy Circus in Gilmore, California. An accident occurred while practicing for the trick riding event, and she was seriously injured. Alice was slipping from the saddle to a position under the running horse's body when a hoof struck her in the side, and she was hurled to the ground. Alice was taken to the hospital, where doctors found she had contusions in her right leg and abdomen and was suffering internal injuries as well. "I'll be riding tomorrow," she told reporters concerned about her condition. "Not to worry."[12]

In February 1939, Alice rode in the Coronado Town Plate Horse Race alongside a handful of other top female equestrians who had graduated from rodeo performer to jockey.[13] She didn't give up competing in rodeos completely, but she spent the bulk of the year racing. The March 31, 1940, edition of the *Los Angeles Times* ranked her as one of the top eight "girl jockeys on the Coast."[14]

Alice's status as an accomplished jockey prompted film directors to hire her for difficult stunts in a series of new B Westerns. One of those stunts called for her to execute a thirty-foot jump across a broken railroad bridge between two mesas. Another called for her to jump a cliff into a river. Alice didn't know how to swim, but she wasn't going to let that stop her from doing the job. Other complications arose early in the stunt that she had to overcome before she hit the water.[15]

When the director gave her the cue to start, she galloped her horse toward them as rehearsed. There was no question she could ride, but the horse balked and landed fifty feet short of the spot he was to go over. The bank was too steep, and the horse reared and veered away. The director kept the cameras rolling through the initial difficulty. The footage was too exciting to miss. Alice led the horse back to the mark set by the director and attempted the jump again. The second time the animal landed where he was supposed to. The horse squealed as they hit the river but was up in a moment, swimming. Alice held on tight to her ride, quickly guiding

Alice Van Springsteen jumping across a dilapidated railroad cut NATIONAL COWGIRL MUSEUM AND HALL OF FAME

him against the raging current to the other bank. Halfway up, Alice was to tumble off and roll back into the water. She did so and the current carried her along. The camera followed her every move.[16]

Downstream a bit sat the cowboy star on his horse, lasso in hand. Alice slapped hard at the river water lapping her chin. The cowboy threw a noose over her. He let his horse pull the other end of the rope, which was tied around the saddle horn. When Alice was out of the water and had managed to make it up the slick embankment safely, the director shouted "cut." He congratulated the stunt woman on her superb work. "You truly looked panicked. Nice acting," he told her. "Who was acting?" she responded.[17]

Alice's fearlessness on camera led to an abundance of stunt double work in the 1940s. She stood in for many leading actresses in a variety of Westerns from *The Cowboy and the Blonde,* starring George Montgomery, to *Man from Cheyenne,* starring Roy Rogers. When she wasn't stunting, she was riding some of the fastest horses in the country to big wins at Agua Caliente Racetrack and the Hollywood Park Racetrack.[18]

Between competing in rodeos, her professional jockey venture, and stunt jobs, Alice was a busy woman. Each area of endeavor had challenges and rewards that she appreciated, but she was most fascinated with being a stunt double. The feats Alice was hired to perform varied from film to film. Sometimes she had to fall off a galloping horse or ride inside a burning stagecoach. At other times, she needed to dodge knives being thrown at her or jump from her horse onto a train.[19]

Alice enjoyed meeting the actors she stood in for as much as performing stunts. In 1944, twenty-five-year-old Alice was introduced to eleven-year-old Elizabeth Taylor. The film that the two would be appearing in was *National Velvet.* Based on the novel by Enid Bagnold, the story was of a teenage girl who won a major horse racing competition. As a trained jockey, Alice rode the horse in the film over hedgerows and stone walls and around the racetrack. Released in January 1945, the movie was an instant family classic, and it earned two Academy Awards.[20]

Republic Pictures capitalized on Alice's talent and hired her to double for a handful of their stars, including Dale Evans. Dale and Alice met on the set of the movie the *Yellow Rose of Texas.* Dale's experience in the saddle was limited. The studio assumed that, because she was from Texas, she could ride. She couldn't. Alice performed the difficult work as Dale looked on. "I learned things watching her," Dale admitted later about Alice. "I watched the way she sat a horse like a man. She would give me tips along the way."[21]

Alice was Dale's stunt double in several of the films she made with Roy Rogers, including *Home in Oklahoma* and *Bells of San Angelo*. The two women became lifelong friends, spending time together off camera as well as on. "We were like sisters," Alice noted later in her career.[22]

No matter how involved she was in stunt work, Alice could never stay away from rodeo life for long. She was a top attraction throughout California in the 1940s, appearing in contests from Sacramento to San Bernadino.[23]

The chance to double for award-winning actresses made stunting all the more attractive to Alice, because they were performers she admired. She stunted for Ingrid Bergman in *Joan of Arc* in 1948, Ginger Rogers in the *Groom Wore Spurs* in 1951, and Doris Day in *Calamity Jane* in 1953.[24]

Westerns continued to be a popular film genre during the 1950s. Not only were audiences going to theaters to see movies such as *High Noon* and *Broken Arrow*, they could also watch Westerns in their homes; the genre made the effortless production jump to television. Alice was not only working as a stunt double in feature films but now on the small screen as well. She stunted for Gail Davis in the series *Annie Oakley,* for various actresses in the series *Trackdown* starring Robert Culp, and again for Dale Evans in the *Roy Rogers Show*.[25]

She met director Robert G. Springsteen at Republic Studios, where he was making B Westerns such as *The Arizona Cowboy* starring Rex Allen and *Oklahoma Annie* starring Judy Canova. Alice was one of the stunt doubles for Canova. They married on August 12, 1962 in Los Angeles. He was fifty-seven and she was forty-four.[26]

Alice remained in high demand during the 1960s, doubling for Jane Wyman in the television series *Wagon Train*, Barbara Stanwyck in the series *Big Valley*, and for Susan Hayward in the feature film *The Revengers*. Robert added to the Westerns he directed for Republic Pictures and expanded the list of Western-themed films he produced for Universal and Paramount, including a series of movies starring Audie Murphy.[27]

When the couple retired from the motion picture industry, they settled on a ranch outside San Diego. There Alice raised Thoroughbred horses and taught horseback riding. She was often invited to film festivals to speak about her career as a stunt double. Like many other cowgirl stunt women, she recalled the number of cracked ribs, bruised arms and legs, and broken body parts she'd suffered at one time or another while on the job.[28]

In January 1999, Alice happily agreed to be interviewed along with Dale Evans for the *Desert Sun* newspaper, talking about the films they made together. The pair reminisced about their longtime friendship and the days of sharing a guesthouse while on location shooting early pictures with Roy Rogers. Alice recalled the time she was expelled from drama school and a conversation she had with Dale not long after the incident. "I told her, Dale, you do the acting and I'll do the stunts," she admitted. "I'm satisfied with that."[29]

Dale was by Alice's side when she was inducted into the Cowgirl Hall of Fame in 1998. "Alice deserves this honor," Dale told the audience during the ceremony. "She made me look good for years."[30]

Alice Van Springsteen died of pneumonia on September 13, 2008, when she was ninety years old.[31]

Notes

Before the Cameras

1. Decennial Census Official Publications, https://www.census.gov/programs-surveys/decennial-census/decade/decennial-publications.1890.html.
2. *Boston Post,* June 19, 1943.
3. *The Evening Post,* August 30, 1943; *Struggles & Triumphs: or, Forty Years' of Recollections of P.T. Barnum,* pp. 94–95.
4. Ibid.
5. *The Wild West: A History of the Wild West Shows,* pp. 31–36.
6. *Buffalo Gals: Women of Buffalo Bill's Wild West Show,* pp. 15–21.
7. Ibid.
8. Ibid.
9. *Along Came a Cowgirl: Daring and Iconic Women of the Rodeo and Wild West Shows,* pp. 116–18.
10. Ibid.
11. *Annie Oakley, Women at Arms,* pp. 59–62; *Annie Oakley of the Wild West,* pp. 39–47.
12. Ibid.
13. Ibid.
14. *The Trials of Annie Oakley,* pp. 3–6.
15. *The Trials of Annie Oakley,* pp. 4–9.
16. Ibid.
17. *The Trials of Annie Oakley,* pp. 6–10.
18. Ibid.
19. *The Trials of Annie Oakley,* pp. 8–11.
20. Ibid.
21. *The Trials of Annie Oakley,* pp. 11–15.
22. Ibid.
23. *Buffalo Gals,* pp. 98–99.
24. *The Trials of Annie Oakley,* pp. 17–20.
25. *The Trials of Annie Oakley,* pp. 147–48.

NOTES

Lucille Mulhall

1. *The Guthrie Daily Leader*, February 13, 1903; *Elizabethville Echo*, September 18, 1903; *America's First Cowgirl Lucille Mulhall,* pp. 28–32.
2. *The Guthrie Daily Leader*, February 13, 1903; *Elizabethville Echo*, September 18, 1903; *America's First Cowgirl*, pp. 28–32.
3. *The Livestock Inspector*, October 15, 1899.
4. *America's First Cowgirl*, pp. 66–67.
5. *The El Paso Herald*, July 21, 1900.
6. *Mountain Gazette*, December 10, 1960.
7. *The St. Louis Republic*, May 17, 1901.
8. *Lucille Mulhall: Wild West Cowgirl*, pp. 125–126; *America's First Cowgirl*, pp. 66–67.
9. *America's First Cowgirl*, pp. 83–86.
10. Ibid.
11. *The Pryor Creek Clipper*, May 17, 1901.
12. *The El Paso Herald*, December 20, 1902.
13. *America's First Cowgirl*, pp. 108–109.
14. Ibid.
15. *America's First Cowgirl*, pp. 108–109; *The El Paso Herald*, December 20, 1902.
16. *Claflin Clarion*, January 29, 1903; *The Neihart Herald*, February 12, 1903; *Oklahoma Rodeo Women*, pp. 33–34.
17. *The Butte Miner*, April 19, 1903.
18. Ibid.
19. Ibid.
20. Ibid.
21. *The St. Louis Dispatch*, January 18, 1907.
22. *The Kansas City Star*, January 21, 1907.
23. *America's First Cowgirl*, pp. 160–162.
24. *America's First Cowgirl*, pp. 163–165.
25. Ibid.
26. *The Chicago Livestock World*, May 19, 1910.
27. Ibid.
28. Ibid.
29. *Manitoba Free Press*, March 31, 1914.
30. Ibid.
31. *America's First Cowgirl*, pp. 132–133.
32. *The Haworth Herald*, May 9, 1919; *Star Tribune*, May 29, 1922.
33. *America's First Cowgirl*, pp. 156–157.
34. *Lubbock Morning Avalanche*, December 24, 1940; *The Daily Oklahoman*, December 27, 1940.
35. *The Livestock Inspector*, October 15, 1899.
36. *The Daily Oklahoman*, December 27, 1940.

Lulu Belle Parr

1. *Harrisburg Telegram*, July 23, 1917.
2. Lulu Bell Parr, ancestry.com.

3. *Elwood Daily Press*, September 23, 1895; *Delphos Daily Herald*, September 25, 1895.
4. Lulu Bell Parr, ancestry.com.
5. Ibid.
6. *The Pittsburgh Press*, May 3, 1903.
7. *Pittston Gazette*, July 24, 1906.
8. *The Standard Union*, June 24, 1906.
9. Ibid.
10. Ibid.
11. Ibid.
12. *The Philadelphia Inquirer*, June 7, 1908.
13. *The Salt Lake Herald Republican*, November 30, 1908.
14. *The Brooklyn Citizen*, May 21, 1910.
15. Ibid.
16. Ibid.
17. *New Orleans Republican*, August 24, 1873.
18. *The Courier*, August 11, 1911.
19. Ibid.
20. Ibid.
21. Ibid.
22. *Evening Times Republican*, July 27, 1912.
23. Ibid.
24. Ibid.
25. U.S. Presbyterian Church Records, 1896–1943, https://www.history.pcusa.org/services/records-management/records-congregations; *Muskogee Daily Phoenix*, November 24, 1914; *The Times Democrat*, November 24, 1914.
26. *Billboard Magazine*, February 21, 1914.
27. Buffalo Bill Wild West Collection at the Center of the West, MS 261 Lulu Bell.
28. Ibid.
29. Ibid.
30. *Weekly Journal Miner*, May 26, 1915.
31. *Pittsburgh Daily Post*, July 16, 1916.
32. *Weekly Journal Miner*, May 26, 1915.
33. Buffalo Bill Wild West Collection at the Center of the West, MS 261 Lulu Bell.
34. Ibid.
35. *Billboard Magazine*, April 4, 1921.
36. *Florence Morning News*, October 20, 1925.
37. *Billboard Magazine*, August 29, 1929.
38. *The La Crosse Tribune*, July 4, 1926.
39. Ibid.
40. *Billboard Magazine*, June 4, 1927.
41. *Billboard Magazine*, March 23, 1929.
42. *Dodge City Journal*, September 19, 1929.
43. *Battle Creek Enquirer*, July 12, 1930.
44. *The Gazette and Daily*, May 17, 1938; *Dodge City Journal*, September 19, 1929.
45. *Dayton Daily News*, May 10, 2001.

46. *Argus Leader*, January 18, 1955; *The Spokesman Review*, January 19, 1955.
47. Ibid.
48. Ibid.

May Manning Lillie

1. *The Times*, Shreveport, Louisiana, June 10, 1885.
2. *Pawnee Bill: A Biography of Major Gordon Lillie,* pp. 100–101.
3. *Pawnee Bill: A Biography of Major Gordon Lillie,* pp. 73, 100–101.
4. Ibid.
5. *The Evening Telegram,* September 1, 1886.
6. *Pawnee Bill: A Biography of Major Gordon Lillie,* pp. 116–17.
7. Ibid.
8. Ibid.
9. Ibid.
10. Ibid.
11. *The Peabody Weekly Republican,* September 16, 1887.
12. *The Boston Journal,* December 10, 1887.
13. *Pawnee Bill: A Biography of Major Gordon Lillie,* pp. 117–18.
14. *Ashland Weekly News,* August 7, 1889.
15. *Oakland Tribune,* January 15, 1928.
16. *Pawnee Bill: A Biography of Major Gordon Lillie,* pp. 199–200, 174–75, 180–81.
17. *The Joliet News,* June 6, 1907.
18. Ibid.
19. Ibid.
20. Ibid
21. *The Weekly Kansas City Star,* September 23, 1936.
22. *Pawnee Bill: A Biography of Major Gordon Lillie,* pp. 122–24.
23. *The El Reno Daily Tribune,* August 31, 1936.
24. Ibid.
25. *The Weekly Kansas City Star,* September 23, 1936
26. *The Rock Island Argus,* September 22, 1936.

Bertha Kaepernik Blanchett

1. *The Sidney Telegraph*, July 1, 1905; *The South Bend Tribune*, July 28, 1906.
2. *The South Bend Tribune*, July 28, 1906.
3. Ibid.
4. *The Sunday Oregonian*, October 22, 1905.
5. Ibid.
6. Bertha Kaepernik, ancestry.com.
7. *The Sunday Oregonian*, October 22, 1905.
8. Ibid.
9. *The South Bend Tribune*, July 28, 1906.
10. Bertha Kaepernik, ancestry.com.
11. Bertha Kaepernik, ancestry.com; *Stockton Evening and Sunday Record*, July 8, 1922.
12. *Stockton Evening and Sunday Record*, July 8, 1922.

13. Ibid.
14. Bertha Kaepernik, ancestry.com; *Tulare Advance Register*, July 6, 1979.

Adele Von Ohl

1. *The Last of the Wild West Cowgirls: A True Story*, pp. 22–24.
2. *Great Falls Tribune*, June 15, 1969; Adele Von Ohl, ancestry.com.
3. *The Courier News*, July 20, 1903.
4. *The Courier News*, August 17, 1904.
5. *The Courier News*, November 15, 1904.
6. Ibid.
7. Ibid.
8. *Buffalo Courier*, April 25, 1905.
9. *The Courier News*, October 26, 1905.
10. *The Minneapolis Journal*, October 27, 1905.
11. *The Courier News*, October 2, 1905.
12. *The Courier News*, September 5, 1902; *The Courier News*, February 8, 1906.
13. *The Courier News*, February 8, 1906.
14. *The Courier News*, April 4, 1908.
15. *The Courier News*, March 18, 1908.
16. *The Courier News*, November 21, 1908.
17. *The Central New Jersey Home News*, December 4, 1908.
18. Ibid.
19. James Letcher Parker, ancestry.com.
20. *Detroit Free Press*, April 30, 1911.
21. *New York Times*, April 29, 1912.
22. *Press Sun Bulletin*, January 8, 1912.
23. *The Courier News*, July 10, 1913.
24. *The Central New Jersey Home News*, June 26, 1913.
25. *Boston Globe*, March 8, 1915; *San Francisco Examiner*, June 24, 1915.
26. *Los Angeles Record*, July 13, 1916.
27. Ibid.
28. Ibid.
29. Ibid.
30. Ibid.
31. *Salt Lake Herald Republican*, June 25, 1917.
32. *Los Angeles Evening Express*, April 9, 1923.
33. *The Courier News,* May 23, 1928; *The Courier News,* April 10, 1928.
34. *The Courier News,* September 9, 1931; *The Courier News,* November 13, 1936.
35. *Great Falls Tribune,* April 25, 1965.
36. *The Courier News,* November 13, 1936.
37. *Akron Beacon Journal,* January 22, 1966; Adele Von Ohl, ancestry.com.

Silent Stunters

1. *Press of Atlantic City*, December 24, 1903; *Funk & Wagnalls New Encyclopedia*, Vol. 17, "Motion Pictures," pp. 8–9.

2. *Kenosha News*, December 29, 1903.
3. *Funk and Wagnalls*, pp. 8–9; *A Pictorial History of the Western Film*, pp. 2–5.
4. *A Pictorial History,* pp. 6–12.
5. "A Knight of the Range," IMDb.com; *The Berlin News Record* (Ontario), March 18, 1916, IMDb.
6. *Buffalo Sunday Morning News*, May 31, 1914; Olive Cary (Carey), ancestry.com.
7. Olive Carey, IMDb; *The Inner Conscience,* IMDb.
8. *The Long Beach Telegram*, October 10, 1914; *The State* (Columbia, South Carolina), August 30, 1914.
9. *The Wilmington* (N.C.) *Morning Star*, August 29, 1917; *The Soul Herder,* IMDb.
10. Olive Cary (Carey), ancestry.com; Olive Carey, IMDb.com.
11. *Los Angeles Times,* March 17, 1988; *Oakland Tribune,* March 16, 1988.
12. Bessie Barriscale, IMDb.
13. Bessie Barriscale, IMDb; *San Francisco Examiner*, July 1, 1965.
14. Ibid.
15. *Rose of the Rancho,* IMDb; *The Washington Post*, December 8, 1914.
16. *Daily Times* (Davenport, Iowa), December 12, 1914.
17. Ibid.
18. *Two-Gun Betty,* IMDb.
19. *Star Tribune* (Minneapolis), December 8, 1918; *The Minneapolis Journal*, December 10, 1918.
20. Bessie Barriscale, IMDb.
21. *San Francisco Bulletin*, December 26, 1924.
22. *San Francisco Examiner*, July 1, 1965; Bessie Barriscale, IMDb.
23. Anita Bush, ancestry.com; Anita Bush, IMDb; *Ebony,* pp. 106–107.
24. *Ebony,* pp. 106–107.
25. *The Bull Dogger*, IMDb.
26. *The Afro American,* April 21, 1922.
27. *The Afro American,* May 5, 1922.
28. Ibid.
29. Ibid.
30. *The Afro American,* May 12, 1922.
31. *Ebony,* pp. 106–107; Anita Bush, IMDb.
32. *Daily News* (N.Y.), February 19, 1974.
33. *Miami Herald,* February 20, 1974; Anita Bush, ancestry.com.

Helen Gibson

1. *Lights, Camera, Action: Helen Gibson, Silent Serial Queen Who Became Hollywood's First Professional Stunt Woman*, pp. 104–105, 109.
2. *Lights, Camera, Action*, pp. 104–105, 109; *Films in Review,* pp. 31.
3. *The Film Encyclopedia,* pp. 480; Rose Wenger, ancestry.com; *Lights, Camera, Action*, pp. 1–5.
4. Ibid.
5. *The Dayton Herald*, April 27, 1910.

6. Ibid.
7. *Lights, Camera, Action*, pp. 8–11; *A Pictorial History of the Western Film*, pp. 23–27.
8. *The Lexington Herald*, May 20, 1912; *The Evening Mail*, May 29, 1912; *The Roanoke Times*, May 25, 1912; Helen Gibson, IMDb.com.
9. *The Salt Lake Tribune*, July 3, 1913; *The Los Angeles Times*, February 18, 1913.
10. *Lights, Camera, Action*, pp. 8–9; Helen Gibson, IMDb.com; *The Bangor Daily News*, February 27, 1913.
11. *Lights, Camera, Action*, pp. 9–11; *Films in Review*, pp. 19–22; Rose Wenger, ancestry.com.
12. *The Winnipeg Tribune*, August 13, 1913.
13. *Lights, Camera, Action*, pp. 9–11; *Films in Review*, pp. 19–22.
14. *East Oregonian*, September 12, 1913; *East Oregonian*, September 15, 1913.
15. *East Oregonian*, September 8, 1913; *Lights, Camera, Action*, pp. 11–12.
16. Rose Wenger, ancestry.com; *East Oregonian*, September 12, 1913; *East Oregonian*, September 15, 1913.
17. Helen Gibson, IMDb.com; *East Oregonian*, September 30, 1913; *East Oregonian*, October 27, 1914.
18. *Los Angeles Times*, April 4, 1915; *Los Angeles Evening Express*, April 28, 1915.
19. *Los Angeles Express*, April 5, 1915.
20. Ibid.
21. *Los Angeles Times*, May 7, 1915.
22. *The Daily Telegram*, April 17, 1915; *Lights, Camera, Action*, pp. 15–20; Helen Gibson, IMDb.com.
23. *Films in Review*, pp. 19–22; *Press of Atlantic City*, October 13, 1915; *Fort Wayne Journal Gazette*, October 24, 1915.
24. *The Allentown Democrat*, October 26, 1915.
25. Ibid.
26. *The Hutchinson Gazette*, February 6, 1916.
27. Ibid.
28. *The West Virginian*, February 15, 1917; Helen Gibson, IMDb.com; *Lights, Camera, Action*, pp. 88–92.
29. Helen Gibson, IMDb.com; *Lights, Camera, Action*, pp. 88–92.
30. Helen Gibson, IMDb.com; *The Chico Enterprise*, December 24, 1917; *Tri-County News*, May 4, 1917.
31. Ibid.
32. Ibid.
33. Ibid.
34. Ibid.
35. *The Logan Republican*, March 27, 1917.
36. *The Sacramento Bee*, November 13, 1917; *Reading Times*, October 29, 1917; *Argus Leader*, October 20, 1917; *The Leavenworth Post*, October 21, 1917; Helen Gibson, IMDb.com.
37. *The Los Angeles Times*, January 10, 1918; *The Los Angeles Times*, January 13, 1918.
38. *East Oregonian*, January 11, 1917.

39. *The Lima Gazette* and *The Lima Republican*, November 30, 1918.

40. *The Bridgeport Times and Evening Farmer*, March 28, 1919; *The Helena Star*, February 27, 1919; *Films in Review*, 31–32.

41. Helen Gibson, IMDb.com; Helen Gibson Scrapbook, pp. 33.

42. *The Billings Gazette*, October 31, 1921; Helen Gibson, IMDb.com; *Films in Review*, 33–34.

43. *Los Angeles Times*, March 16, 1922; *Los Angeles Evening Express*, March 20, 1922.

44. *The Ponca City News,* August 24, 1924; *The Times Leader,* October 1, 1924.

45. *The Ponca City News*, August 24, 1924; *The Times Leader*, October 1, 1926; *Seattle Union Record*, June 30, 1927.

46. *Clinton Daily Journal and Public*, September 26, 1936.

47. Helen Gibson Scrapbook, pp. 37; Rose Wenger, ancestry.com.

48. *The Lawless Nineties*, IMDb.com.

49. *The Enid Morning News*, March 20, 1938; *Vallejo Evening News*, March 30, 1938.

50. Helen Gibson; IMDb.com.

51. *Sacramento Bee*, August 14, 1957.

52. Ibid.

53. Ibid.

54. *Lights, Camera, Action*, pp. 223–25.

55. *Lights, Camera, Action*, pp. 227–28; Rose Wenger, ancestry.com.

Tillie Baldwin

1. *Elmore County Republican,* September 7, 1912; *Los Angeles Evening Express,* March 25, 1912.

2. *Hartford Courant,* August 23, 1925.

3. *Kennebec Journal,* March 12, 1910.

4. *Hartford Courant,* October 19, 1930.

5. *The Daily Report* (Ontario, Calif.), March 20, 1912.

6. Ibid.

7. Ibid.

8. Ibid.

9. Ibid.

10. Ibid.

11. *Monterey Daily Cypress,* January 11, 1913.

12. *The Tacoma Times,* July 3, 1913; *The Winnipeg Tribune,* August 15, 1913; *The Spokesman Review,* August 2, 1913.

13. *The Times,* September 10, 1916.

14. Ibid.

15. *Fitchburg Sentinel,* September 28, 1917; *The Manchester Journal,* September 2, 1920; *Norwich Bulletin,* May 26, 1917.

16. *Calgary Herald*, August 28, 1919.

17. *Bennington Banner*, September 10, 1920; *The Boston Globe*, September 28, 1921; *Independent Observer*, June 21, 1923.

18. *Independent Observer,* June 21, 1923.

19. *Hartford Courant,* August 23, 1925.

20. Ibid.
21. Ibid.
22. Ibid.
23. *Hartford Courant*, August 18, 1957.
24. *Hartford Courant*, February 4, 1930.
25. *The Oklahoma News,* August 18, 1935.
26. *Daily News,* August 23, 1936.
27. *Scranton Tribune,* September 29, 1946.
28. *Hartford Courant,* August 18, 1957.

Allene Ray

1. *San Antonio Evening News*, June 7, 1919; Allene "Alene Ray" Burch, ancestry.com.
2. *Moving Picture World*, Vol. 76, pp. 45–50.
3. Allene "Alene Ray" Burch, ancestry.com; *Moving Picture World*, Vol. 76, October 21, 1925, pp. 45–50; *Monrovia News Post*, March 5, 1978; *The San Bernardino County Sun*, November 4, 1923.
4. Allene "Alene Ray" Burch, ancestry.com; *San Antonio Evening News*, November 27, 1920.
5. *Fort Scott Daily Tribune*, December 7, 1920.
6. *The Los Angeles Times*, August 27, 1922.
7. *San Antonio Evening News*, February 4, 1922.
8. *The Perils of Pauline,* IMDb.com; Allene "Alene Ray" Burch, ancestry.com.
9. *The San Bernardino County Sun*, November 4, 1923; *Film Serials and the American Cinema*, pp. 6–10.
10. *Film Serials and the American Cinema*, pp. 6–10, Allene "Alene Ray" Burch, ancestry.com.
11. *Times Union*, October 11, 1925; *Evening Star*, October 4, 1925.
12. *Moving Picture World*, Vol. 76, pp. 45–50.
13. Ibid.
14. *The Lincoln Star*, April 19, 1925; *Evening Star*, May 20, 1925; *Moving Picture World*, Vol. 82, September 18, 1926, pp. 27–32.
15. *Detroit Free Press*, May 23, 1926.
16. *San Francisco Examiner*, July 30, 1925.
17. *The Newcastle Sun*, August 15, 1930.
18. *State Journal,* August 3, 1930; *The Overlook Film Encyclopedia*, pp. 22–23; *Daily News*, September 12, 1930; *Tracy Press*, September 30, 1930.
19. *The Los Angeles Times*, September 30, 1930.
20. *The Overlook Film Encyclopedia*, pp. 22–23.
21. *Cavern City Chronicle*, January 16, 1931; *Valley Morning Star*, March 19, 1931.
22. *Monrovia News Post*, March 5, 1978.
23. Allene "Alene Ray" Burch, ancestry.com.

Bonnie Gray

1. *Monte Vista Tribune*, August 1, 1929.
2. *Monte Vista Tribune*, August 1, 1929; Bonnie Gray Papers, Box 2.

3. Verna Grace Harris, ancestry.com; Bonnie Gray Papers, Box 2.
4. Ibid.
5. United States Military Record, Bonnie Gray Papers, Box 2.
6. Verna Grace Harris, ancestry.com; Bonnie Gray Paper, Box 2.
7. *The Salt Lake Tribune*, September 28, 1927.
8. *The Signal*, May 6, 1921; *Evening World Herald*, July 29, 1921; *Casper Star Tribune*, July 29, 1929.
9. *Okmulgee Daily Times*, September 6, 1921.
10. *Arizona Republic*, December 11, 1921.
11. *El Paso Herald*, December 29, 1921; *The Billboard*, November 25, 1922.
12. *Las Cruses Sun News*, January 19, 1922; *Falls City Daily News*, July 30, 1922.
13. *Oakland Tribune*, August 9, 1922; *Salt Lake Telegram*, August 18, 1922; *The Standard Union*, October 31, 1922; *New York Times*, November 12, 1922.
14. *Cheyenne State Leader*, July 20, 1922.
15. *San Fernando Valley Times*, January 10, 1946.
16. Verna Grace Harris, ancestry.com; Bonnie Gray Papers, Box 2.
17. *The Des Moines Register*, July 12, 1928; *The Gazette*, July 11, 1928.
18. *The Burbank Pathfinder*, January 22, 1924.
19. Ibid.
20. *The Overlook Film Encyclopedia*, pp. 15–16; *The Cincinnati Enquirer*, December 27, 1925.
21. Bonnie Gray Papers, Box 2.
22. Ibid.
23. *Reno Evening Gazette*, June 14, 1927; Bonnie Gray Papers, Box 1.
24. *Riverside Daily Press*, June 1, 1926.
25. *Gazette and Telegraph*, August 15, 1926.
26. Ibid.
27. *The Stroud Messenger*, August 13, 1926.
28. *Psychology Magazine*, pp. 37–39; Bonnie Gray Papers, Box 1.
29. *Burbank Daily Evening Review*, March 12, 1928; *Los Angeles Times*, April 29, 1928; Bonnie Gray Papers, Box 1.
30. *Statesman Journal*, June 9, 1929.
31. *The Sacramento Bee*, June 20, 1930; *The Bellingham Herald*, June 20, 1930.
32. *Los Angeles Evening Post Record*, June 20, 1930; *San Francisco Examiner*, June 20, 1930; *Martinez News Gazette*, June 24, 1930; Bonnie Gray Papers, Box 2.
33. *The Payson Chronicle*, August 1, 1930; *The Pomona Progress Bulletin*, September 22, 1930; *Anaheim Bulletin*, September 17, 1930.
34. *The Sunday Star*, March 10, 1929.
35. *The Modesto Bee*, May 8, 1931; *The Modesto Bee*, May 13, 1931.
36. *Los Angeles Evening Post Record*, August 4, 1932.
37. *The Spokesman Review*, August 27, 1932.
38. *The Morning Press*, August 27, 1932; *The Long Beach Sun*, August 27, 1932; *Statesmen Journal*, September 20, 1932; *Ventura Weekly Post*, November 18, 1932.
39. *The Valley Times*, November 27, 1959; *Los Angeles Evening Citizen*, August 15, 1936; *Lincoln Nebraska State Journal*, July 26, 1936; *The Valley Times*, November 27, 1959.

40. *San Fernando Valley Times,* January 10, 1946.
41. Ibid.
42. Verna Grace Harris, ancestry.com; Bonnie Gray Papers, Box 2.
43. *The Valley Times,* November 27, 1959.
44. Ibid.
45. Verna Grace Harris, ancestry.com; Bonnie Gray Papers, Box 2.

Mildred Douglas

1. *Six-Shooter Andy,* IMDb.com.
2. *Six-Shooter Andy,* IMDb.com; Mildred May McConnell Douglas Chrisman, ancestry.com; *The Houston Post,* February 24, 1918.
3. Mildred May McConnell Douglas Chrisman, ancestry.com; *The Fox Film Corporation,* pp. 85–92; *Detroit Free Press,* June 4, 1922.
4. Mildred May McConnell Douglas Chrisman, ancestry.com; Mildred Douglas Scrapbook.
5. Mildred May McConnell Douglas Chrisman, ancestry.com; Mildred Douglas Scrapbook; *Kansas City Journal,* October 8, 1916.
6. Mildred May McConnell Douglas Chrisman, ancestry.com; Mildred Douglas Scrapbook.
7. *The Kansas City Star,* October 1, 1916.
8. *East Oregonian,* September 27, 1917; *The Oregonian,* July 1, 1918; *The Idaho Statesman,* October 6, 1917.
9. *The News Tribune,* June 29, 1918.
10. Ibid.
11. *The Gordon Journal,* July 17, 1919.
12. Ora Nelson "Pat" Chrisman, IMDb.com; Mildred May McConnell Douglas Chrisman, ancestry.com; Mildred Douglas Scrapbook.
13. *The Daily Oklahoman,* November 26, 1978.
14. Mildred Douglas Scrapbook; *The Daily Oklahoman,* November 26, 1978.
15. *The Daily Oklahoman,* March 15, 1953; *The Daily Oklahoman,* November 26, 1978; Mildred May McConnell Douglas Chrisman, ancestry.com.
16. *The Daily Oklahoman,* March 15, 1953; *The Daily Oklahoman,* November 26, 1978; Mildred May McConnell Douglas Chrisman, ancestry.com; Mildred Douglas Scrapbook.
17. *The Daily Oklahoman,* January 26, 1982; Mildred May McConnell Douglas Chrisman, ancestry.com.

Lorena Trickey

1. *The Queen of Sheba,* IMDb.com.
2. *The South Bend Tribune,* June 30, 1921; *The Tacoma Daily Leader,* April 24, 1921.
3. *Through the Back Door,* IMDb.com.
4. Lorena Mickey Peterson, ancestry.com; *The West,* pp. 36–38.
5. Lorena Mickey Peterson, ancestry.com; *The West,* pp. 36–38, *Morning Register,* September 3, 1910.
6. *The Capital Journal,* May 28, 1937; *East Oregonian,* October 14, 1921.
7. *Bozeman Daily Chronicle,* August 9, 1919; *The Spokesman Review,* April 27, 1917.

8. *The West*, pp. 38–39; *Casper Star Tribune*, August 1, 1926.

9. *The Missoula Sentinel*, July 4, 1918; *East Oregonian*, October 14, 1921, Pendleton, Oregon; *Bozeman Daily Chronicle*, August 9, 1919.

10. *The West*, pp. 38–39; Lorena Trickey Papers: "Fame Sought for Tonopah Cowgirl Lorena Trickey."

11. *The Idaho Republican*, October 8, 1918.

12. *The Mount Hope Clarion*, July 25, 1919.

13. *Bozeman Daily Chronicle*, August 9, 1919.

14. *The Idaho Stateman*, September 19, 1919; *The Oregon Daily Journal*, September 20, 1919.

15. *The Hood River Glacier*, April 29, 1920.

16. *Idaho Daily Statesman*, September 29, 1920, The Calhoun Chronicle, March 3, 1921.

17. *The Kansas City Star*, July 13, 1921.

18. Ibid.

19. *Casper Star Tribune*, July 27, 1922.

20. *The Spokesman Review*, July 4, 1923.

21. "Fame Sought for Tonopah Cowgirl Lorena Trickey."

22. *Spokane Chronicles*, September 3, 1927.

23. *Corvallis Gazette Times*, September 3, 1927; *The Sacramento Bee*, September 5, 1927; *The Spokesman Review*, September 5, 1927.

24. *The Great Falls Leader*, September 7, 1927; *Red Bluff News*, September 9, 1927; *The Fresno Morning Republican*, September 13, 1927.

25. *The Idaho Statesman*, September 13, 1927; *The Sacramento Bee*, September 14, 1927; *Times Monitor*, September 15, 1927; *The Klamath News*, September 14, 1927.

26. *The Klamath News*, September 14, 1927.

27. *The News Review*, November 7, 1927; *Star Herald*, November 9, 1927.

28. Ibid.

29. *The St. Louis Star and Times*, November 8, 1927.

30. Ibid.

31. Ibid.

32. *The St. Louis Star and Times*, November 8, 1927; *Miles City Star*, November 8, 1927.

33. *The Everett Daily Herald*, November 12, 1927; *The Sacramento Bee*, November 12, 1927.

34. Ibid.

35. *The Pittsburgh Press*, November 14, 1927; *The Sacramento Bee*, November 14, 1927.

36. *The Bulletin*, December 27, 1927; *The Eugene Guard*, December 28, 1927.

37. *La Grande Observer*, December 28, 1927; *Daily News*, January 29, 1928; Nevada State Journal, May 31, 1928.

38. *The Columbus Telegram*, June 16, 1928; *The Bulletin*, June 30, 1928.

39. *The Billings Gazette*, July 12, 1928.

40. *The Sacramento Bee*, August 30, 1928; *The Klamath News*, August 24, 1928; *The Independent Record*, September 25, 1928; *The Tacoma Daily Leader*, October 29, 1928.

41. *Nevada State Journal*, April 15, 1934.

42. *Reno Gazette Journal*, June 14, 1946.

43. "Fame Sought for Tonopah Cowgirl Lorena Trickey"; Lorena Mickey Peterson, ancestry.com; *The West*, pp. 58–60.

44. *Reno Gazette Journal*, September 11, 1948; *Nevada State Journal*, January 5, 1951.

45. *Nevada State Journal*, January 5, 1951.

46. Ibid.

47. *Reno Gazette Journal*, October 24, 1956.

48. Ibid.

49. Ibid.

50. *The Kansas City Times*, November 16, 1961; *The Spokesman Review*, November 16, 1961; Lorena Mickey Peterson, ancestry.com.

Stunting in the Talkies

1. *New York Times*, June 22, 1926.

2. *Funk & Wagnalls New Encyclopedia*, pp. 15–16.

3. *A Pictorial History of the Western Film*, pp. 14–17.

4. *The Overlook Film Encyclopedia*, pp. 16–21; *Buffalo Jewish Review*, January 18, 1929; *The Buffalo Times*, January 20, 1929.

5. Ibid.

6. *Republic Confidential*, pp. 241–42; Mildred Nell "Nellie" Roach "O'Day," ancestry .com.

7. Ibid.

8. *Fort Worth Star Telegram*, March 12, 1933; *Standard Speaker*, June 11, 1938; *The Ithaca Journal*, November 27, 1931.

9. *Republic Confidential*, pp. 241–42; Mildred Nell "Nellie" Roach "O'Day," ancestry .com.

10. *Los Angeles Evening News*, April 25, 1941, IMDb.com.

11. *Los Angeles Evening News*, April 25, 1941.

12. *Los Angeles Evening News*, April 25, 1941, IMDb.com.

13. *Santa Maria Times*, January 30, 1941; *The Driftin' Kid* (Monogram Press Booklet), 1941.

14. *The Driftin' Kid* (Monogram Press Booklet), 1941.

15. *Modesto Bee*, June 12, 1992.

16. Polly Burson, ancestry.com.

17. *The Eugene Guard*, November 7, 1929; *Press & Sun Bulletin*, April 21, 1943; *Daily News*, October 22, 1941.

18. *Republic Confidential*, pp. 183–84.

19. *Republic Confidential*, pp. 183–84; *Valley Times*, September 18, 1947.

20. *Ventura County Star*, April 8, 2006.

21. Polly Burson, ancestry.com.

Vera McGinnis

1. *Cimarron*, IMDb.com; *The Los Angeles Times*, November 3, 1930.

2. *Cimarron*, IMDb.com; *The Los Angeles Times*, November 3, 1930; *Rodeo Road*, pp. 158–65.

3. *Cimarron*, IMDb.com; *The Los Angeles Times*, November 3, 1930; *Rodeo Road*, pp. 158–65; *Los Angeles Post Record*, November 22, 1930; *Visalia Times Delta*, November 17, 1930.

4. *Los Angeles Evening Express*, January 3, 1931.

5. *Rodeo Road*, pp. 10–11; Vera McGinnis, ancestry.com; *Warrensburg Daily Star*, February 22, 1899; *The Standard Herald*, February 24, 1899.

6. *Rodeo Road*, pp. 14–15; *The Journal Democrat*, August 18, 1905, Vera McGinnis, ancestry.com.

7. *Rodeo Road*, pp. 16–19; *The Hardin News*, September 21, 1905.

8. Ibid.

9. *Rodeo Road*, pp. 16–19.

10. *Rodeo Road*, pp. 18–19; *The Southwest Mail*, January 21, 1910; *The Weekly Post*, April 15, 1910; *Daily Star Journal*, November 8, 1911; *The Standard Herald*, February 16, 1912.

11. *Rodeo Road*, pp. 21–23; *The Salt Lake Herald Republican*, July 9, 1913.

12. *The Oregon Daily Journal*, September 13, 1913.

13. *Rodeo Road*, pp. 26–32.

14. *Rodeo Road*, pp. 38–41; *The Winnipeg Tribune*, August 11, 1913.

15. *Rodeo Road*, pp. 38–41.

16. *Rodeo Road*, pp. 57–58.

17. *Rodeo Road*, pp. 59–60.

18. *Bakersfield Morning Echo*, April 20, 1914; *Rodeo Road*, pp. 59–61.

19. *The Californian*, April 29, 1914; *The Salt Lake Herald Republican*, August 23, 1914; *East Oregonian*, September 12, 1914.

20. *Rodeo Road*, pp. 68–72 and 91–93; *The Los Angeles Times*, May 4, 1915; *The Los Angeles Times*, May 7, 1915.

21. *The Northern Wyoming Herald*, July 15, 1915; *Billings Evening Journal*, July 3, 1915; *Rodeo Road*, pp. 109–112, 121–123; *Idaho County Free Press*, September 30, 1915; *Great Falls Tribune*, June 4, 1916.

22. *The Montana Progressive*, June 11, 1916; *Rodeo Road*, pp. 121–23.

23. *Nevada County Tribune*, July 6, 1916, *Rodeo Road*, pp. 127–28.

24. *Rodeo Road*, pp. 120–21, 133.

25. *Rodeo Road*, pp. 144–46; *Arizona Daily Star*, October 26, 1916.

26. *Rodeo Road*, pp. 144–46.

27. *San Francisco Examiner*, September 10, 1917; Vera McGinnis, ancestry.com; *Arizona Republic*, October 4, 1918.

28. *Rodeo Road*, pp. 157–59.

29. Vera McGinnis, IMDb.com; *Record Journal*, August 30, 1919.

30. *Rodeo Road*, pp. 161–63; *Reno Gazette Journal*, June 30, 1919.

31. *The Bulletin*, August 21, 1919.

32. Ibid.

33. *Rodeo Road*, pp. 164.

34. *Honolulu Star Bulletin*, January 20, 1922; *Honolulu Star Bulletin*, January 24, 1922.

35. *Rodeo Road*, pp. 164–65.

36. *Rodeo Road*, pp. 164–66; *Honolulu Star Bulletin*, February 9, 1922; *Honolulu Star Bulletin*, February 18, 1922.

37. *Rodeo Road*, pp. 172–73; *Honolulu Star Bulletin*, February 26, 1922.

38. *Daily News*, March 24, 1923; *Rodeo Road*, pp. 176–78.

39. *Rodeo Road*, pp. 179–80; *Riverside Daily Press*, January 29, 1924.

40. *Ventura Daily Post*, February 27, 1924; *The Dalby Herald*, August 8, 1924.

41. *Rodeo Road*, pp. 184–85.

42. *The Guardian*, July 2, 1924; *The Daily Telegraph*, July 29, 1924; *Rodeo Road*, pp. 189–90.

43. *The Honolulu Advertiser*, April 7, 1925.

44. *The Van Nuys News*, April 3, 1925; *Rodeo Road*, pp. 206–8.

45. *Rodeo Road*, pp. 206–8.

46. *Riverside Daily News*, June 1, 1926; *Stockton Evening and Sunday Record*, June 23, 1926; *Oakland Tribune*, July 4, 1926; *The Waco Times Herald*, August 6, 1926; *Rodeo Road*, pp. 210–12; *Calgary Herald*, September 19, 1927.

47. *Rodeo Road*, pp. 211–12.

48. Ibid.

49. Ibid.

50. *Rodeo Road*, pp. 221-225; *Oakland Tribune*, June 11, 1934; *The Oakland Post Enquirer*, June 11, 1934.

51. *Arizona Daily Star*, March 8, 1935.

52. *The Signal*, April 28, 1940.

53. Vera McGinnis, ancestry.com.

Marie Walcamp

1. Marie E. Walcamp, ancestry.com; *Der Deutsche Beobachter*, November 22, 1900.

2. *Buffalo Courier*, May 23, 1909; *Buffalo Courier*, May 30, 1909.

3. *The Lexington Herald*, October 28, 1912; Marie Walcamp, IMDb.com.

4. Ibid.

5. Marie Walcamp, IMDb.com; *The Fresno Tribune*, August 19, 1912; *San Francisco Chronicle*, December 23, 1912; *The Register*, August 6, 1912.

6. *Los Angeles Evening Express*, February 17, 1913.

7. Ibid.

8. Marie Walcamp, IMDb.com.

9. *Newport Daily Independent*, September 19, 1913.

10. Marie Walcamp; IMDb.com; *The Werewolf*, IMDb.com.

11. *The Werewolf*, IMDb.com; *Arkansas Democrat*, December 22, 1913; *Hartford Courant*, December 13, 1913; *The Tulsa Tribune*, December 21, 1913.

12. *Los Angeles Evening Express*, March 2, 1914; *Honolulu Star Bulletin*, March 2, 1914.

13. *Santa Cruz Evening News*, December 28, 1914.

14. Ibid.

15. *Motion Picture Magazine*, March 1915; *The Fort Wayne News* and *The Fort Wayne Sentinel*, March 8, 1915.

16. Ibid.

17. *The Girard Press*, September 5, 1918.

18. *The Ottowa Journal*, June 14, 1919; *The Buffalo News*, May 31, 1919.

19. *The Muscatine Journal*, September 3, 1919; *The Arizona Republic*, October 26, 1919; *The Daily Notes*, October 8, 1919.

20. *Motion Picture Journal*, August 1920.

21. *Pensacola Journal*, December 11, 1920; *Norfolk Daily News*, August 16, 1920; *The Oklahoma News*, August 6, 1920.

22. *The Oregon Daily Journal*, May 28, 1922; *The Connecticut Labor News*, September 30, 1921.

23. *The Blot*, IMDb.com.

24. Marie Walcamp, IMDb.com; *The Kansas City Star*, September 18, 1921.

25. *Los Angeles Evening Express*, September 21, 1922; *Oakland Tribune*, January 1, 1922; *The Wichita Eagle*, September 29, 1922.

26. *The Tampa Times*, September 19, 1925.

27. *The Kentucky Post*, April 18, 1925; *The Herald Statesman*, November 29, 1927.

28. *San Franisco Bulletin*, March 26, 1928.

29. *San Francisco Examiner*, July 3, 1933; *The Sun News Pictorial*, January 26, 1938, *Spokane Chronicle*, January 3, 1933.

30. *San Francisco Examiner*, May 7, 1934.

31. *The Morning Press*, November 19, 1936; *Kansas City Times*, November 18, 1936.

32. Marie E. Walcamp, ancestry.com; *The Montgomery Advertiser*, July 27, 1941.

Mary Wiggins

1. *Call of the Wild*, IMDb.com.

2. Mary Lois Wiggins, ancestry.com; *The Tampa Tribune*, April 26, 1927; *The Tampa Times*, July 26, 1927.

3. Mary Wiggins, IMDb.com; *The Film Encyclopedia*, pp. 1039–40.

4. *Visalia Times Delta*, July 30, 1929; *Auburn Journal*, August 1, 1929.

5. *The Overlook Film Encyclopedia*, pp. 25–26.

6. *The Hartford Sentinel*, April 30, 1932; Mary Lois Wiggins, ancestry.com.

7. *The Bakersfield Californian*, April 30, 1932; "The Ninety-Nines from 1920 to 1989," www.ninety-nines.org/sixty-years.htm.

8. *The Bakersfield Californian*, April 16, 1932; *The Bakersfield Californian*, April 30, 1932.

9. *Ventura County Star*, November 3, 1932; *Ventura Weekly Post*, November 11, 1932; *Central Airport*, IMDb.com; *Tucson Daily Citizen*, April 22, 1933.

10. *Central Airport*, IMDb.com; *Tucson Daily Citizen*, April 22, 1933.

11. *Tucson Daily Citizen*, April 22, 1933.

12. *San Francisco Examiner*, April 24, 1933.

13. Mary Wiggins, IMDb.com, *It Happened One Night*, IMDb.com.

14. Mary Wiggins, IMDb.com; *Atlanta Journal*, October 14, 1934.

15. *The Buffalo News*, November 8, 1933; *The Oakland Post Enquirer*, November 8, 1933.

16. *The Tampa Times*, October 16, 1934; *Atlanta Journal*, October 14, 1934.

17. *Atlanta Journal*, October 14, 1934.

18. Ibid.

19. Ibid.

20. Mary Wiggins, IMDb.com; *Hell Ship Morgan*, IMDb.com.
21. *Los Angeles Evening Citizen News*, March 4, 1936.
22. *The Ottawa Citizen*, June 13, 1936.
23. *Daily News*, July 17, 1936; *Stunt: The Story of the Great Movie Stuntmen*, pp. 62–67.
24. *Richmond Times Dispatch*, October 25, 1936; *Mountain Justice*, IMDb.com.
25. *Covington Virginian*, October 31, 1936; *The Roanoke Times*, November 2, 1936.
26. Ibid.
27. *The Washington Post*, October 31, 1936.
28. *Long Beach Press Telegram*, February 23, 1937; *The York Dispatch*, April 10, 1937; *The Morning Call*, September 30, 1937.
29. *Kitsap Sun*, February 10, 1938; *Torchy Blane . . . Playing with Dynamite*, IMDb.com; Mary Wiggins, IMDb.com.
30. *The Daily News*, February 8, 1938.
31. Ibid.
32. *Calgary Herald*, May 30, 1938; *The Vinita Daily Journal*, May 31, 1938.
33. *The Times*, July 23, 1938; *The Los Angeles Times*, July 23, 1938.
34. *Wilkes-Barre Times Leader*, September 22, 1938.
35. Ibid.
36. Mary Wiggins, IMDb.com; *The Overlook Film Encyclopedia*, pp. 99–100.
37. *The Ogden Standard Examiner*, November 10, 1938; *The Salt Lake Tribune*, November 13, 1938.
38. Mary Wiggins, IMDb.com; *The San Bernardino County Sun*, January 8, 1939.
39. *Press Telegram*, January 8, 1939; *The Daily Nonpareil*, June 24, 1939; *The Independent Record*, April 19, 1940; *The Selma Times Journal*, April 26, 1940.
40. Mary Wiggins, IMDb.com; *The Greensboro Record*, May 11, 1942.
41. Mary Wiggins, IMDb.com; *The Salt Lake Tribune*, November 1, 1942.
42. *Fort Worth Star Telegram*, May 3, 1943.
43. *San Francisco Examiner*, August 19, 1943; *Salisbury Evening Post*, October 30, 1943.
44. *San Fernando Valley Times*, September 18, 1944; *Abilene Reporter News*, December 6, 1944.
45. *Los Angeles Evening Citizens News*, October 12, 1945; *The Los Angeles Times*, December 21, 1945.
46. *Los Angeles Evening Citizens News*, October 12, 1945; *The Los Angeles Times*, December 21, 1945; *The Daily Herald*, December 21, 1945; *Star Tribune*, December 21, 1945; *The Tampa Tribune*, December 21, 1945.
47. *Star Tribune*, December 21, 1945; *The Tampa Tribune,* December 21, 1945.
48. *Star Tribune*, December 21, 1945; *The Tampa Tribune*, December 21, 1945; Mary Lois Wiggins, ancestry.com.

Texas Guinan

1. *The White Squaw*, IMDb.com.
2. Ibid.
3. Texas Guinan, IMDb.com.
4. Texas Guinan, ancestry.com; Texas Guinan, IMDb.com.

5. *Star Tribune*, February 1, 1910; *"Hello, Sucker!": The Story of Texas Guinan*, pp. 11–12.
6. *"Hello, Sucker!"*, pp. 11–13; Texas Guinan, IMDb.com.
7. *The Arizona Republic*, August 13, 1918; *Salt Lake Herald*, January 26, 1918.
8. Texas Guinan, IMDb.com; *"Hello, Sucker!"*, pp. 20–22.
9. *"Hello, Sucker!"*, pp. 38–41.
10. *The Buffalo Times*, August 31, 1924.
11. Ibid.
12. Ibid.
13. *St. Louis Globe Democrat*, November 6, 1933.
14. Ibid.
15. *"Hello, Sucker!"*, pp. 56–69.
16. *St. Louis Globe Democrat*, November 6, 1933.
17. *Los Angeles Times*, August 4, 1929.
18. *Los Angeles Times*, August 4, 1929; Texas Guinan, IMDb.com.
19. *Warren Times Mirror*, May 29, 1931; Texas Guinan, IMDb.com.
20. *St. Louis Globe Democrat*, November 6, 1933.
21. Texas Guinan, ancestry.com; *Courier Post*, November 25, 1933.

Ruth Roland

1. *San Francisco Chronicle*, December 12, 1920 *Courtland Journal*, October 7, 1920; *The Wichita Beacon*, December 26, 1920.
2. Ruth R. Roland, ancestry.com; Ruth Roland, IMDb.com.
3. *The Film Encyclopedia*, pp. 989; Ruth R. Roland, ancestry.com.
4. *The Kansas City Star*, September 27, 1937.
5. Ibid.
6. *The Kansas City Star*, September 27, 1937; *The Film Encyclopedia*, pp. 989; Ruth R. Roland, ancestry.com; Ruth Roland, IMDb.com.
7. Ibid.
8. *The Film Encyclopedia*, pp. 989.
9. *The Kansas City Star*, September 27, 1937.
10. Ibid.
11. Ibid.
12. Ruth R. Roland, ancestry.com; Ruth Roland, IMDb.com.
13. *The Kansas City Star*, September 27, 1937.
14. Ibid.
15. Ibid.
16. Ibid.
17. Ruth R. Roland, ancestry.com; Ruth Roland, IMDb.com.
18. Ruth R. Roland, ancestry.com; Ruth Roland, IMDb.com.
19. Ruth R. Roland, ancestry.com; *The Holbart Democrat-Chief*, September 24, 1937; *Telegram Forum*, September 23, 1937.

Alice Van Springsteen

1. *The Overlook Film Encyclopedia*, pp. 157.
2. Alice Van Springsteen, IMDb.com.

NOTES

3. Alice G. Van Derveen, ancestry.com; *Los Angeles Evening Post Record*, July 30, 1932; *Ventura County Star*, May 27, 1933; *The Californian*, July 19, 1932.
4. *Daily News*, July 6, 1932.
5. Alice G. Van Derveen, ancestry.com; *Riverside Daily Press*, September 10, 1934.
6. *The Sacramento Union*, September 8, 1934.
7. Alice Van Springsteen, IMDb.com; *The News and Observer*, November 24, 1935.
8. Alice Van Springsteen; IMDb.com.
9. Alice Van Springsteen, IMDb.com; *Salinas Morning Post*, July 20, 1937.
10. Alice Van Springsteen, IMDb.com; *Vallejo Evening News*, September 11, 1937.
11. Alice Van Springsteen, IMDb.com; *The Overlook Film Encyclopedia*, pp. 68–73.
12. *The Daily Breeze*, August 13, 1938; *Daily News,* August 9, 1938; *The Los Angeles Times*, August 14, 1938.
13. *The San Diego Sun*, February 3, 1939.
14. *The Los Angeles Times*, March 31, 1940.
15. *Daily News*, March 27, 1940.
16. *New York Daily News*, March 10, 1940; *Daily News*, March 27, 1940.
17. *Daily News*, March 10, 1940.
18. *The Whittier News*, April 14, 1941; *The Tribune*, April 14, 1941; *The Los Angeles Times*, July 27, 1941.
19. Alice Van Springsteen, IMDb.com.
20. *The Windsor Star*, October 14, 1943.
21. *The Desert Sun*, January 19, 1999; *Republic Confidential,* pp. 22–23.
22. *The Desert Sun*, January 19, 1999.
23. *Hanford Morning Journal,* April 25, 1946; *Tulare Register*, March 19, 1944.
24. Alice Van Springsteen, IMDb.com.
25. *The Overlook Film Encyclopedia*, pp. 188; *Big Bear Grizzly*, July 20, 1951; *Merced Sun Star,* April 15, 1950; *The Complete Directory to Prime Time Network TV Shows, 1946–Present*, pp. 808.
26. Alice Van Springsteen, IMDb.com; *The Desert Sun*, January 19, 1999.
27. Ibid.
28. *The Desert Sun*, January 19, 1999.
29. Ibid.
30. Ibid.
31. Alice G. Van Derveen, ancestry.com; *The Hollywood Reporter*, September 16, 2008.

Bibliography

Books

Barnum, P. T. *Struggles & Triumphs: or, Forty Years of Recollections of P. T. Barnum.* Agawam, Massachusetts, 2011.

Baxter, John O. *Stunt: The Story of the Great Movie Stuntmen.* Doubleday, 1974.

Brasch, Ilka. *Film Serials and the American Cinema, 1910–1940.* Netherland Amsterdam University Press, 2018.

Brooks, Tim and Earle F. Marsh. *The Complete Directory to Prime Time Network TV Shows 1946–Present.* Ballentine Books, 1979.

Collings, Ellsworth and Alma Miller England. *The 101 Ranch.* University of Oklahoma, 1971.

Cooper, Courtney Ryley. *Annie Oakley: Woman at Arms.* Duffield & Company, 1927.

Day, Beth. *American's First Cowgirl Lucille Mulhall.* Julian Messner, Inc., 1957

Enss, Chris. *Along Came a Cowgirl: Daring and Iconic Women of the Rodeo and Wild West Shows.* Farcountry Press, 2022

Enss, Chris. *Buffalo Gals: Women of Buffalo Bill's Wild West Show.* TwoDot Books, 2006.

Enss, Chris. *The Trials of Annie Oakley.* TwoDot Books, 2018.

Everson, William K. *A Pictorial History of the Western Film.* Citadel Press, 1969.

Flood, Elizabeth Clair. *Women of the Wild West.* Zon International Publishing Company, 2000.

Granlund, Nils T. *Blondes, Brunettes, and Bullets.* Dave McKay Publishing, 1957.

Gregory, Mollie. *Stuntwomen: The Untold Hollywood Story.* University Press of Kentucky, 2015.

Hanshew, Tracey. *Oklahoma Rodeo Women.* The History Press, 2020.

Hardy, Phil. *The Overlook Film Encyclopedia: The Western.* Overlook Press, 1994.

Havighurst, Walter. *Annie Oakley of the Wild West.* Macmillan Company, 1954.

Katz, Ephraim. *The Film Encyclopedia.* Perigee Books, 1979.

Mathis, Jack. *Republic Confidential, Volume 2: The Players.* Jack Mathis Advertising, 1992.

McGinnis, Vera. *Rodeo Road: My Life as a Pioneer Cowgirl.* Hastings House, 1974.

Place, J. A. *The Western Films of John Ford.* Citadel Press, 1973.

Russell, Don. *The Wild West: A History of the Wild West Shows.* Amon Carter Museum of Western Art, 1970.

Shirley, Glenn. "*Hello, Sucker!": The Story of Texas Guinan.* Eakin Press, 1989.
Shirley, Glenn. *Pawnee Bill: A Biography of Major Gordon W. Lillie.* University of Nebraska Press, 1958.
Solomon, Aubrey. *The Fox Film Corporation, 1915–1935.* McFarland, 2011.
Stansbury, Kathryn. *Lucille Mulhall: Wild West Cowgirl.* Homestead Heirlooms Publishing, 1992.
Telles, Larry. *Lights, Camera, Action: Helen Gibson, Silent Serial Queen Who Became Hollywood's First Professional Stunt Woman.* Bitterroot Mountain Publishing, 2013.

Encyclopedias, Journals, Magazines, Pamphlets

The Billboard (magazine), February 1914
The Billboard, April 1921
The Billboard, November 25, 1922
The Billboard, June 4, 1927
The Billboard, March 23, 1929
The Billboard, August 1929
Bonnie Gray Papers, Box 1-3, DRC National Cowboy and Western Heritage Museum, Oklahoma City, Oklahoma
Buffalo Bill Wild West Collection at the Center of the West, MS 261 Lulu Bell
The Driftin' Kid (Monogram Press Booklet), 1941
Ebony, Vol. 28, April 1973
Films in Review (magazine), January 1968 (published by the National Board of Review of Motion Pictures
Films in Review, May 1968
Funk & Wagnalls New Encyclopedia, Vol. 17, "Motion Pictures"
Helen Gibson Scrapbook, from the Helen Gibson collection, Vancouver, Washington
Lorena Trickey Papers: "Fame Sought for Tonopah Cowgirl Lorena Trickey" by Teresa Trickey Jacobsen, Tonopah Historical Society Archives, Tonopah, Nevada
Mildred Douglas Scrapbook, Museum of the Great Plains Archives, Lawton, Oklahoma
Motion Picture Magazine, Vol. 9, March 1915
Motion Picture Magazine, Vol. 20, August 1920
Moving Picture World, Vol. 76, October 21, 1925
Moving Picture World, Vol. 82, September 18, 1926
Moving Picture World, Vol. 84, February 5, 1927
Psychology Magazine, September 1927
United States Military Records, Washington State Archives, Olympia, Washington
The West, Vol. 7, no. 4, September 1967. "Lorena Trickey—Rodeo's Bonanza Queen" by Sam Henderson

Newspapers

Abilene Reporter News, Abilene, Texas, December 6, 1944
The Afro American, Baltimore, Maryland, April 21, 1922
The Afro American, Baltimore, Maryland, May 5, 1922
The Afro American, Baltimore, Maryland, May 12, 1922
The Akron Beacon Journal, Akron, Ohio, January 22, 1966

BIBLIOGRAPHY

The Allentown Democrat, Allentown, Pennsylvania, October 26, 1915
Anaheim Bulletin, Anaheim, California, September 17, 1930
Arizona Daily Star, Tucson, Arizona, October 26, 1916
Arizona Daily Star, Tucson, Arizona, March 8, 1935
The Arizona Republic, Phoenix, Arizona, August 13, 1918
The Arizona Republic, Phoenix, Arizona, October 4, 1918
The Arizona Republic, Phoenix, Arizona, October 26, 1919
The Arizona Republic, Phoenix, Arizona, December 11, 1921
Arkansas Democrat, Little Rock, Arkansas, December 22, 1913
Argus Leader, Sioux Falls, South Dakota, October 20, 1917
Argus Leader, Sioux Falls, South Dakota, January 18, 1955
*Asbury Park Pres*s, Asbury Park, New Jersey, December 28, 1936
Ashland Weekly News, Ashland, Wisconsin, August 7, 1889
The Atlanta Constitution, Atlanta, Georgia, December 6, 1942
The Atlanta Journal, Atlanta, Georgia, October 14, 1934
Auburn Journal, Auburn, California, August 1, 1929
The Bakersfield Californian, Bakerfield, California, April 16, 1932
The Bakersfield Californian, Bakerfield, California, April 30, 1932
Bakersfield Morning Echo, Bakersfield, California, April 20, 1914
The Bangor Daily News, Bangor, Maine, February 27, 1913
Battle Creek Enquirer, Battle Creek, Michigan, July 12, 1930
The Bellingham Herald, Bellingham, Washington, June 20, 1930
Bennington Banner, Bennington, Vermont, September 10, 1920
The Berlin News Record, Kitchner, Ontario, Canada, March 18, 1916
Big Bear Grizzly, Big Bear Lake, California, July 20, 1951
Billings Evening Journal, Billings, Montana, July 3, 1915
The Billings Gazette, Billings, Montana, October 31, 1921
The Billings Gazette, Billings, Montana, July 12, 1928
The Billings Gazette, Billings, Montana, July 27, 2009
The Boston Globe, Boston, Massachusetts, March 8, 1915
The Boston Globe, Boston, Massachusetts, September 28, 1921
The Boston Journal, Boston, Massachusetts, December 10, 1887
The Boston Post, Boston, Massachusetts, June 19, 1943
Bozeman Daily Chronicle, Bozeman, Montana, August 9, 1919
Bozeman Daily Chronicle, Bozeman, Montana, September 6, 1927
The Bridgeport Times & Evening Farmer, Bridgeport, Connecticut, March 28, 1919
The Brooklyn Citizen, Brooklyn, New York, May 21, 1910
Buffalo Courier, Buffalo, New York, April 25, 1905
Buffalo Courier, Buffalo, New York, May 23, 1909
Buffalo Courier, Buffalo, New York, May 30, 1909
Buffalo Courier Express, Buffalo, New York, April 2, 1939
Buffalo Jewish Review, Buffalo, New York, January 18, 1929
The Buffalo News, Buffalo, New York, November 8, 1933
The Buffalo Sunday Morning News, Buffalo, New York, May 31, 1919
The Buffalo Times, Buffalo, New York, August 31, 1924

The Buffalo Times, Buffalo, New York, January 13, 1929
The Buffalo Times, Buffalo, New York, January 20, 1929
The Bulletin, Bend, Oregon, December 27, 1927
The Bulletin, Bend, Oregon, June 30, 1928
The Bulletin, San Francisco, California, August 21, 1919
Burbank Daily Evening Review, Burbank, California, March 12, 1928
The Burbank Pathfinder, Burbank, California, January 22, 1924
The Butte Miner, Butte, Montana, April 19, 1903
Calgary Herald, Calgary, Alberta, Canada, August 28, 1919
Calgary Herald, Calgary, Alberta, Canada, September 19, 1927
Calgary Herald, Calgary, Alberta, Canada, May 30, 1938
The Calhoun Chronicle, Grantsville, West Virginia, March 3, 1921
The Californian, Salinas, California, April 29, 1914
The Californian, Salinas, California, July 19, 1932
Camarillo Star, Camarillo, California, August 5, 1938
The Capital Journal, Pierre, South Dakota, May 28, 1937
Casper Star Tribune, Casper, Wyoming, July 27, 1922
Casper Star Tribune, Casper, Wyoming, August 1, 1926
Casper Star Tribune, Casper, Wyoming, July 29, 1929
Casper Star Tribune, Casper, Wyoming, October 15, 2000
Cavern City Chronicle, Carlsbad, New Mexico, January 16, 1931
The Central New Jersey Home, New Brunswick, New Jersey, December 4, 1908
The Central New Jersey Home, New Brunswick, New Jersey, June 26, 1913
Cheyenne State Leader, Cheyenne, Wyoming, July 20, 1922
The Chicago Livestock World, Chicago, Illinois, May 19, 1910
The Chico Enterprise, Chico, California, December 24, 1917
The Cincinnati Enquirer, Cincinnati, Ohio, December 27, 1925
Claflin Clarion, Claflin, Kansas, January 29, 1903
Clinton Daily Journal & Public, Clinton, Illinois, September 26, 1936
The Columbus Telegram, Columbus, Nebraska, June 16, 1928
The Commercial Appeal, Memphis, Tennessee, September 23, 1937
The Connecticut Labor News, New Haven, Connecticut, September 30, 1921
Corvallis Gazette Times, Albany, Oregon, September 3, 1927
Council Bluffs Nonpareil, Council Bluff, Iowa, June 24, 1939
The Courier News, Bridgewater, New Jersey, September 5, 1902
The Courier News, Bridgewater, New Jersey, July 20, 1903
The Courier News, Bridgewater, New Jersey, August 17, 1904
The Courier News, Bridgewater, New Jersey, November 15, 1904
The Courier News, Bridgewater, New Jersey, October 2, 1905
The Courier News, Bridgewater, New Jersey, October 26, 1905
The Courier News, Bridgewater, New Jersey, February 8, 1906
The Courier News, Bridgewater, New Jersey, March 18, 1908
The Courier News, Bridgewater, New Jersey, April 4, 1908
The Courier News, Bridgewater, New Jersey, April 14, 1908
The Courier News, Bridgewater, New Jersey, November 21, 1908

BIBLIOGRAPHY

The Courier News, Bridgewater, New Jersey, August 11, 1911
The Courier News, Bridgewater, New Jersey, July 10, 1913
The Courier News, Bridgewater, New Jersey, April 10, 1928
The Courier News, Bridgewater, New Jersey, May 23, 1928
The Courier News, Bridgewater, New Jersey, September 9, 1931
The Courier News, Bridgewater, New Jersey, November 13, 1936
Courier Post, Camden, New Jersey, November 25, 1933
Courtland Journal, Courtland, Kansas, October 7, 1920
Covington Virginian, Covington, Virginia, October 31, 1936
The Daily Breeze, Torrance, California, August 13, 1938
The Daily Bulletin, Marysville, Kentucky, June 12, 1905
The Daily Herald, Provo, Utah, December 21, 1945
Daily News, New London, Connecticut, August 23, 1936
Daily News, Canonsburg, Pennsylvania, February 8, 1938
The Daily News, New York, New York, March 24, 1923
The Daily News, New York, New York, January 29, 1928
The Daily News, New York, New York, September 12, 1930
The Daily News, New York, New York, July 6, 1932
The Daily News, New York, New York, July 17, 1936
The Daily News, New York, New York, August 9, 1938
The Daily News, New York, New York, March 27, 1940
The Daily News, New York, New York, September 10, 1940
The Daily News, New York, New York, October 22, 1941
The Daily News, New York, New York, February 19, 1974
The Daily Nonpareil, Council Bluff, Iowa, June 24, 1939
The Daily Notes, Canonsburg, Pennsylvania, October 8, 1919
The Daily Notes, Canonsburg, Pennsylvania, February 8, 1938
The Daily Oklahoman, Oklahoma City, Oklahoma, December 27, 1940
The Daily Oklahoman, Oklahoma City, Oklahoma, March 15, 1953
The Daily Oklahoman, Oklahoma City, Oklahoma, December 4, 1977
The Daily Oklahoman, Oklahoma City, Oklahoma, November 26, 1978
The Daily Oklahoman, Oklahoma City, Oklahoma, January 26, 1982
The Daily Report, Ontario, California, March 20, 1912
Daily Star Journal, Warrensburg, Missouri, November 8, 1911
The Daily Telegram, Adrian, Michigan, April 17, 1915
The Daily Telegraph, London, England, July 29, 1924
The Daily Times, Davenport, Iowa, December 12, 1914
The Dalby Herald, Queensland, Australia, August 8, 1924
Dayton Daily News, Dayton, Ohio, May 10, 2001
The Dayton Herald, Dayton, Ohio, April 27, 1910
Delphos Daily Herald, Delphos, Ohio, September 25, 1895
The Desert Sun, Palm Springs, California, January 19, 1999
The Des Moines Register, Des Moines, Iowa, July 12, 1928
Detroit Free Press, Detroit, Michigan, April 30, 1911
Detroit Free Press, Detroit, Michigan, December 12, 1912

Detroit Free Press, Detroit, Michigan, June 4, 1922
Detroit Free Press, Detroit, Michigan, May 23, 1926
Detroit Free Press, Detroit, Michigan, August 2, 1936
Der Deutsche Beobachter, New Philadelphia, Ohio November 22, 1900
Dodge City Journal, Dodge City, Kansas, September 19, 1929
East Oregonian, Pendleton, Oregon, September 8, 1913
East Oregonian, Pendleton, Oregon, September 12, 1913
East Oregonian, Pendleton, Oregon, September 15, 1913
East Oregonian, Pendleton, Oregon, September 30, 1913
East Oregonian, Pendleton, Oregon, September 12, 1914
East Oregonian, Pendleton, Oregon, October 27, 1914
East Oregonian, Pendleton, Oregon, January 11, 1917
East Oregonian, Pendleton, Oregon, September 24, 1917
East Oregonian, Pendleton, Oregon, September 27, 1917
East Oregonian, Pendleton, Oregon, September 19, 1918
East Oregonian, Pendleton, Oregon, October 14, 1921
El Paso Herald, El Paso, Texas, July 21, 1900
El Paso Herald, El Paso, Texas, December 20, 1902
El Paso Herald, El Paso, Texas, December 29, 1921
El Paso Times, El Paso, Texas, March 8, 1917
The El Reno Daily Tribune, El Reno, Oklahoma, August 31, 1936
Elizabethville Echo, Elizabethville, Pennsylvania, September 18, 1903
Elmore County Republican, Mountain Home, Idaho, September 7, 1912
Elwood Daily Press, Elwood, Indiana, September 23, 1895
The Enid Morning News, Enid, Oklahoma, March 20, 1938
The Eugene Guard, Eugene, Oregon, December 28, 1927
The Eugene Guard, Eugene, Oregon, November 7, 1929
The Evening Mail, Stockton, California, May 29, 1912
The Evening Post, New York, New York, August 30, 1943
Evening Standard, London, England, June 24, 1924
Evening Star, Washington, D.C., February 26, 1918
Evening Star, Washington, D.C., May 20, 1925
Evening Star, Washington, D.C., October 4, 1925
The Evening Telegram, Providence, Rhode Island, September 1, 1886
Evening Times Republican, Marshalltown, Iowa, July 27, 1912
Evening World Herald, Omaha, Nebraska, July 29, 1921
The Everett Daily Herald, Everett, Washington, November 12, 1927
Falls City Daily News, Falls City, Nebraska, July 30, 1922
Fitchburg Sentinel, Fitchburg, Massachusetts, September 28, 1917
The Flathead Monitor, Kalispell, Montana, September 15, 1927
Florence Morning News, Florence, South Carolina, October 20, 1925
Fort Scott Daily Tribune and *Fort Scott Daily Monitor*, Fort Scott, Kansas, December 7, 1920
Fort Wayne Journal Gazette, Fort Wayne, Indiana, October 24, 1915
The Fort Wayne News and *The Fort Wayne Sentinel*, Fort Wayne, Indiana, March 8, 1915

BIBLIOGRAPHY

Fort Worth Star Telegram, Fort Worth, Texas, March 12, 1933
Fort Worth Star Telegram, Fort Worth, Texas, May 3, 1943
The Fresno Morning Republican, Fresno, California, September 13, 1927
The Fresno Tribune, Fresno, California, August 19, 1912
The Gazette, Cedar Rapids, Iowa, July 11, 1928
The Gazette and Daily, York, Pennsylvania, May 17, 1938
Gazette and Telegraph, Colorado Springs, Colorado, August 15, 1926
The Girard Press, Girard, Kansas, September 5, 1918
The Gordon Journal, Gordon, Nebraska, July 17, 1919
The Grand Rapids Press, Grand Rapids, Michigan, July 13, 1921
The Great Falls Leader, Great Falls, Montana, September 7, 1927
Great Falls Tribune, Great Falls, Montana, June 4, 1916
Great Falls Tribune, Great Falls, Montana, April 25, 1965
Great Falls Tribune, Great Falls, Montana, June 15, 1969
The Greensboro Record, Greensboro, North Carolina, May 11, 1942
The Guardian, Kings Place, London, July 2, 1924
The Guthrie Daily Leader, Guthrie, Oklahoma, February 13, 1903
Hanford Morning Journal, Hanford, California, April 25, 1946
The Hardin News, Hardin, Missouri, September 21, 1905
Harrisburg Telegram, Harrisburg, Pennsylvania, July 23, 1917
Hartford Courant, Hartford, Connecticut, December 13, 1913
Hartford Courant, Hartford, Connecticut, August 23, 1925
Hartford Courant, Hartford, Connecticut, February 4, 1930
Hartford Courant, Hartford, Connecticut, October 19, 1930
Hartford Courant, Hartford, Connecticut, August 18, 1957
The Hartford Sentinel, Hartford, Connecticut, April 30, 1932
The Haworth Herald, Haworth, Oklahoma, May 9, 1919
The Helena Star, Helena, Oklahoma, February 27, 1919
The Herald Statesman, Yonkers, New York, July 19, 1922
The Herald Statesman, Yonkers, New York, November 29, 1927
The Hobart Democrat-Chief, Hobard, Oklahoma, September 24, 1937
Hollywood Citizen News, Hollywood, California, July 28, 1943
The Hollywood Reporter, Hollywood, California, September 16, 2008
The Honolulu Advertiser, Honolulu, Hawaii, April 7, 1925
Honolulu Star Bulletin, Honolulu, Hawaii, March 2, 1914
Honolulu Star Bulletin, Honolulu, Hawaii, January 20, 1922
Honolulu Star Bulletin, Honolulu, Hawaii, January 24, 1922
Honolulu Star Bulletin, Honolulu, Hawaii, February 9, 1922
Honolulu Star Bulletin, Honolulu, Hawaii, February 18, 1922
Honolulu Star Bulletin, Honolulu, Hawaii, February 26, 1922
The Hood River Glacier, Hood River, Oregon, April 29, 1920
The Houston Post, Houston, Texas, February 24, 1918
The Hutchinson Gazette, Hutchinson, Kansas, February 6, 1916
Idaho County Free Press, Grangeville, Idaho, September 30, 1915
The Idaho Republican, Blackfoot, Idaho, October 8, 1918

The Idaho Statesman, Boise, Idaho, October 6, 1917
The Idaho Statesman, Boise, Idaho, September 19, 1919
The Idaho Statesman, Boise, Idaho, September 29, 1920
The Idaho Statesman, Boise, Idaho, September 13, 1927
Independent Observer, Conrad, Montana, June 21, 1923
The Independent Record, Helena, Montana, September 25, 1928
The Independent Record, Helena, Montana, April 19, 1940
The Ithaca Journal, Ithaca, New York, November 27, 1931
The Joliet News, Joliet, Illinois, June 6, 1907
The Journal Democrat, Warrenburg, Missouri, August 18, 1905
Kansas City Journal, Kansas City, Missouri, October 8, 1916
The Kansas City Star, Kansas City, Missouri, January 21, 1907
The Kansas City Star, Kansas City, Missouri, October 1, 1916
The Kansas City Star, Kansas City, Missouri, July 13, 1921
The Kansas City Star, Kansas City, Missouri, September 18, 1921
The Kansas City Star, Kansas City, Missouri, September 27, 1937
The Kansas City Times, Kansas City, Missouri, June 12, 1905
The Kansas City Times, Kansas City, Missouri, November 18, 1936
The Kansas City Times, Kansas City, Missouri, November 16, 1961
Kennebec Journal, Augusta, Maine, March 12, 1910
Kenosha News, Kenosha, Wisconsin, December 29, 1903
The Kentucky Post, Covington, Kentucky, April 18, 1925
Kitsap Sun, Bremerton, Washington, February 10, 1938
The Klamath News, Klamath Falls, Oregon, September 14, 1927
The Klamath News, Klamath Falls, Oregon, August 24, 1928
The Klamath News, Klamath Falls, Oregon, September 4, 1929
The La Crosse Tribune, La Crosse, Wisconsin, July 4, 1926
Las Cruses Sun News, Las Cruses, New Mexico, January 19, 1922
La Grande Observer, La Grande, Oregon, December 28, 1927
The Lawton Constitution, Lawton, Oklahoma, February 21, 1974
The Leavenworth Post, Leavenworth, Kansas, October 21, 1917
The Leavenworth Times, Leavenworth, Kansas, March 26, 1915
Lewiston Daily News, Lewiston, Montana March 30, 1921
The Lexington Herald, Lexington, Kentucky, May 20, 1912
The Lexington Herald, Lexington, Kentucky, October 28, 1912
The Lima Gazette and *Lima Republican*, Lima, Ohio, November 30, 1918
The Livestock Inspector, Woodward, California, October 15, 1899
Lincoln Nebraska State Journal, Lincoln, Nebraska, August 3, 1930
Lincoln Nebraska State Journal, Lincoln, Nebraska, July 26, 1936
The Lincoln Star, Lincoln, Nebraska, April 19, 1925
The Logan Republican, Logan, Utah, March 27, 1917
The Long Beach Press Telegram, Long Beach, California, May 10, 1914
The Long Beach Press Telegram, Long Beach, California, October 10, 1914
The Long Beach Press Telegram, Long Beach, California, February 23, 1937
The Long Beach Telegram, October 10, 1914

The Long Beach Sun, Long Beach, California, August 27, 1932
Los Angeles Citizen News, Los Angeles, California, August 15, 1936
Los Angeles Citizen News, Los Angeles, California, October 12, 1945
Los Angeles Evening Citizen, Los Angeles, California, March 4, 1936
Los Angeles Evening Citizen, Los Angeles, California, August 15, 1936
Los Angeles Evening Express, Los Angeles, California, March 21, 1912
Los Angeles Evening Express, Los Angeles, California, February 17, 1913
Los Angeles Evening Express, Los Angeles, California, March 2, 1914
Los Angeles Evening Express, Los Angeles, California, April 28, 1915
Los Angeles Evening Express, Los Angeles, California, January 2, 1920
Los Angeles Evening Express, Los Angeles, California, March 20, 1922
Los Angeles Evening Express, Los Angeles, California, September 21, 1922
Los Angeles Evening Express, Los Angeles, California, April 9, 1923
Los Angeles Evening Express, Los Angeles, California, January 3, 1931
Los Angeles Evening News, Los Angeles, California, April 25, 1941
Los Angeles Evening Post, Los Angeles, California, June 20, 1930
Los Angeles Evening Post Record, Los Angeles, California, August 4, 1932
Los Angeles Evening Post Record, Los Angeles, California, November 22, 1930
Los Angeles Evening Post Record, Los Angeles, California, July 30, 1932
Los Angeles Express, Los Angeles, California, April 5, 1915
Los Angeles Record, Los Angeles, California, July 13, 1916
Los Angeles Times, Los Angeles, California, February 18, 1913
Los Angeles Times, Los Angeles, California, April 4, 1915
Los Angeles Times, Los Angeles, California, May 4, 1915
Los Angeles Times, Los Angeles, California, May 7, 1915
Los Angeles Times, Los Angeles, California, January 10, 1918
Los Angeles Times, Los Angeles, California, January 13, 1918
Los Angeles Times, Los Angeles, California, March 16, 1922
Los Angeles Times, Los Angeles, California, August 27, 1922
Los Angeles Times, Los Angeles, California, April 29, 1928
Los Angeles Times, Los Angeles, California, August 4, 1929
Los Angeles Times, Los Angeles, California, September 30, 1930
Los Angeles Times, Los Angeles, California, November 3, 1930
Los Angeles Times, Los Angeles, California, November 6, 1933
Los Angeles Times, Los Angeles, California, July 23, 1938
Los Angeles Times, Los Angeles, California, August 14, 1938
Los Angeles Times, Los Angeles, California, March 31, 1940
Los Angeles Times, Los Angeles, California, April 14, 1941
Los Angeles Times, Los Angeles, California, July 27, 1941
Los Angeles Times, Los Angeles, California, December 21, 1945
Los Angeles Times, Los Angeles, California, March 17, 1988
Lubbock Morning Avalanche, Lubbock, Texas, December 24, 1940
The Manchester Journal, Manchester, Vermont, September 2, 1920
Manitoba Free Press, Winnipeg, Manitoba, Canada, March 31, 1914
Martinez News Gazette, Martinez, California, June 24, 1930

BIBLIOGRAPHY

Merced Sun Star, Merced, California, April 15, 1950
The Miami Herald, Miami, Florida, February 20, 1974
Miles City Star, Miles City, Montana, November 8, 1927
The Minneapolis Journal, Minneapolis, Minnesota, October 27, 1905
The Minneapolis Journal, Minneapolis, Minnesota, December 10, 1918
The Missoula Sentinel, Missoula, Montana, July 4, 1918
The Modesto Bee, Modesto, California, May 8, 1931
The Modesto Bee, Modesto, California, May 13, 1931
The Modesto Bee, Modesto, California, June 12, 1992
Monrovia News Post, Monrovia, California, March 5, 1978
The Montana Progressive, Helena, Montana, June 11, 1916
Monte Vista Tribune, Monte Vista, Colorado, August 1, 1929
Monterey Daily Cyprus, Monterey, California, January 11, 1913
The Montgomery Advertiser, Montgomery, Alabama, July 27, 1941
The Morning Call, Allentown, Pennsylvania, September 30, 1937
The Morning Press, Santa Barbara, California, August 27, 1932
The Morning Press, Santa Barbara, California, November 19, 1936
Morning Register, Eugene, Oregon, September 3, 1910
The Mount Hope Clarion, Mount Hope, Kansas, July 25, 1919
Mountain Gazette, Jefferson, Vermont, December 10, 1960
The Muscatine Journal, Muscatine, Iowa, September 3, 1919
Muskogee Daily Phoenix, Muskogee, Oklahoma, November 24, 1914
The Neihart Herald, Neihart, Montana, February 12, 1903
Nevada County Tribune, Carson City, California, July 6, 1916
Nevada State Journal, Reno, Nevada, May 31, 1928
Nevada State Journal, Reno, Nevada, April 15, 1934
Nevada State Journal, Reno, Nevada, October 5, 1948
Nevada State Journal, Reno, Nevada, January 5, 1951
Nevada State Journal, Reno, Nevada, May 19, 1951
New Orleans Republican, New Orleans, Louisiana, August 24, 1873
The News Journal, Wilmington, Delaware, November 6, 1933
The News and Observer, Sacramento, California, November 24, 1935
News and Record, Greensboro, North Carolina, March 16, 1988
The News Review, Roseburg, Oregon, November 7, 1927
The News Tribune, Tacoma, Washington, June 29, 1918
The Newcastle Sun, New South Wales, Australia, August 15, 1930
Newport Daily Independent, Newport, Arkansas, September 19, 1913
New York Times, New York, New York, April 29, 1912
New York Times, New York, New York, June 22, 1926
New York Times, New York, New York, November 12, 1922
The Nome Nugget, Nome, Alaska, April 9, 1925
Norfolk Daily News, Norfolk, Nebraska, August 16, 1920
North Hollywood Valley Times, North Hollywood, California, January 10, 1944
The Northern Wyoming Herald, Cody, Wyoming, July 15, 1915
Norwich Bulletin, Norwich, Connecticut, May 26, 1917

BIBLIOGRAPHY

The Oakland Post Enquirer, Oakland, California, November 8, 1933
The Oakland Post Enquirer, Oakland, California, June 11, 1934
Oakland Tribune, Oakland, California, January 1, 1922
Oakland Tribune, Oakland, California, August 9, 1922
Oakland Tribune, Oakland, California, July 4, 1926
Oakland Tribune, Oakland, California, January 15, 1928
Oakland Tribune, Oakland, California, June 11, 1934
Oakland Tribune, Oakland, California, November 27, 1938
Oakland Tribune, Oakland, California, March 16, 1988
The Ogden Standard Examiner, Ogden, Utah, November 10, 1938
The Oklahoma News, Oklahoma City, Oklahoma, August 6, 1920
The Oklahoma News, Oklahoma City, Oklahoma, August 18, 1935
Okmulgee Daily Times, Okmulgee, Oklahoma, September 6, 1921
The Oregon Daily Journal, Portland, Oregon, September 13, 1913
The Oregon Daily Journal, Portland, Oregon, September 20, 1919
The Oregon Daily Journal, Portland, Oregon, May 28, 1922
The Oregonian, Portland, Oregon, July 1, 1918
The Ottawa Citizen, Ottawa, Ontario, Canada, June 13, 1936
The Ottawa Journal, Ottawa, Ontario, Canada, June 14, 1919
The Payson Chronicle, Payson, Utah, August 1, 1930
The Peabody Weekly Republican, Peabody, Kansas, September 16, 1887
Pensacola Journal, Pensacola, Florida, December 11, 1920
The Philadelphia Inquirer, Philadelphia, Pennsylvania, June 7, 1908
The Philadelphia Inquirer, Philadelphia, Pennsylvania, August 24, 1924
Pittsburgh Daily Post, Pittsburgh, Pennsylvania, July 16, 1916
The Pittsburgh Press, Pittsburgh, Pennsylvania, May 3, 1903
The Pittsburgh Press, Pittsburgh, Pennsylvania, November 14, 1927
The Pittston Gazette, Pittston, Pennsylvania, July 24, 1906
The Pomona Progress Bulletin, Pomona, California, September 22, 1930
The Pomona Progress Bulletin, Pomona, California, February 3, 1937
The Payson Chronicle, Payson, Utah, August 1, 1930
The Ponca City News, Ponca City, Oklahoma, August 24, 1924
Press of Atlantic City, Atlantic City, New Jersey, March 11, 1915
Press of Atlantic City, Atlantic City, New Jersey, October 13, 1915
Press of Atlantic City, Atlantic City, New Jersey, December 24, 1903
Press and Sun Bulletin, Binghamton, New York, January 8, 1912
Press and Sun Bulletin, Binghamton, New York, April 21, 1943
Press Telegram, Long Beach, California, January 8, 1939
The Province, Vancouver, British Columbia, Canada, September 3, 1927
The Province, Vancouver, British Columbia, Canada, November 6, 1933
The Pryor Creek Clipper, Pryor, Oklahoma, May 17, 1901
The Quinton Times and *The McCurtain Leader*, Quinton, Oklahoma, September 4, 1924
Reading Times, Reading, Pennsylvania, October 29, 1917
Record Journal, Meriden, California, August 30, 1919
Red Bluff News, Red Bluff, California, September 9, 1927

The Register, Santa Ana, California, August 6, 1912
The Register, Santa Ana, California, September 8, 1934
Reno Evening Gazette, Reno, Nevada, June 14, 1922
Reno Evening Gazette, Reno, Nevada, June 14, 1927
Reno Gazette Journal, Reno, Nevada, June 30, 1919
Reno Gazette Journal, Reno, Nevada, June 14, 1946
Reno Gazette Journal, Reno, Nevada, September 11, 1948
Reno Gazette Journal, Reno, Nevada, October 24, 1956
Richmond Times Dispatch, Richmond, Virginia, October 25, 1936
Riverside Daily Press, Riverside, California, January 29, 1924
Riverside Daily Press, Riverside, California, June 1, 1926
Riverside Daily Press, Riverside, California, September 10, 1934
The Roanoke Times, Roanoke, Virginia, May 25, 1912
The Roanoke Times, Roanoke, Virginia, November 2, 1936
The Rock Island Argus, Rock Island, Illinois, September 22, 1936
The Sacramento Bee, Sacramento, California, November 13, 1917
The Sacramento Bee, Sacramento, California, September 5, 1927
The Sacramento Bee, Sacramento, California, September 14, 1927
The Sacramento Bee, Sacramento, California, November 12, 1927
The Sacramento Bee, Sacramento, California, November 14, 1927
The Sacramento Bee, Sacramento, California, August 30, 1928
The Sacramento Bee, Sacramento, California, June 20, 1930
The Sacramento Bee, Sacramento, California, August 14, 1957
The Sacramento Bee, Sacramento, California, March 16, 1988
The Sacramento Union, Sacramento, California, September 8, 1934
The Sacramento Union, Sacramento, California, May 8, 1938
Salinas Morning Post, Salina, California, July 20, 1937
Salisbury Evening Post, Salisbury, North Carolina, October 30, 1943
The Salt Lake Herald Republican, Salt Lake, Utah, November 30, 1908
The Salt Lake Herald Republican, Salt Lake, Utah, July 9, 1913
The Salt Lake Herald Republican, Salt Lake, Utah, August 24, 1914
The Salt Lake Herald Republican, Salt Lake, Utah, June 25, 1917
The Salt Lake Herald Republican, Salt Lake, Utah, January 26, 1918
Salt Lake Telegram, Salt Lake City, Utah, September 22, 1937
The Salt Lake Tribune, Salt Lake City, Utah, July 3, 1913
The Salt Lake Tribune, Salt Lake City, Utah, August 23, 1914
The Salt Lake Tribune, Salt Lake City, Utah, August 18, 1922
The Salt Lake Tribune, Salt Lake City, Utah, September 28, 1927
The Salt Lake Tribune, Salt Lake City, Utah, November 13, 1938
The Salt Lake Tribune, Salt Lake City, Utah, November 1, 1942
San Antonio Evening News, San Antonio, Texas, June 7, 1919
San Antonio Evening News, San Antonio, Texas, November 27, 1920
San Antonio Evening News, San Antonio, Texas, February 4, 1922
The San Bernardino County Sun, San Bernardino, California, November 4, 1923
The San Bernardino County Sun, San Bernardino, California, February 4, 1937

BIBLIOGRAPHY

The San Bernardino County Sun, San Bernardino, California, January 8, 1939
The San Diego Sun, San Diego, California, February 3, 1939
San Fernando Valley Times, San Fernando, California, September 18, 1944
San Fernando Valley Times, San Fernando, California, January 10, 1946
San Francisco Bulletin, San Francisco, California, March 26, 1928
San Francisco Chronicle, San Francisco, California, December 12, 1920
San Francisco Examiner, San Francisco, California, June 24, 1915
San Francisco Examiner, San Francisco, California, September 10, 1917
San Francisco Examiner, San Francisco, California, July 30, 1925
San Francisco Examiner, San Francisco, California, July 1, 1965
San Francisco Bulletin, San Francisco, California, June 4, 1914
San Francisco Bulletin, San Francisco, California, December 26, 1924
San Francisco Bulletin, San Francisco, California, March 26, 1928
San Francisco Chronicle, San Francisco, California, December 23, 1912
San Francisco Chronicle, San Francisco, California, December 20, 1920
San Francisco Examiner, San Francisco, California, February 1, 1885
San Francisco Examiner, San Francisco, California, September 10, 1917
San Francisco Examiner, San Francisco, California, July 30, 1925
San Francisco Examiner, San Francisco, California, June 20, 1930
San Francisco Examiner, San Francisco, California, April 24, 1933
San Francisco Examiner, San Francisco, California, July 3, 1933
San Francisco Examiner, San Francisco, California, May 7, 1934
San Francisco Examiner, San Francisco, California, August 19, 1943
San Francisco Examiner, San Francisco, California, July 1, 1965
Santa Cruz Evening News, Santa Cruz, California, December 28, 1914
Santa Maria Times, Santa Maria, California, January 30, 1941
Scranton Tribune, Scranton, Pennsylvania, September 29, 1946
Seattle Union Record, Seattle, Washington, June 30, 1927
The Selma Times Journal, Selma, Alabama, April 26, 1940
The Sidney Telegraph, Sidney, Nebraska, July 1, 1905
The Signal, Santa Clarita, California, May 6, 1921
The Signal, Santa Clarita, California, April 28, 1940
The South Bend Tribune, South Bend, Indiana, July 28, 1906
The South Bend Tribune, South Bend, Indiana, June 30, 1921
The Southwest Mail, Nevada, Missouri, January 21, 1910
The Spokane Chronicle, Spokane, Washington, September 3, 1927
The Spokane Chronicle, Spokane, Washington, January 3, 1933
The Spokesman Review, Spokane, Washington, August 2, 1913
The Spokesman Review, Spokane, Washington, April 27, 1917
The Spokesman Review, Spokane, Washington, August 6, 1921
The Spokesman Review, Spokane, Washington, July 4, 1923
The Spokesman Review, Spokane, Washington, September 5, 1927
The Spokesman Review, Spokane, Washington, August 27, 1932
The Spokesman Review, Spokane, Washington, January 19, 1955
The Spokesman Review, Spokane, Washington, November 16, 1961

BIBLIOGRAPHY

The St. Louis Dispatch, St. Louis, Missouri, January 18, 1907
St. Louis Globe Democrat, St. Louis, Missouri, November 6, 1933
The St. Louis Republic, St. Louis, Missouri, May 17, 1901
The St. Louis Star and Times, St. Louis, Missouri, November 8, 1927
The Standard Herald, Warrensburg, Missouri, February 24, 1899
The Standard Herald, Warrensburg, Missouri, February 16, 1912
Standard Speaker, Hazleton, Pennsylvania, June 11, 1938
The Standard Union, Brooklyn, New York, June 24, 1906
The Standard Union, Brooklyn, New York, October 31, 1922
Star Herald, Scottsbluff, Nebraska, November 9, 1927
Star Tribune, Minneapolis, Minnesota, February 1, 1910
Star Tribune, Minneapolis, Minnesota, December 8, 1918
Star Tribune, Minneapolis, Minnesota, May 29, 1922
Star Tribune, Minneapolis, Minnesota, July 9, 1938
Star Tribune, Minneapolis, Minnesota, December 2, 1945
State Journal, Lincoln, Nebraska, August 3, 1930
The State, Columbia, South Carolina, August 30, 1914
Statesman Journal, Salem, Oregon, June 9, 1929
Statesman Journal, Salem, Oregon, September 20, 1932
Stockton Evening and Sunday Record, Stockton, California, July 8, 1922
Stockton Evening and Sunday Record, Stockton, California, June 23, 1926
The Stroud Messenger, Stroud, Oklahoma, August 13, 1926
The Stuart News, Stuart, Florida, May 8, 1983
The Sun News Pictorial, Melbourne, Victoria, Australia, January 16, 1933
The Sun News Pictorial, Melbourne, Victoria, Australia, January 26, 1938
The Sunday Oregonian, Portland, Oregon, October 22, 1905
The Sunday Star, Washington, D.C., March 10, 1929
The Tacoma Daily Leader, Tacoma, Washington, April 24, 1921
The Tacoma Daily Leader, Tacoma, Washington, October 29, 1928
The Tacoma Times, Tacoma, Washington, July 3, 1913
The Tampa Times, St. Petersburg, Florida, September 19, 1925
The Tampa Times, St. Petersburg, Florida, April 26, 1927
The Tampa Times, St. Petersburg, Florida, July 26, 1927
The Tampa Times, St. Petersburg, Florida, October 16, 1934
The Tampa Times, St. Petersburg, Florida, August 12, 1943
The Tampa Tribune, Tampa, Florida, April 26, 1927
The Tampa Tribune, Tampa, Florida, December 21, 1945
Telegram Forum, Bucyrus, Ohio, September 23, 1937
The Times, San Mateo, California, July 23, 1938
The Times, Shreveport, Louisiana, June 10, 1885
The Times, Shreveport, Louisiana, December 11, 1914
The Times, Shreveport, Louisiana, September 10, 1916
The Times Democrat, Davenport, Iowa, November 24, 1914
The Times Leader, Wilkes-Barre, Pennsylvania, October 1, 1926
Times Monitor, Kalispell, Montana, September 15, 1927

Times Union, Brooklyn, New York, October 11, 1925
Tracy Press, Tracy, California, September 30, 1930
The Tribune, San Luis Obispo, California, April 14, 1941
The Tribune, Scranton, Pennsylvania, September 21, 1888
The Tri-County News, Kiel, Wisconsin, May 4, 1917
Tucson Daily Citizen, Tucson, Arizona, April 22, 1933
Tulare Advance Register, Visalia, California, March 19, 1944
Tulare Advance Register, Visalia, California, July 6, 1979
The Tulsa Tribune, Tulsa, Oklahoma, December 21, 1913
Vallejo Evening News, Vallejo, California, September 11, 1937
Vallejo Evening News, Vallejo, California, March 30, 1938
Valley Morning Star, Harlington, Texas, March 19, 1931
The Valley Times, Valley, Alabama, September 18, 1947
The Valley Times, Valley, Alabama, November 27, 1959
The Van Nuys News, Van Nuys, California, April 3, 1925
Ventura County Star, Camarillo, California, April 16, 1932
Ventura County Star, Camarillo, California, April 30, 1932
Ventura County Star, Ventura, California, November 3, 1932
Ventura County Star, Ventura, California, November 27, 1933
Ventura County Star, Ventura, California, March 10, 1940
Ventura County Star, Camarillo, California, April 8, 2006
Ventura Daily Post, Ventura, California, February 27, 1924
Ventura Weekly Post, Ventura, California, November 11, 1932
Ventura Weekly Post, Ventura, California, November 18, 1932
The Vicksburg Post, Vicksburg, Mississippi, November 22, 1922
The Vinita Daily Journal, Vinta, Oklahoma, May 31, 1938
Visalia Times Delta, Visalia, California, July 30, 1929
Visalia Times Delta, Visalia, California, November 17, 1930
The Waco Times Herald, Waco, Texas, August 6, 1926
Warren Times Mirror, Warren, Pennsylvania, May 29, 1931
Warrensburg Daily Star, Warrensburg, Missouri, February 22, 1899
The Washington Post, Washington, D.C., December 8, 1914
The Washington Post, Washington, D.C., October 31, 1936
Weekly Journal Miner, Prescott, Arizona, May 26, 1915
The Weekly Kansas City Star, Kansas City, Missouri, September 23, 1936
The Weekly Post, Nevada, Missouri, April 15, 1910
The Weekly Post, Nevada, Missouri, January 6, 1911
The West Virginian, Fairmont, West Virginia, February 15, 1917
The Whittier News, Whittier, California, April 14, 1941
The Wichita Beacon, Wichita, Kansas, December 26, 1920
The Wichita Eagle, Wichita, Kansas, November 28, 1920
The Wichita Eagle, Wichita, Kansas, September 29, 1922
Wilkes-Barre Times Leader, Wilkes-Barre, Pennsylvania, September 22, 1938
The Wilmington Morning Star, Wilmington, North Carolina, August 29, 1917
The Windsor Star, Windsor, Ontario, Canada, October 14, 1943

The Winnipeg Tribune, Winnipeg, Manitoba, Cananda, August 11, 1913
The Winnipeg Tribune, Winnipeg, Manitoba, Cananda, August 13, 1913
The Winnipeg Tribune, Winnipeg, Manitoba, Cananda, August 15, 1913
The York Dispatch, York, Pennsylvania, April 10, 1937

Websites

Bertha Kaepernik, https://ancestors.familysearch.org/en/L5XF-PN7/bertha-marie-kaepernick-1863-1950

Decennial Census Official Publications, https://www.census.gov/programs-surveys/decennial-census/decade/decennial-publications.1890.html

Journal of the Illinois State Historical Society, https://www.encyclopedia.com/women/encyclopedias-almanacs-transcripts-and-maps/weber-lois-1881-1929

The Ninety-Nines from 1929 to 1989, https://www.ninety-nines.org/sixty-years.htm

Screening the Past, https://web.archives.org/web/20130504141404/http://tlweb.latrobe.edu.au/humanities/screeningthepast/firstrelease/fr0301/wr1fr12ahm

U.S. Presbyterian Church Records, 1896–1943, https://www.history.pcusa.org/services/records-management/records-congregations

www.ancestry.com:

Adele Von Ohl
Alice G. Van Derveen
Allene "Alene Ray" Burch
Anita Bush
Bertha Kaepernik
Elizabeth "Bessie" Mary Barriscale
James Letcher Parker
Lorena Mickey Peterson
Lulu Bell Parr
Marie E. Walcamp
Mary Lois Wiggins
Mildred May McConnell Douglas Chrisman
Mildred Nell "Nellie" Roach "O'Day"
Olive Cary (Carey)
Polly Burson
Rose Wenger
Ruth R. Roland
Texas Guinan
Vera McGinnis
Verna Grace Harris

Internet Movie Database (IMDb.com):

Alice Van Springsteen, https://www.imdb.com/name/nm1116276/
Anita Bush, https://www.imdb.com/name/nm0124090/
Bessie Barriscale, https://www.imdb.com/name/nm0057585/
Betty Miles, https://www.imdb.com/name/nm0587062/
The Blot, https://www.imdb.com/title/tt0011979/

BIBLIOGRAPHY

The Bull Dogger, https://www.imdb.com/title/tt0129804/
Call of the Wild, https://www.imdb.com/title/tt0026164/
Central Airport, https://www.imdb.com/title/tt0023878/?ref_=fn_all_ttl_1
Cimarron, https://www.imdb.com/title/tt0021746/
Helen Gibson, https://www.imdb.com/name/nm0316993/
Hill Ship Morgan, https://www.imdb.com/title/tt0027731/
The Inner Conscience, https://www.imdb.com/title/tt0483660/?ref_=nm_flmg_job_1_cdt_t_78
It Happened One Night, https://www.imdb.com/title/tt0025316/
A Knight of the Range, https://www.imdb.com/title/tt0006901/
The Lawless Nineties, https://www.imdb.com/title/tt0027876/
Marie Walcamp, https://www.imdb.com/name/nm0906942/
Mary Wiggins, https://www.imdb.com/name/nm0927798/
Mountain Justice, https://www.imdb.com/title/tt0029263/
Olive Carey, https://www.imdb.com/name/nm0137010/
Ora Nelson "Pat" Chrisman, https://www.imdb.com/name/nm0159643/?ref_=tt_cst_t_8
The Perils of Pauline, https://www.imdb.com/title/tt0004465/
The Queen of Sheba, https://www.imdb.com/title/tt0012600/
Rose of the Rancho, https://www.imdb.com/title/tt0004545/
Ruth Roland, https://www.imdb.com/name/nm0738082/
Six-Shooter Andy, https://www.imdb.com/title/tt0009621/
The Soul Herder, https://www.imdb.com/title/tt0008605/?ref_=ttfc_fc_tt
Spook Ranch, https://www.imdb.com/title/tt0016387/
Texas Guinan, https://www.imdb.com/name/nm0347345/
Through the Back Door, https://www.imdb.com/title/tt0012755/
Torchy Blane, https://www.imdb.com/title/tt0032044/
Two-Gun Betty, https://www.imdb.com/title/tt0190100/
Vera McGinnis, https://www.imdb.com/name/nm0569381/
The Werewolf, https://www.imdb.com/title/tt0049944/
The White Squaw, https://www.imdb.com/title/tt0379016/

Index

INDEX

INDEX

INDEX